AN END TO HIERARCHY! AN END TO COMPETITION!

NEW VIEWPOINTS  A DIVISION OF FRANKLIN WATTS, INC., NEW YORK

FREDERICK C. THAYER

an end to hierarchy! an end to competition!

ORGANIZING THE POLITICS AND ECONOMICS OF SURVIVAL

Text design by Hermann Strohbach

Library of Congress Cataloging in Publication Data

Thayer, Frederick C
  An end to hierarchy!

  Bibliography: p.
  1. Organization. 2. Organizational change.
3. United States–Civilization. I. Title.
HM131.T44   301.24′3   73-1815
ISBN 0-531-05351-2
ISBN 0-531-05552-3 (pbk)

LIST OF FIGURES

his book is a search for an alternative we have assumed impossible up to now. Especially in the West, we believe that organization *means* hierarchy, and that the only alternative is anarchy. We look upon ourselves as "naturally" atomistic human beings who can come together to do socially useful work, whether in families or corporations, only if our natural tendencies are rearranged into relationships between "superiors" and "subordinates." This has the effect of making all formally organized interactions, including marriage, seem unnatural. Unlike other books which address the possibilities of transforming organizations into more "natural" or "humanistic" communities, this one argues that instead of compromising with hierarchy, *we must end it,* that this is both possible and quite easy to do, and that there is a workable alternative which is not anarchy. In thinking through the logic and developing the argument, it has been necessary to challenge the basic tenets of politics and economics, for this seemed the only way to deal with the complex relationships between hierarchy as the base of politics, competition as the ideal of economics, and alienation as the inexorable outcome of both. The argument cannot be separated into parts; we cannot choose to abandon hierarchy *or* competition, only to abandon both. There is no other way to break the cycle of ever-increasing alienation.

Because of the long period of socialization we have endured, what we are searching for will itself appear unnatural to us for a time. Our future probably will be an even *more structured* one than any we have imagined to now, and even to hint at more structure is to raise the specter of more and more conventional bureaucracy. But this instills fear in us only because we are conditioned to equate organization with hierarchy; over time, *structured nonhierarchy* will come to feel natural because it is free of alienation. We will have no reason to turn away from it or reject it, and every reason to seek more of it. Admittedly, it will take some effort to get used to organization and structure as worthy of our

INTRODUCTION

love because of what they enable us to *become* as the outcome of *intensive interaction with others,* but we will come to realize that a uniquely fulfilling combination of individual autonomy and interdependence holds the key to our only possible future. What we are searching for, I argue, is a formal theory of structured non-hierarchical social interaction, and this is an attempt to outline it.

Contemporary commentators suggest that we are approaching a "great divide" of sorts, and that only after we have crossed it will we be able to describe where we have been. Some are mentioned herein, and it should be clear where my views parallel, or diverge from, theirs. My objective is to be as specific as possible about *how* to reach that vague new world nobody can yet describe with precision, for that is the most critical question asked of authors who speculate about the future. This much is certain: if we attempt to wait until we have "proved" something will work, we will be extinguished. Indeed, the notion of "scientific proof" has blinded social scientists to its most obvious contradiction, the impossibility of "proving" something *will* work until it *has* worked. Since the world must be transformed in ways it never has been transformed, all we can do is seek a basis for agreeing to what we must do, and "proof" cannot be that basis.

None of this is meant to suggest that we can survive the future only by abandoning technology. On the contrary, technology will be needed as never before, but we need new intellectual frameworks to help us devise systems in which humans can interact with technology and not be devoured by it. We suffer from assembly-line thinking in almost every technological design we use, even if the first encouraging signs of change are now appearing. That we are almost stymied is due not to the "needs" of technology, but to the theories of social intercourse and human nature which are imbedded as deeply in technologists as in the rest of us.

Despite its outright attack on the established wisdom of politics and economics, this is an optimist book which sees our future as survivable, decent, and more humane than our present and any part of our past. It is an optimism tinged with fear, however, for we do not have much time left to us unless we begin to disconnect technology from hierarchy. Those officially designated as our leaders will soon have available to them a series of drugs and computer-connected devices having the capability to profoundly alter their behavior. A recent president of the American Psychological Association proudly announces that we seem

on the threshold of that type of scientific biochemical intervention which could stabilize and make dominant the moral and ethical propensities of man and subordinate, if not eliminate, his negative and primitive behavioral tendencies.[1]

The leader, faced with prescriptions for drugs which allegedly could make him more "humane" or, alternatively, could for a short period increase his mental capability by some extraordinary amount, might be tempted to say to us, "I am doing this for *you*," especially if he believes that competing leaders are about to do the same thing. This technological trend contains within it a degrading assumption and a terrible contradiction, both of which are important to the themes of this book.

The psychologist's remarks include the old but ever popular notion that human beings left to themselves are dangerous beasts of prey whose only objective is to kill one another; to paraphrase philosopher Thomas Hobbes and management engineer Frederick Taylor, people are just no damned good. The contradiction, on the other hand, goes to the heart of our political theories, and we cannot resolve it within the confines of hierarchy: if a President takes a mind-altering drug prescribed for him by a "psychotechnical expert" who *knows* how the President will behave while under the drug's influence, *who is President?* Perhaps, just perhaps, we will begin to see the choice we must make if we begin to ask such questions.

Some readers may instantly react to the arguments in this book by branding them wildly utopian, "impractical," or "unrealistic." I emphasize here only that my own operational experience (24 years in government service, many of them spent managing complex organizational systems and interacting with and within various policy processes in Washington) convinces me that everything argued herein either exists already or can easily be accomplished. Indeed, the only truly impractical and unrealistic theory is the hierarchical and competitive one we attempt to maintain.

However imperfectly, I should like to thank a number of people who have made direct or indirect contributions to this book. They were indispensable, for there is no truly systematic way of approaching the themes argued herein, hence even a casual reference to an interesting item in a newspaper is likely to be critical to the entire process. Those named in alphabetical order include individuals who have typed or reproduced drafts with greater alacrity than I have ever witnessed, provided brief or extended criticism, edited with care and precision, advanced ideas I found incredibly perceptive, and outlined their own relevant experiences: June Abelman, Mary Ellen Bayuk, Peter Bouvier, Gerald Brown, Catherine Carrubba, John Chapman, Edward Dolbow, William Dunn, James Elden, Lionel Feldman, Bahman Fozouni, Colin Freebury, Bruce Gates, David Gloss, Janet Good, John Graham, Sandra Haber, David K. Hart, John Inman, Saul Katz, Mary Lumpkin, Harvey Mansfield, Sr., Harvey Mansfield, Jr., Frank Marini, Gene Mason, Margaret McKenzie, Frankie Miles, Allyn Morrow, Candace Neller, Marie Nigro, Henrietta Pons, Wilma Richman, Gilles Rondeau, Patricia Sands, R. L. Scott, William G. Scott, Morley Segal, Mildred Simpson, Sheila Smith, David Spitz, Gail Starrs, Katherine Stewart, Daniel Straub, Eloise Taylor, Louise Taylor, Linda Thomas, Dwight Waldo, Kenneth Wedel, Scott Wheeler, Orion White, Francis X. Winters, Susan Woolfson, and Arthur Wright. My apologies to any I have overlooked.

Finally, two additional apologies, the first to those in libraries who will have to catalog this book within the confines of existing index systems. While I *hope* it is relevant to a number of academic "fields," I would not attempt to list them in any order. Second, to those who might feel uncomfortable with the lack of an index, I have attempted to be reasonably thorough in the use of footnotes; readers are encouraged to consult them often.

AN END TO HIERARCHY! AN END TO COMPETITION!

McDonald's sells hamburgers, billions of them. In its own way McDonald's is also part of an emerging organizational revolution which, before it is finished, will transform our political and economic systems in ways we cannot yet fully describe. This book examines the implications of that organizational revolution, as important as any revolution ever recorded. It offers us a combination of individual freedom and mutual dependence that we have dreamed about, on occasion, but never have been able to realize. If we do not grasp this opportunity, we shall probably perish. In order to grasp it, however, we must sweep away the conventional baggage of what we know as "politics" and "economics." Our system of representative government is designed only to preserve *hierarchy,* and our economic system is based upon the ideal of *competition.* Yet neither hierarchy nor competition has a place in our future, for both compel us to repress ourselves and each other. The organizational revolution is an attempt to end repression, and the alienation that accompanies it.

What does this have to do with McDonald's hamburgers? McDonald's executives, in common with those of many other corporations, decided to move from downtown (Chicago) to the suburbs, but, unlike most others, these executives decided they needed a somewhat radical office design. Their architects used a concept of "open planning," which groups departmental functions into unpartitioned areas. Each area is defined clearly enough so a person knows which area he or she "belongs" to, but the same individual is free to mingle with others in adjacent areas. No one is isolated in an old-fashioned cage-type office. Instead, each person works in a "task response module," a unit made up of phone booth, room divider, desk, table, set of drawers, closet, and bul-

THE ORGANIZATIONAL REVOLUTION

letin board. It contains its own electrical and phone wiring, and can be quickly moved to wherever it is needed. The "walls" are only five feet high, and the instant an employee stands up, he is a part of the entire floor. The fluidity and flexibility of this type of modular office furniture (which is being advertised more and more in *Fortune*) enables an organization to restructure itself almost immediately, depending upon the groupings of employees that it needs at a given moment. The McDonald's executive who was instrumental in planning the new layout argues, "If you're going to hire young people, you've got to motivate them, and these days little cubicles and superficial status symbols like northeast corner offices don't motivate people." On the other hand, if some employees are to be believed, the open design makes "people seem more open and less bitchy," and "you always know what's going on."

McDonald's has on its seventh floor a sealed-off "think tank," in two sections. One is a soundproof workroom with dimmable lights, a hassock, a beanbag chair, a desk adjustable in height for sitting or standing positions, and walls, floor, and ceiling covered in beige pseudosuede. The other section is a "meditation room" covered in the same "suede" material; it has concealed loudspeakers hooked to stereo equipment, and a floor consisting of nothing but a water bed nine feet wide. Because there are no vertical or solid horizontal reference points in this water-bed room, those entering it are "unconsciously encouraged to think differently" and "forced into a change configuration." The room is available—to any employee who reserves it—for thinking, resting, or staff conferences. There is only one ground rule: it cannot be used by mixed couples.[1]

Many aspects of the emerging organizational revolution are embodied in this building. Work areas offer a combination of privacy, openness, and interaction; related small groups overlap each other but have recognizable geographical boundaries. Each individual is inside an office but always aware of not only the adjacent offices but the outside world and the weather as well. (How many of us toil all day under fluorescent lights in impenetrable dungeons?) The design assumes not only that small-group interaction is the most significant factor in organizational life, but also that it can be so intensive upon occasion that some locale for respite and total privacy is needed. There is also a certain sensuality and eroticism associated with the psychedelic and disorienting atmosphere of the "meditation room"; if this were not the case, there would be no reason to discourage couples from using it. And so a dollop of fear is added to the sensuality of McDonald's design, signaling the nature of the ultimate revolution.

There is nothing uncommon about "office sex" in today's organizational world. A great deal of it goes on, especially in large cities where those in downtown office buildings can slip away for a few hours or adjust their commuting schedules to accommodate it. Contrary to what we usually think, however, the discomfort, pain, and demeaning nature of today's office sex seem less traceable to the violation of traditional moral codes, including marriage vows, than to the association of sex with repressive models of organizational hierarchy. Women who do office work are attracted to the city because that is where they can "meet people." But they meet them within a hierarchical framework—superiors and subordinates, bosses and secretaries. This transforms the sex aspects of such relationships into those of repression and alienation, and women come to consider themselves not only slaves of the organization, but sexual slaves to boot.[2] Two worlds of hierarchy come together to make things intolerable: the male executive dominating the female secretary in the old culture of male supremacy, as well as the old organizational design of superiors and subordinates.

When the organizational revolution has run its course, and when societies have been transformed as they must be if we are to survive, the world of organizations will be one of innumerable small face-to-face groups characterized by openness, trust, and intensive interpersonal relations. If these groups are to be democratic in structure and operation, a person's sex will play no part in their makeup. Most groups—whether in offices or in factories

—will include both men and women. When no one is compelled to fight to attain and preserve status, prestige, or success, the atmosphere may become more erotic and sensual, and even office sex may be a natural thing. The operational restriction on McDonald's water-bed room may be a casualty of the overarching social revolution we must experience.

The remainder of this chapter outlines the organizational revolution now under way, one which is causing the pyramidal hierarchical walls of formal organizations to "wither away" (in a non-Marxist sense). Because the revolution is being impeded by our outmoded theories of politics and economics, it is necessary to strip away the sham of "democracy" (Chapter 2) and "competition" (Chapter 3), for we cannot survive unless we find a non-hierarchical meaning for democracy and substitute cooperation and sharing for competition. The need to limit economic growth, on a global basis, probably will make this obvious to most of us before this year ends. Chapter 4 outlines the framework of a non-hierarchical social theory, or paradigm; any attempt in 1973 can only be filled with assertions whose only claim to "truth" lies in the *plausibility* of the reasoning behind them. Chapter 5 endeavors to fill in this theory for the policy-making system which constitutes the U.S. government; everything proposed herein conforms to the U.S. Constitution, which, indeed, we seem to have misinterpreted all along. The final chapter is devoted to futuristic and, to some extent, frightening speculation, carrying the logic of the argument as far as is possible now.

The entire book argues for a *different* way of looking at the world in which we live, and especially at the organizations (nation-states, universities, public agencies, corporations, and whatever) which dominate the world's activity. The initial premise, which may seem extremely disorienting at first glance, is that formal organizations as we think of them either *do not exist* or are *dysfunctional*. The most useful work is accomplished only through *other* processes for which we now have no accepted explanation or theory. To put it simply, we do not yet know *how* we do useful work. When we discover an explanation or theory—and this book is an attempt to suggest how we might begin—we will apply the same organizational principles to all social structures, from families to corporations to nation-states. All distinctions between public and private, national and international will be erased as we learn that democracy cannot exist anywhere unless it exists everywhere—though in ways we cannot yet completely understand, predict in detail, or design. The reader must be willing to assume that an intellectual leap is at least possible, and that a revised view of the world might conform more closely both to how useful things *are* done and how they *should be* done. The change we seek is, first and foremost, *a different way of seeing things as they are today*. Much of the organizational revolution is invisible because we cannot see it within the intellectual frameworks we use. Thus, change must begin in a way we usually do not think of as change, because everything remains the same except the way we look at it. Later change will follow, of course, but only after this first step. As a starting point for understanding the nature of the intellectual leap, the world of organizations provides two research and operational approaches which seldom are directly compared.

Hierarchical Span of Control Versus the Small Group

In formal organizations, no principle of management remains more significant than "span of control," i.e., the number of subordinates one supervisor can effectively manage. The superior-subordinate relationship is vertical. The superior must evaluate subordinates, moreover, on a periodic basis (often through the use of "efficiency reports"), a system which gives the superior massive leverage, in that his evaluations of subordinates determine who is promoted and who is fired. The precise ratio of subordinates to superiors has never been scientifically determined, but management literature recommends spans of control between three and nine subordinates in most environments, four being considered most desirable. At lower levels of routinized work, spans of control can expand, so it is thought, to about thirty.[3]

Turn quickly now to different research, based upon small-group processes which do not include superior-subordinate relationships. The small group is conventionally defined as one in which each member must receive an impression or perception of each other member that is distinct enough to enable the member to react or give some opinion of each of the others—and to recall later one or more impressions of each of the others.[4] Research into the processes of "action-taking groups" (where decisions are made), subcommittees in legislative bodies which do the toughest detailed work (both in Western and non-Western cultures), experiments with various-sized groups of youngsters, and the observations, of, for example, sociologist Georg Simmel and bureaucratic commentator C. Northcote Parkinson all reach the same conclusion: *the size of effective small groups is precisely the same as that prescribed for vertical spans of control.* It is possible to be almost mystical about the problem of "numbers," in that some of our current organizational problems may be traceable to the shift from "hunting" to "agricultural" societies many centuries ago, and our social hierarchies seem to date from that shift. When people hunted together in bands, their languages seldom had words for numbers over five, which is still the most desirable size for an effective small group. While common sense would seem to dictate that there can be no "magic" number, five appears so often in so many environmental situations as to carry persuasion with it.[5] *

These results come from research shaped by two theories which, by definition, determine the researchers' interpretations of those results. Only the theories and the interpretations differ, *not the results themselves.* Which theory conforms to organizational reality? Do groups produce effective outcomes because one indi-

---

* For reasons not spelled out now, my *feeling* is that the most ideal group is two women and three men.

vidual is armed with authority to direct the work of four subordinates, or because five individuals interact in a nonhierarchical process in which no individual is "boss" of the others? Even two "classical" theorists of administration, Chester Barnard and Lyndall Urwick, were reluctant to use the vertical pattern to describe their experiences. Barnard acknowledged hierarchy on grounds that it was forced upon organizations from without, thus implying it was unnatural, and Urwick surrounded his views on spans of control with explicit caveats which interpreters often overlook.[6] Both seem to have distorted their observations to make them fit conventional wisdom.

Is it possible that the effective conduct of social business occurs *in spite of* hierarchy, not because of it? This should not be too startling a question. Theorists have admitted for years that a principal objective of any permanent organization is its own survival —a finding which holds for corporations, nation-states, and public agencies. Many organizations, in other words, spend their time exacerbating the problems they supposedly want to solve. This is why welfare agencies behave in ways which perpetuate poverty instead of removing it, and why the Federal Bureau of Investigation pours money and people into the Communist party. To ensure survival ("boundary maintenance" in the jargon of administration, "security" in that of the nation-state), hierarchical leaders direct a competitive struggle for resources (corporations for markets, universities and public agencies for funds, armies for territory). This requires that organizational members be kept under strict discipline, through the dispensing of rewards and punishments. This is why organizations use the military stereotype for selecting leaders, searching for "decisive," "hard-nosed," "tough-minded" executives who can "ruthlessly" cut away "deadwood" in the name of effectiveness. Organizations select those who excel at repressing others, place them in positions they cannot handle because reality does not correspond to the theory, and thus operationalize the "Peter Principle."[7] The error lies not in those who select leaders, nor in the leaders themselves, but in the conventional wisdom that both use. The vertical theory, then, explains only how we create problems; in solving them, we use another theory, yet to be articulated in detail, that has the effect of eliminating the typical formal organization as an agent of social purpose.

The "Withering Away" of Organizations

"Withering away" may be a frightening phrase, but no other will quite do. A reanalysis of past trends and an assessment of current ones make it possible to view all effective social interaction through horizontal, rather than vertical, lenses. Conventional organization theory concentrates on the permanent formal organization. But we have entered an era of interdependence in which autonomous organizations, including nation-states, can do little of importance alone, unless one considers the disciplining of employees an achievement. Everything useful is done in cooperation with other organizations and individuals, and in most cases these broader relationships cannot be twisted into superior-subordinate patterns.

The four organizational trends outlined in this chapter can make little sense to anyone who insists upon retaining the notion that only individuals can make decisions. Trends can best be visualized by relating them to the traditional hierarchical pyramid of any typical organization (Figure 1). Sectioning the pyramid into three levels—top management, middle management, and workers/employees—provides a framework for analyzing the trends; most organizations of any consequence are experiencing one or more of them. *Transorganizational processes* cut across permanent organizational boundaries, compelling us to think of "open systems" of action. Within organizations, especially in middle management, activities grouped under the title "Organization Development" (OD) seek the democratization of decision processes. From the outside come *demands from clients, customers, or citizens,* those affected by organizational decisions, for

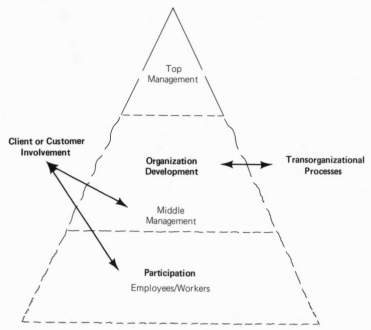

Figure 1: The "Withering Away" of Organizations

involvement in the making of decisions. Finally, an increasing *malaise among low-level employees,* especially assembly-line workers, is forcing *the redesign of industrial technology.*

Taken together, the trends suggest the emergence of a larger overall theory which now focuses on organizations, but inevitably will transform politics and economics. Its most important underlying premise lies in the nexus of *conflict* and *consensus.* Conflict is perceived as a positive stimulus, *provided* it is brought to the surface, confronted, and resolved through the creation of consensus. The best environments for reaching consensus are those in which no individual or group can impose a solution upon others. This violates the ancient conventional wisdom of administration which viewed conflict as dysfunctional and disruptive, but most organization theorists have discarded that view; they now look upon conflict within and between organizations and individuals as the first step toward improvement. In politics and economics, theorists remain behind the times. Even when they speak glibly of "conflict resolution," they do not mean consensus; they refer instead to *conflict-perpetuating* devices such as *majority* rule, the use of *power,* and *increased competition* in a "win-lose" setting. Our conventional approaches to politics and economics are dedicated to *preventing* consensus, which is to say they prevent us from agreeing with each other. Since political and economic theories were derived from a social (or organization) theory of hierarchy, a normal preliminary step is for a revised organization theory of consensus-building to point the way toward newer political and economic theories. Our principal concern, then, is with the *implications* of these organizational trends for our entire political and economic framework—implications which many who are involved in the process of change cannot yet see. We begin with transorganizational processes.

Transorganizational Processes

There is nothing mysterious about the word "transorganizational." It refers to the innumerable occasions when individuals from different organizations or suborganizations work together to solve an existing problem. Policemen and firemen do this all the time, usually in situations not covered by the rules under which they separately work. A consumer affairs bureau or a health department can do little on its own, but together they can do much. At the national level, the same can be said of the Department of Housing and Urban Development and the Department of Health, Education, and Welfare. The effective functions are performed partly inside each separate organization and partly outside, for the cooperative venture is itself a new organization created almost in an instant. The emphasis on the "trans" helps us see that things occur both *through* and *beyond* individual permanent organizations, and that we can no longer visualize each such organization as a closed system. Most practitioners, whether policemen or Cabinet officers, realize instinctively that they cannot accomplish much by themselves or with only the assistance of those directly subordinate to them. All of us were brought up to believe we should make organizational boundaries clear so as to control what is inside them. Now we must get used to the idea that every organization is an open system with ambiguous, fluid, and constantly changing boundaries.[8]

Examples of transorganizational processes are everywhere. Some designs became prominent during the heyday of the U.S. space program, when the National Aeronautics and Space Administration (NASA) was known as the first full-scale collection of postindustrial organizations described by one author as "adaptive, problem-solving, temporary systems of diverse specialists, linked together by coordinating and task-evaluating specialists . . . which replace bureaucracy as we know it." [9] Project and matrix designs came to fill textbooks on organization and, as indicated in Figure 2, the designs only clarified what had been happening in many organizations, not just those involved in advanced technology.

The project manager has a grant of formal authority which legitimizes his need to cut across organizational lines, but this is not the important ingredient. Indeed, the very design vitiates conventional wisdom. It is a classic rule of administration that organizations cannot function with divided authority, but even the simplest matrix model designates two superiors for a single individual. By conventional wisdom's own logic, then, authority cannot be the thrust of the project design; it makes sense only as a nonhierarchical arrangement which includes a range of skills wider than any one person can possess. This tends to make collegiality inevitable, especially if one individual is a member of several such processes. The shift away from rigid, permanent lines to fluid, temporary networks expresses the reality of the functions and interactions in which individuals are engaged. The permanent vertical structure churns out efficiency reports, related more to its view of discipline than to what actually goes on, but it often has little to do with the

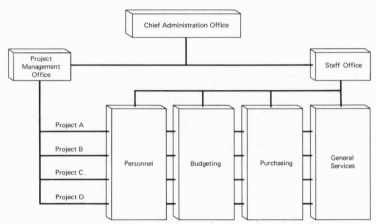

Figure 2: A Simple Model of the Matrix Format

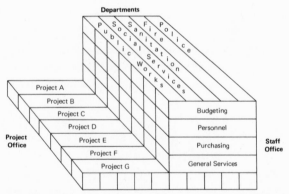

Figure 2A: A More Complex Model of the Matrix Format

Source: H. George Frederickson, *Recovery of Structure in Public Administration* (Washington: Center for Governmental Studies, 1970), p. 10.

work performed. This inevitably produces conflict between the vertical permanent structure and the horizontal temporary one. When a vertical structure resolves conflict by exerting its authority, things usually deteriorate.

Most administrators in government agencies spend their time "clearing" matters with people whom they cannot order around and who cannot order them around. Decisions emerge from a continuous "web of tensions" which sustains "fruitful friction" on a problem-to-problem basis.[10] This occurs within the single large organization, so large that it really is many organizations, but we often talk vaguely about coordination and then forget about it. The same thing happens across organizations, as between the State and Defense Departments, in which a group of persons engaged on an issue at a given moment acts as a temporary problem-solving organization. This would happen just as often in the private sector were it not for our doctrine of competition, which prevents interaction between producers of the same product. Even there, corporations increasingly farm out to each other the performance of specialized functions, thus shifting away from autonomy toward interdependence.[11]

Public and private agencies combine their efforts in urban "enterprises," a term coined a decade ago to describe the processes of urban renewal.[12] The more elaborate "conjoin" is a collaboration of many organizations, often hundreds, to achieve objectives in urban development that no one of them could accomplish alone.[13] The same thing occurs in transnational environments. The "miracle rice" program in the Philippines included two U.S. foundations, the Agency for International Development, and, within the host country, a semiautonomous central bank, rural private banks, a special agency in the President's office, commercial fertilizer companies, the National Agricultural Extension Service, the church, and 4-H groups; no one of these agencies could have been designated as "in command" of the others.[14] An effective process, in this instance one of inestimable benefit to Philippine agriculture, often seems to work almost by accident, for we have no suitable theory to guide us.

That we do not have thousands of documented examples is due to the conventional organizational assumption that the only important actions are those of authoritative decision-makers. We condemn committees as the worst form of organization, failing to note that in so doing we imply that individuals should act only in total isolation from one another—never, never together. Yet just the opposite is true: nothing of any significance can be, or should be, done alone. Committees were one of the first responses to the need to bring people together in groups. They deserve an honored place in the history of organizations, even if we have done our best to ensure they do not work. Herewith is one example of how vertical structures prevent committees from becoming as effective as they might be.

In the mid-1960's the U.S. government formed a transagency (or interagency) committee to begin planning for the air transport agreement later signed by the United States and the Soviet Union. (Pan American now flies regularly to Moscow, and Aeroflot, the Soviet airline, flies to New York.) The committee included members of the Defense Department, the State Department, the Civil Aeronautics Board, the Federal Aviation Administration, and the Commerce Department, among others. They met weekly to develop the positions to be negotiated with the Soviet Union. For some months, however, things remained stalemated because the Defense Department "representative" was ordered each week by his superiors to announce to the committee that any agreement must allow the United States to search within the Soviet Union any time a Pan American jet was overdue or not heard from. Paraphrased, the Defense Department view went like this:

We of the United States cannot rely upon the shoddy air rescue facilities of the Soviet Union. We must be assured we can initiate a search without delay. Because we do not have enough unarmed rescue aircraft to cover the route, the agreement must permit us to send into Soviet airspace, immediately and automatically, all U.S. military aircraft now assigned to our NATO forces in Europe.

Each time this statement was advanced, the other members of the committee would groan aloud and mutter something about the "inflexibility of the military mind," and the meeting would adjourn forthwith. Of course, the Soviets never were asked to agree to such a provision, and the proposal was absurd to begin with, but it stalemated that committee for some time.* But insofar as relationships between committees and their parent organizations are concerned, what is it that makes some committees effective and others ineffective? Experience suggests that committees function in one of three ways:

[1] Committee members form a task force separated from their parent organizations, and work out their own solution to a problem. Given the isolation, the solution comes as a surprise to the organizations, so each committee member must set about selling it to his superiors. By the time this begins, the task force feels committed to its own proposal, but, more to the point, the organizations instantly oppose any proposal which is unexpected. This approach cannot be expected to produce much, primarily because the committee has sealed itself off.

[2] Each committee member functions as an instructed delegate of his organization, much in the manner of a diplomat who cannot speak at an international meeting unless every word has been cleared by his government. With the members thus restricted, their meetings usually lead either to meaningless agreements on insignificant matters or to stalemates on important ones. We refer to the former as "lowest-common-denominator" solutions. As for the latter, the air transport experience was the typical stalemate that can be overcome only by higher-level intervention.

[3] Each member starts out as an instructed delegate, but everyone in the several organizations assumes that interaction within the committee, and between its members and the organizations,

---

* Then a military officer, I was directed by my civilian superiors to take this position. Numerous attempts to secure different instructions were to no avail.

will evolve into a solution acceptable to all. Consensus emerges principally because many individuals and suborganizations are involved, but it emerges so gradually that its significance often goes unnoticed. Furthermore, most of us are conditioned to believe that we should begin a committee meeting with the idea of winning out over other organizations, thereby improving our status. Yet consensus, which often produces outcomes different from, and better than, all those initially proposed by the separate organizations, is the only approach that makes sense.

This third outcome seldom occurs—not only because departments give strict instructions to their delegates, but also because we insist upon structuring committees along hierarchical lines. The common practice is to designate one member as chairman and to cast him in the role of an authoritative decision-maker whose choices are binding upon all organizations represented on the committee. Other members feel compelled to resist, inferring that to accept the chairman's decisions is to acknowledge the subordination of their organizations to his. No organization, especially a Cabinet department, willingly subordinates itself to another, yet conventional wisdom insists that a committee cannot proceed unless someone is in charge of it.

For committee processes which do work—and a number of them do, even in government—the logic of the process is signifi-

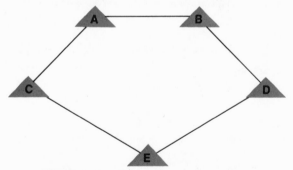

Figure 3: The Transagency Committee

cant.[15] Any such committee, task force, or whatever, can be charted as in Figure 3).

Assume officials A through E are members of organizations A through E and are designated as members of the committee. Each person actually belongs to at least six organizations: the one to which he is permanently assigned, the four other permanent organizations, and the committee. Interactions within the committee enable each individual to directly influence all six organizations.

Assuming that, whatever the outcome, it causes something to happen within organization E, individual A is part of the *internal* processes of that organization; the same can be said of individuals B through D. Officials A through D, in other words, are temporary members of organization E without being in its chain of command. Assuming still further that the outcome will have some effect upon society, this involvement is *political* in character. As transorganizational processes expand, and they inevitably will, one thing should become obvious: to allow "outsiders" to influence what goes on in an organization, while refusing to allow "insiders" to do more than obey orders, is to deny the insiders a *political right of involvement as important as any now in the Bill of Rights.* Such denial will be seen (as many see it now without being able to articulate it) as discriminatory and active repression, which cries out for new theory and new practice. The point may be emphasized that modern organizations cannot function without this organizational activity, but the activity cannot be carried on according to conventional wisdom. Only a theory of nonhierarchy can accommodate it.

It follows that a transorganizational process is likely to be effective only when the committee chairman's role is one of facilitation—*not* one of personal responsibility for, and authority over, outcomes. This suggests a law for such processes, which turns conventional wisdom inside out: *The effectiveness of group processes is inversely proportional to the amount of formal decision authority assigned to chairmen; the less the authority assigned an individual chairman, the more likely an effective outcome.*[16]

This does not imply that chairmen cannot be or should not be responsible for outcomes; they can be, indeed, and they should be, but the same can be said for all other members. The individualistic perspective thus gives way to a collective one which assumes that each individual makes, or can make, a unique contribution to the small-group outcome. Foreshadowing the arguments in the remainder of this book, there are and can be no exceptions to this law—not for presidents, governors, generals, or university presidents. Achieving effective outcomes requires *collective responsibility,* and further requires that we pay attention to the number of individuals involved in each group—something for which the literature on span of control and small groups provides broad guidelines. If a problem requires the involvement of many individuals from many organizations, we must create enough groups to keep each one small enough to be effective. Groups can then be linked together through overlapping memberships. The skills required of chairmen, of those holding overlapping memberships, and indeed of all members are not the skills of giving and carrying out orders; they are the skills associated with a second trend which, at the moment, focuses on the internal workings of permanent organizations.

Organization Development (OD)

OD is a social movement, or a passing fad that cannot last much longer, or an important profession, depending upon one's perspective. At its best, it may already have given us a fundamental addition to our repertoire of skills and knowledge about the behavior of organizations and the individuals within them. Those who consider themselves leaders of the movement cite impressive statistics: a "network" of consultants and practitioners numbers 400, and a "division" of the American Society for Training and Development includes 750.[17] As in the case of transorganizational processes, a high-sounding title—OD—masks activities well known to many people in organizations, especially middle-level executives. They are the ones who dash around the country at company expense to participate in "group experiments," "experiences," or "laboratories," variously labeled as "sensitivity training," "encounter groups," "T-groups," or "executive development." Alternatively, they attend "training" sessions on company premises and company time. One approach involves "stranger groups" (made up of persons who have not met each other before coming together in the group experience, and who may never meet again). Another leads to "family groups" (persons who work together within the organization and who will continue to do so). These distinctions are important to the controversies that surround the OD phenomenon, and they come up later in this discussion. Our first interest lies in why corporations spend their money on this activity, and what is likely to happen as a result.

In ruminating aloud about the executives who attend his sessions, one associate of the National Training Laboratories, the leading provider of such programs, observes:

Competition and status is [sic] bred into these men, and we try to show them there's a different way. They come here as managers who are also people, and hopefully they leave as managers in search of the people they are.[18]

If the individuals seek to discover themselves, any organization that pays for the experience is seeking its own improvement or "development." If the objectives are not always compatible—and they seldom are in most organizations—the very attendance of these persons means that they and their organizations agree that *something* is wrong and that the experience, if it does not completely "cure" that something, may at least alleviate it. That something, mutually recognized if not always articulated, is the malaise of our society so often described as *alienation* from our *selves,* our *work,* and *others.* In words that parallel a simplistic version of Karl Marx's definition of alienation, one observer of training programs finds himself startled to discover that corporate executives in group experiences almost never talk about the products their organizations sell, nor do they think of themselves as individuals who assist in the manufacture of those products.[19] Humans, in other words, find themselves separated from what they produce at work and see themselves only as "roles" or "functions." This attitude cannot be overcome so long as we retain our current theories of politics, economics, and organizations. (The deeper wellsprings of alienation are explored in Chapter 2.) But for now, how does OD attempt to remove alienation?

OD is oriented to *process;* it stresses interpersonal competence, collaboration, teamwork, and group dynamic skills. It seeks to instill humanistic value systems in work units in the hope that open and authentic personal relationships will improve the persons involved as well as their organizations.[20] The immediate objective is an organizational environment in which decision-making is democratized through sharing of authority and responsibility in group processes.[21] This can happen, so it is thought, in one or more of these ways: (1) Executives go to "stranger group" sessions, then return as "change agents" who disseminate what they have learned. (2) Executives come together in "family groups" and, with the assistance of a "training leader," are transformed as a group. (3) The OD practitioner, who brings with him the skills and techniques acquired from a background in industrial psychology, consulting experience, and counseling, is inserted as the "change agent" into the mainstream of the organization itself. Or (4) the same practitioner performs as a consultant who diagnoses and recommends. All these activities follow two paths which, if related, are nonetheless different, for they involve the individual and the organization.

On the individual side, OD is an outgrowth of the late Abraham Maslow's humanistic psychology and his efforts to help individuals achieve "self-actualization." In his "hierarchy of needs" theory, Maslow concluded that once the requirements of hunger, thirst, sex, and safety were satisfied, people would be ready to search for "belongingness," "esteem," and "self-actualization" (shorthand for becoming all they are capable of becoming). As Maslow described self-actualized people, and he did it in a very personal way by nominating specific individuals who conformed to his definitions, he noted that all of them, *without exception,* were "involved in a cause outside their own skin, in something outside of themselves . . . something . . . very precious to them—some calling or vocation." [22] While our traditions encourage us to seek self-fulfillment apart from our work, Maslow directly related the *self* and *work,* and even though he saw the individual as the unit of psychological improvement, his attempt to remove the boundaries between a person and his work was an attack upon alienation.

As psychologists have tended to get involved in group therapy and related undertakings, so has the OD movement increasingly tended to emphasize the "team" or "work group" rather than the individual. If executives who attend sensitivity training programs engage in a form of group therapy, other OD efforts focus on the redesigning or revisualizing of decision processes within organizations. Some efforts are small in scale, as when an OD consultant intervenes in a process involving only a few people, if only to assist in overcoming interpersonal problems that individuals cannot recognize. The more elaborate efforts involve extensive research, and have led to far-reaching proposals for the redesign of entire organizations. The intellectual leader here is Rensis Likert, who sees a range of possible management "styles" from *System 1* (exploitative-authoritative), through *System 2* (benevolent-authoritative), and *System 3* (consultative), to *System 4* (participative). He makes a convincing case that organizations become increasingly effective as they progress from 1 toward 4—a system which relies upon supportive relationships (individuals see that their experiences are building and maintaining a sense of personal worth), group decision-making (through conflict-resolving consensus), and high performance goals (productivity). To operationalize System 4, one must consciously create a network of interlocking, interde-

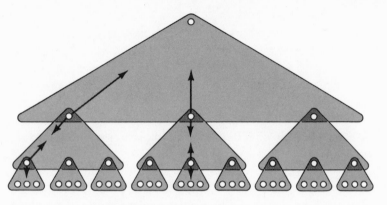

(The arrows indicate the linking-pin function)

Figure 4: The linking pin (*From Rensis Likert. New patterns of management. New York: McGraw-Hill Book Company, 1961. By permission of the publishers.*)

pendent, overlapping work groups, as in Likert's simplest design (Figure 4). Each shaded area outlines a work group, and the "linking pins" are individuals whose overlapping memberships keep groups synchronized.

The Likert design attempts to transform vertical span-of-control relationships into a network of nonhierarchical small groups. In his more elaborate designs, all "informal" and "coordinating" relationships are spelled out in detail. This erases distinctions between formal and informal,* and it attempts to account for all interactions which affect organizational outcomes. Any such contact is a part of Likert's scheme. The design thus includes two types of group processes. One combines a superior and his subordinates, as in the chart; the second brings together those who deal with one another but have no "chain of command" relationships.[23]

---

* The idea of informal organization was forced upon us by traditional theory, but it otherwise made little sense. Any individual interacting with another who was neither his superior nor his subordinate was thought to be part of an "informal" relationship. Since most human interaction is of this sort, that theory explained only a very small part of what went on.

Many of the transorganizational relationships mentioned earlier, however, remain invisible because we are not used to searching for them. Thus OD focuses primarily on democratizing the vertical structure, and this is both a strength and a weakness of the OD movement. If every group made up of one superior and three to five subordinates were transformed into a problem-solving process in which no individual could ever exercise authority over the others, that would conform in part to what is argued in this book. The fact that OD practitioners work within the system as we see it, however, raises practical difficulties, theoretical problems, and potential dangers worth spelling out:

[1] If everything useful is done in ways other than through formal hierarchical relationships, OD may harm important transorganizational processes. When it succeeds in sensitizing superiors and subordinates to each other within a single organization, the distance between those individuals and "outsiders" is increased, especially those with whom they are involved in transorganizational processes.[24]

[2] In part because of its intellectual origins, advocates of OD attempt to reconcile their efforts with pyramidal models of organization. Maslow defined self-actualization and success in conventional terms, arguing that self-actualized people are superior people who should become leaders of all the others. He assumed that competition would bring out the best, not the worst, in people. He seemed not to notice that the individuals who met his criteria were public officials, artists, and intellectuals for the most part (not businessmen), even if he did observe that complete self-actualization seems to emerge at an advanced age (sixty-five, when persons have no further need to compete).[25] *We must, in other words, search for something better than Maslow.* Where groups are concerned, OD's roots are in the "human relations" school of management which began with the Hawthorne experiments at the Western Electric Company in the late 1920's and 1930's. The company, as well as researchers from Harvard, was interested in relationships between productivity and the work environment.

There was no interest in democratizing factories, only in finding out how to meet objectives set by corporate hierarchies.[26] Most human relations and motivation theories have sought to manipulate workers and middle managers, and they have been validly criticized on those grounds. OD, despite the excitement surrounding it, remains open to the charge that it, too, seeks only to manipulate. Even Rensis Likert, dedicated to making vertical groups more horizontal, insists that "the superior is accountable for all decisions, for their execution, and for the results," and hence is free to impose his decision upon the group whenever he thinks it necessary.[27] *We must also move beyond Likert.* The extent of the potential danger can best be understood by recalling the close ties between OD and individual or group therapy. When hierarchy and intensive psychological involvement are combined, it becomes relatively easy to advance from manipulation to out-and-out brainwashing (without realizing it).[28]

[3] Some OD efforts make this all too clear by crossing a frightening line. Where OD techniques usually put a group of people under stress, then encourage them to cooperate in solving their problems, some organizations create the same situations in order to evaluate competing candidates for promotion. Those who want to advance must troop into an "assessment center" where they know that only a few in the group will "succeed" and be promoted. All of them are subjected to long hours of stress (perhaps an unbroken twenty-four hours), during which "assessment experts" choose among them. The atmosphere resembles the training establishments used during World War II by the Office of Strategic Services; the objective then was to discover the most likely nominees for parachuting behind enemy lines and committing sabotage.[29] Perhaps today's activist corporate hierarchy, engaged in its own struggle for survival, feels compelled to search for this type of effectiveness. Assessment centers hardly encourage openness, for one individual cannot trust another who, by the rules of the game, must attempt to destroy him. Within a hierarchical structure, then, the techniques of OD *can* be antithetical to the

professed objectives of most OD practitioners. Instead of discovering himself, a person finds out only what makes him "break."

[4] Even when OD programs make every effort to change organizational behavior, the norms of hierarchy tend to offset any gains. Some practitioners, for example, contend that while all the executives of a given corporation benefit from OD training, those who work together should not train together, because the togetherness of the training experience will undercut the "social distance" which (in their view) must be maintained within permanent organizations.[30] This is an understandable argument. Certainly, when a superior and his subordinates return to the organization, the subordinates know they must resume competing against each other for the favors of the superior, and he knows he must continue writing the efficiency reports that make or break them. And so the necessity to compete for survival erases the cooperative relationships engendered by the training.[31]

[5] While some federal agencies have financed OD programs for middle-level administrators, and the government has provided the same thing for foreign administrators (through contracts with outside institutions), the notion of training elected leaders and their appointed administrators raises important questions. Political leaders cannot admit they make decisions collectively with their administrative subordinates, nor are many of them willing to admit they may need training. In the only reported example of its kind, one OD practitioner conducted a "team-development" program for members of the Kansas City, Missouri, city council. The program included confidential interviews followed by a "retreat," where the interview information was discussed with council members. One of them, refusing to participate, condemned the whole thing as insulting. This councilwoman saw no reason to substitute consultation with a psychologist for "conferring and meeting people in the district." [32] Thus the OD version of democratic decision-making may not square with what we call "democratic" government, a problem that is the focus of the following chapter. For the moment we are concerned with one emerging

phenomenon in the public sector which resembles OD and which is making headway in some urban communities.

Citizen Participation and the "Charrette"

Participation disorients many of the elite managers who dominate organizational systems. It means they must face demands from lower-class citizens whose capabilities they have denigrated for years. When this occurs, the elites argue that involvement is dangerous because the outsiders are not well enough educated to deal with the expert professionals who make day-to-day decisions. For other elites who face demands from affluent suburbanites and sophisticated college students, the same arguments do not apply. In these cases, the elites insist that they are the only ones with legal authority to make decisions. Both arguments make them uncomfortable. Either they must stress their own inherent superiority or tell citizens that what happens to them or their children is none of their business, even if those citizens are, by conventional wisdom's own standards, as qualified as the professionals. Having no consistent argument to advance, the elites feel trapped within a theory from which they see no escape. Meanwhile, the trend toward involvement has advanced far beyond the "maximum feasible participation" of the 1960's, which turned into an old-fashioned power struggle; those in authority defined participation as something that would destroy them, and those on the outside did indeed seek control. Only after intense discomfort on all sides has it become clear that the issue is not a *transfer* of authority but a *sharing* of it.[33] This shift has not been a noisy one, but it is revolutionary, and it is happening in countless organizations. Here is one black principal's description of how he manages an elementary school:

. . . The secret . . . is not to get upset about the power struggle. The old-line principals are fighting like mad because the parents want some power. You see, I don't care, quite frankly. I really don't. . . . There are certain decisions that have to be made. I can share the decision-making process with all the people who want power. I would do it anyway. I want to know what the parents feel. I feel it's essential that teachers tell me how they feel. . . . The PTA president recently came in and told me she had just hired someone. I said, "Fine, who did you hire?" Well, the thing is she can't hire anybody. But she had somebody she wanted me to hire, and it was a good person . . . an aide . . . and we needed one. The old-line principals would have got uptight and started a long discussion about how you can't hire her, how dare you, and all of this kind of thing. But the new-style principal has to share all this power. . . . You have all these various elements to deal with, and you have to get them to cooperate with one another, and you have to share power with them. Everyone is jealous of what everyone else is doing, and you've got to move and circulate and get the whole thing working. If you're going to be uptight about power, then you're going to be in trouble.[34]

The "charrette" is the best example we have yet. A word used to describe horse-drawn carts which carried prisoners to the guillotine, and also the carts used later to gather up the plans the Beaux Arts architectural students submitted for the annual Paris competition, "charrette" has acquired a new meaning for school and other forms of community planning. In contemporary settings, the charrette is a process vehicle (without wheels), systematically constructed to collect and sort out as many ideas as possible generated by individuals directly interested in a given project. In Brooklyn, residents, community organizations, consulting architects and educators, university students, and neighborhood schoolchildren (180 people at one time) came together in a several-month-long process which designed an educational center for 10,000 students, and for others as well, by arranging that a school cafeteria become a community restaurant at night.[35] A similar process in Toronto produced a new school in the downtown area with a rooftop playground and a community dental clinic staffed by University of Toronto dental students.[36] The Department of Housing and Urban Development has financed a number of charrettes, knowing in advance that they may not succeed.[37]

The only known way to begin is to assemble in one place, say a large auditorium or arena, people whose perspectives encompass the major conflicts within a community. These may include ghetto residents, policemen and police chiefs, elected and appointed public officials, professional civil servants, affluent suburbanites, businessmen, and others. All they have in common when they begin is a temporary agreement that there is a problem to be solved, that they want to explore it, and that they will bring in professional process-facilitators.[38] If the process survives an initial period of intense hostility, subcommittees are formed, consultants are attached to each one, and interaction is continued. Each group is structured to include persons whose interests are diametrically opposed. Periodic progress is reported to the entire body, or to the steering committee, so that conflicts between subcommittees can be worked out. Individuals move back and forth between groups until they find the one of greatest concern to them, or until they decide to leave.

The charrette combines certain features of the OD movement which seldom are brought together. Each subcommittee is a "stranger group," in that its members may not have met before; yet individuals enter each group with reasonably well-defined perspectives on their own roles and on the problems. In this sense, they are a "family group," but one in which a formal pattern of hierarchy could not be designed even if someone attempted to do so. While personal growth can be a by-product, the objective is to solve community problems. The facilitator can add yet other dimensions. He must be conscious of subcommittee tasks and linkages between subcommittees, finances, relations with news media, and even the types of buildings needed (churches are out because people are reluctant to vent their anger there). He becomes a System 4 manager, one who must be well versed in group dynamics and sensitivity skills, one who can cope with an environment more fluid and unsettling than the kind faced by the usual OD consultant.

The mechanics of the charrette directly contradict conventional politics. Those who come together are, at the beginning, the typically large and competing power groups we associate with politics. The assumption behind the charrette is that it is nonsense to have the large groups continue their struggle until some win and others lose. Intentional fragmentation of large groups and the creation of heterogeneous small groups become initial steps toward progress. The ghetto black and the white suburbanite search together for the identity of their "new" group. The charrette places its faith in round-the-clock, operational sensitivity sessions which give everyone, not simply the leaders of monolithic groups, an opportunity to contribute:

Citizens who attend the charrette have gone through three basic facets of group dynamics. At the beginning of the charrette they purge themselves of as many emotional hangups as possible to adequately communicate with one another. They have moved from that process to the process of individual role definition, proceeding to build alliances with people who were previously complete strangers. Within these alliances are found new strengths to deal with the neighborhood or community problems.[39]

Decision-makers learn much about themselves and their effects upon others:

A decision-maker participating in charrette proceedings finds himself in an unprecedented position. He is on grounds he did not create and responding on a level never before considered . . . that of direct confrontation on any given matter and unable to employ any method of coercion previously used as favorite tools. The decision-maker receives a first-hand appraisal of his leadership capabilities as viewed by the community and must reevaluate his own position.[40]

In a different way, ghetto blacks and poor whites view a world previously kept from them:

The groups I have worked with have experienced a resounding change in attitudes when black brothers and sisters feel that maybe, for the first time, they have an opportunity to plan their own lives.[41]

If citizens are apathetic about conventional political participation, this cannot be said of the charrette, or of other participatory forms as well. Once people become convinced that an opportunity is genuine, there is more response than can be handled.[42] Sixty-two community planning boards, first appointed in New York City in 1963 and 1964, now must be notified by the City Planning Commission before important decisions are made which affect their areas; while only advisory, they show signs of increasing vitality.[43] Some laws require consumer involvement in comprehensive health-planning programs, and consumers have had much to do with the organization of neighborhood health centers.* The participatory framework for national health programs is bound to be a major issue when further legislation is passed.[44] The drive for consumer involvement in corporate decisions and the attempts of priests and nuns to gain a voice in church affairs are only two examples of the trends which cannot be detailed here. Nor are military organizations immune to these trends.[45]

Regrettably, even those who shout the loudest in praise of charrettes assume that such processes are, and must remain, temporary undertakings. Once an agreed plan is developed, the assumption is that the charrette should be disbanded and the "official" government should get on with implementation. In Toronto, where the city's director of education has predicted that "never again will the Board of Education build a neighbourhood school without the active involvement and participation of the neighbourhood residents," [46] there is no evidence that charrette supporters see the process as a quasi-official addition to the formal structure of government. Yet it seems obvious that no plan ever can be implemented precisely as written, and that changes in a plan should be "fed back" and worked out with those who developed it in the first place. Therefore the charrette which is abandoned at this early stage can become only another temporarily satisfying "expe-

* A consumer can be defined as anyone who does not earn a living in the health field and this, unfortunately, can be used to *include* the chairman of a hospital's board of trustees while *excluding* others.

rience" which, over time, leads to long-term disillusion. Once again, the problem is in the way we look at things. If we can visualize a charrette sound enough and strong enough to develop a workable plan, we ought to be able to regard it as an ongoing process which sees things through. To get to that point, however, we will first have to examine our theories of political government.

Worker and Employee Participation

Solving this problem will require changes in technology as well as in collective bargaining, but a promising trend is under way, at least in the former. The Hawthorne experiments provide the background for understanding this new trend. They began with an assumption that if plant illumination were increased to some optimum point, productivity would increase, and that if illumination were decreased, productivity would fall off. This seemed only common sense, but it did not turn out that way. Changes in productivity bore no relation to lighting changes: productivity was maintained even when workers could scarcely see what they were doing. A confused Western Electric joined with Harvard University, this time to experiment with all sorts of variations, among them rest pauses of different lengths and frequencies, lunches in midmorning, shorter working days, and shorter working weeks. After manipulating conditions for two years and carefully studying the results, the researchers still could not discover relationships between their manipulations and productivity. They finally concluded that productivity increases were *not* due to the effect of rest periods upon workers' fatigue, to a relief from monotony by virtue of the experiment itself, to changes in the piece-rate system, or to superior working conditions in the relay assembly test room. Despite an exceedingly tedious job (each worker assembled five hundred relays daily), absenteeism decreased by 80 per cent during the experiment, and workers became round-the-clock friends.
   The more widely known bank wiring room experiment then fol-

lowed, because the researchers were eager to prove *something*. The outcomes of this second experiment became staples of sociological literature:

1. Levels of production are set by informal social norms.
2. Noneconomic rewards and sanctions do affect workers' behavior: those who produce more or less than the norms tend to lose their colleagues' respect.
3. Workers do not act or react as individuals, but as members of groups.[47]

Paul Blumberg's reanalysis [48] of the relay test room experiment demonstrates how conventional analysts made a fundamental error which they repeated again and again in a quarter-century of textbook writing. They assumed that the reason for the high morale and productivity of the first experiment had been an informal network of interpersonal relations among the workers, which increased productivity instead of lowering it. Blumberg's reanalysis shows that in the six-worker relay test room experiment every change—in work days, work weeks, meal schedules, and rest periods—was made by the researchers *in agreement with the workers themselves,* because the researchers did not want to antagonize the workers. The theory the researchers used did not enable them to realize that they transformed the six workers into a self-managing, collegial small group in which no single individual was in charge. Their theory, in other words, *prevented* them from seeing what they had done. Only the second experiment (bank wiring room) provided them with evidence to fit the conclusions they had reached before they began.*

But even Blumberg may have missed the most important evidence in the second experiment. Here the group was much larger (fourteen), and it was subdivided by status and wages into three smaller groups (wiremen, soldermen, inspectors).[49] Both the size

* Blumberg's effort demonstrates the importance of looking again at older research in the light of new or different theories. "Participation" and "involvement" did not enter anyone's mind in the 1920's or 1930's.

of the group and the subdivisions would have made it practically impossible for a collegial atmosphere to emerge, and it did not. By the very definition of the experiment itself, the fourteen workers could not have come to share responsibility and authority. The Hawthorne experiments, in retrospect, bear out precisely the evidence from both span-of-control and small-group experience. Even today, those now involved in the trend toward industrial redesign do not realize they are using the same-sized groups that functioned best at Hawthorne.

The trend in various countries is to replace assembly lines with partly autonomous small groups which perform as teams whose members rotate from one task to another. The groups plan their own work, time schedules, and objectives, and they do their own recruiting. The Saab-Scandia Corporation has a new plant in Sweden which has abandoned the assembly line; the makers of Volvo automobiles are attempting to abandon the line. Several plants in Norway are being organized in similar fashion, and in the United States at least one food-processing plant and a paper products plant have been so designed. In the paper products plant, a training consultant has prepared a confidential summary of what happens when groups are exposed to low-intensity training and when team leaders or foremen train workers to get along without them. One outcome is the same increase in workers' morale and socializing that marked the first Hawthorne experiment.[50] *

It seems contradictory to deal secretively with a trend which seeks to "open up" work processes but, given today's situation, those involved have reason to be careful. If conservative managers look with suspicion at nonhierarchical forms of management, organized labor must also feel threatened. If work groups, and small ones at that, set standards, schedules, and recruitment policies, important tasks of union leaders and negotiators will disappear. Indeed, big labor in the United States has traditionally argued

* Had the initial Hawthorne experiments been correctly interpreted, we would have discovered that collective bargaining between "big" labor and "big" business is a step backward.

against any sort of "worker participation" in management, and it feels uncomfortable with this aspect of current trends.[51] Management and labor, however, are being pushed inexorably in that direction, for the boredom and alienation associated with assembly lines are too pronounced to ignore. If some corporate executives indulge themselves in three-martini luncheons which make them impervious to the frustrations of the afternoon, so do assembly-line workers gulp quarts of wine on their lunch break because they don't even want to realize where they are on the second half of their shift. Big labor has yet another problem here.

If work can be made satisfying to the individual worker, increases in productivity may follow. Labor unions argue, however, that unless increases in productivity lead to wage increases, workers are being exploited. But raising wages simply reminds workers that they work only for economic sustenance, not for personal fulfillment; thus alienation is reinforced and the humanistic gains of participation are wiped out. Worker participation makes sense from almost any perspective, and in both industrial and nonindustrial enterprises. If the objective is to increase productivity, participation helps; if the objective is to improve quality, participation helps; if the objective is to transform work into something which does not alienate the individual performing it, participation helps. Economic rewards and general working conditions, the goals of collective bargaining up to now, pale in significance when placed alongside participation. This is nothing new; students of organization have known for years that economic rewards are no answer, and they have so reported, but our dominant theory says otherwise. Instead of using the evidence to construct new theories, we attempt to live with the contradictions, and managers and labor leaders become inadvertent allies in the repression of workers. We must at least face the possibility that to *tie wages to productivity, and perhaps to tie income to employment, is to perpetuate alienation*. On this issue, more later.

If worker participation is to make any sense, it will have to be accompanied by the widespread reshaping of factories themselves.

Among those now involved in the reshaping, the term "socio-technical" is used to describe the combination of factors that must be taken into account. Any scheme of participation that does not redesign the work environment to emphasize the interactive small group really is not worthy of the name; yet most forms of participation—whether called "codetermination," "joint consultation," "self-management," or something else—do not deal with the structure of factories and assembly lines themselves.[52] This is because those who, with the best of intentions, seek to help workers do not realize that conventional approaches (e.g., electing workers to serve on governing bodies) have nothing to do with meaningful democratization. This issue will reappear in Chapter 2's analysis of politics and Chapter 3's discussion of economics, especially the Yugoslav experiment.

A New Definition for Citizenship

All of these trends, and perhaps others we cannot yet see, are indispensable to each other, for each tends to fill in the gaps and resolve the contradictions of the others. Transorganizational processes enable individuals to influence what goes on within organizations other than those to which they permanently "belong," but this does nothing for individuals who work totally *within* a single organization. OD seeks to democratize decision processes within organizations, where the formal barriers of hierarchy remain strongest. Both of these approaches, however, concentrate on middle-level professional executives, to the neglect of both lower-level employees and citizens on the outside who are affected by organizational decisions. If no one trend solves anything by itself, all of them together do offer considerable promise. While a number of metaphors might be used to describe what is happening, "withering away" remains most persuasive. If the trends expand, the walls of organizational pyramids will crumble and the permanent organizations we know now will vanish. Status differences between managers and employees, producers and consumers, professionals and citizens, will begin to disappear along with the pyramids. After all, the pyramids are only artifacts created by our theory and, as such, they will vanish if the theory does. To focus on the professional-citizen dichotomy is to illustrate how this might happen.

The professional administrator in a public agency owes his status to his two roles—as an individual placed where he is by a hierarchy which tells him what to do, and as a member of a group of people who possess recognized skills. In both roles he is perceived, and he perceives himself, as standing "above" those affected by the decisions he makes. If, on the other hand, he is perceived, and perceives himself, as an individual who brings his skills to bear on the problem but whose skills give him no authority to impose his solution upon the citizens with whom he deals, the hierarchical distinction vanishes. This makes it possible for professionals and citizens to realize that the latter bring important skills with them also, primarily an understanding of how decisions are likely to affect them. It is difficult to accept the notion that the collective outcome is likely to be better than any that an individual could produce alone, and it is just as difficult to become accustomed to the idea that outcomes improve as processes become more nonhierarchical. Yet it is increasingly known that as members of a group "experience" each other more and more, they develop more effective ways of dealing with internal conflict, and they become more effective at decision-making.[53]

Both administrators and citizens (and superiors and subordinates in any organization) will have to become "professional citizens," for the creative act of building a consensus can be defined as the *primary act of citizenship* for each individual, wherever he or she is *now*—in schools, families, corporations, public agencies —or wherever affected by the decisions of one or more of them. The driving thrusts of such a definition are face-to-face interaction, small group processes, multiple or overlapping memberships, and a combination of collective and individual responsibility for outcomes. Any consensus-building or problem-solving process should include such steps as these: identifying the problem, defining criteria for a satisfactory solution, listing as many alternative solutions as possible, gathering whatever data are needed to evaluate each alternative, conducting the evaluation, selecting the solution which best meets the criteria, and checking that solution against the problem itself.* To the typically impatient U.S. administrator, making certain that every member is a party to a consensus at every step of the sequence seems a frustrating, laborious, and time-wasting way of doing things, but there is another way of looking at such processes.

We commonly assume that participative processes would add substantially to the cost of government, if only because of the extra time required. But it can be argued that before long all of us will recognize that participative decisions can be uniquely "cost effective"—to use a favorite phrase of recent years. One of the major problems in the United States is that a great many decisions are made solely to overcome the unintended consequences of earlier decisions; i.e., only when an attempt is made to implement certain decisions is it discovered that something prevents their being implemented, something the decision-makers did not know when they decided what to do. Most of the time, the unintended consequences affect individuals and groups who were not consulted before decisions were made. There could be no better way of discovering as many such problems as possible than to include in decision processes those individuals most likely to be affected by them. Although this would slow down the processes, it would produce more effective decisions which, because hidden consequences had been discovered in advance, would become cost-effective through *cost avoidance*. For those addicted to more scientific decision-making approaches, this possibility is easily testable

* This should not be construed as an argument that a rigid checklist can be used to solve every problem. All it can do is provide some guidelines for inserting some discipline into the process. Learning how to interact without relying upon authority remains more important.

through empirical research.[54] Even more important, if the individual's involvement is the highest act of citizenship, it follows that *to deprive the individual of such involvement is to remove his or her political franchise.* There is little doubt that virtually every decision in every social process can be defined as a political decision, for there are few decisions which do not bear upon the future of society as a whole.[55] Perhaps the most operational model is the one the Japanese use, even if it remains substantially hierarchical.*

To the Japanese, "the important element in decision-making is defining the question," [56] an observation that reinforces the significance of the first step in the consensus-building sequence outlined above (page 39). The crux of the Japanese approach is the notion that the only things of ultimate importance are the action and behavior which follow from the decision. This makes it crucial to spend considerable time deciding whether a decision is needed and what the decision should be about. Once that idea is grasped, nobody need be in a hurry to speculate about the precise shape of the answer. This makes it possible for everyone to avoid taking sides and setting up a win-lose confrontation. The method seems cumbersome, for it involves many people in decision-making; to Westerners who must negotiate corporate or other agreements, it seems redundant in that they find themselves interacting with different groups of Japanese over a long period of time, thus making Japanese involvement seem indifferent or disorganized. On the contrary, by exposing several groups to the problem, the Japanese demonstrate their interest in making certain everyone is involved. Furthermore, they demonstrate their seriousness. They would not spend all that time and effort if they thought a decision unimportant. By the same token, the cumbersomeness of the method forces them to make truly big decisions, for the system is too complex to be wasted on trivia. We in the United States, conversely, are more experienced in making large numbers of unimportant decisions.

* The Japanese system has some characteristics of paternalism, or feudalism, a problem taken up in Chapter 2.

When Japanese groups finally reach agreement with their Western counterparts, the differences become manifest. Nobody on the Japanese side remains to be "sold," for all of them are already part of the consensus. The Westerners, on the other hand, must now *begin* "selling" the plan to their organizations. At the moment of agreement, then, the Japanese are prepared to move, and quickly, while their Western counterparts are not. In the West, moreover, one reason so many people resist the "selling" is that they were excluded to begin with. This is not to argue that the Japanese never make mistakes. The attack on Pearl Harbor is a case in point, even if it was made when Japanese processes were more closed than they are now. Nevertheless, the Japanese rarely produce the "right answer to the wrong problem."

To suggest that citizenship itself consists, or should consist, of an individual's involvement in decision processes—and to add that the governance of organizations is best visualized as a series of group processes in which no individual is identified as "in charge" of any process—is to begin to come to grips with the enormity of the intellectual obstacles which inhibit the full flowering of the organizational revolution. People everywhere are trying to make organizations more attractive to those who work in them, to remove the alienation which affects all of us, and to behave in more humane fashion toward each other. That they have yet to succeed is because none of us completely understands how much change is needed in the way we look at things. The unfortunate probability is that the fundamental causes of our alienation from our work and from each other are deeply imbedded in our theories of political government and economic activity.

Those described as "administrators" of public agencies are supposed to "take orders" from elected political leaders who must, in turn, worry about their survival as leaders and the survival of their political systems. Leaders of nation-states do not interact extensively except in crisis, and then only when they are allies. We accepted without question an intricate Anglo-American transnational management structure during World War II, but today we would consider the same arrangement an infringement upon our sovereignty. Nation-states which are enemies, or potential enemies, interact hardly at all until it is time for one to surrender to the other. This has been a common problem of international politics, the classic example being the grotesque scenario which launched World War I. Those who manufacture products for sale must compete against each other in a marketplace where it is agreed from the beginning that some producers (and their employees) must fail while others succeed. As with the nation-state, the only test is survival at whatever cost to organization members (or anyone else, for that matter); this requires that everyone "unite" behind corporate leaders in the struggle for "victory."

All this is changing, and at a more rapid rate than we can now see. The Washington-Moscow communications link, which we hope will prevent thermonuclear disaster, appears to be only a first step toward regularized interaction among leaders of nation-states which heretofore presumed themselves enemies. The heating up of the Cold War in the 1960's seems in retrospect only a temporary setback to an interaction already underway before that time. This trend, which follows the pattern of the organizational revolution, is far more significant than the supposed inability of the United Nations to become a powerful force in the world. It can, in time, become a facilitative mechanism, but we have become too accustomed to hoping it would be the equivalent of a world government (provided it would run things the way *we* wanted them run). The economic growth crisis will lead before long to similarly regularized interaction among the managers of large enterprises, and on a global basis; we will regard it nonsensical that producers of the same product should remain prohibited from talking with each other. This does not mean, of course, that we will continue to look upon such organizations as wholly private.

The emphasis in today's organizational revolution centers on middle managers, workers and employees, and those who are outside organizations (customers and citizens) but who are affected by them. Little has been said of top managers or elected political leaders, except to note how deeply they are affected by the notion that the organizations entrusted to their care must survive. Contrary to what we often think, they are more trapped within the rigidities of chain-of-command principles than everyone else. It has not been unusual for some of them, especially in corporations, to endorse the idea of OD training for everyone in their organizations except themselves. They live under greater psychological strain than most of us, even if we do not correctly perceive why that is so. They know, to begin with, that no single individual can possibly *know* as much as he would have to know if he were really to control the organizational behemoth for which he is responsible, and they implicitly understand that whatever happens (success or failure) is not the result of their *personal* contributions. They intuitively realize that in managing survival they make decisions which damage others, and by their actions they damage themselves, much as any executioner is damaged by what society asks him to do. They have been socialized to believe, finally, that the only significant interactions they have are with subordinates, not with peers. While the problem of corporate managers who cannot interact with similar managers has been mentioned, most of us still believe that a President's Cabinet officers should spend their time running their departments instead of engaging in structured group processes which include Cabinet colleagues. (That is why so much attention is given in Chapter 5 to outlining a different approach to what we call high-level policy processes.) There will be plenty to do in the future for those we now term leaders, but not the traditional function of issuing orders. They will feel disoriented and threatened for a time, until it is clear to them that this revolution seeks not merely to overthrow them in favor of other elites, but to transform *relationships* between individuals and groups so that none dominates others. This revolution cannot be understood as a threat, only as an opportunity. The first step toward a livable future is to understand how our conventional theories of politics and economics stand in the way of attaining it.

2 If the organizational revolution is to expand its frontiers and help show us the way to a meaningful future, we must sweep aside the conventional wisdom of politics and economics which contributes so much to the alienation the revolution seeks to remove. That task will be undertaken in this chapter and the next by focusing on two seminal concepts which form the core of that conventional wisdom—hierarchy and competition. Challenging the viability of economic competition is the easier task; most of us admit to begin with that competition is the driving thrust of our economic system. We are less accustomed to thinking of "democracy" * and hierarchy as unalterably wedded to each other, for we tend to see "democracy" as something which has liberated us from the oppressive rulers of the past. True enough, Henry VIII does not stalk the earth any more, but Hitler came to power in a "democratic" setting. Even at its best, "democracy" has tended only to *limit* the power of rulers, without changing the fundamental *relationship* between those who rule and those who are ruled. This is because all theories of "democracy" contain within them the pervasive assumption that hierarchy is inevitable, desirable, and necessary, the assumption that *no organization (family, church, corporation, public agency, nation-state) can achieve its social purposes other than through the interaction of those designated "superiors" and those labeled "subordinates."*

* "Democracy" refers throughout to our conventional approach to government. It implies that we must transform ourselves if the quotation marks are to be removed.

"DEMOCRACY" AS HIERARCHY AND ALIENATION

We have lost sight of this long-term association of "democracy" and hierarchy, in part because "democracy" developed as a reaction to more oppressive forms of government and in part because most "democracies" began as limited governments—that is, most of the activities of individuals and groups took place outside the control of political leaders. These activities, however, were also based upon the assumption of hierarchy; and, as modern governments take on more and more of them, we feel increasingly alienated from those activities without understanding why.

This does not mean that alienation is *solely* a modern phenomenon; it is caused by hierarchy, and social hierarchies existed long before anyone began thinking of political "democracy." If alienation is traceable to hierarchy, as argued herein, the association of "democracy" with hierarchy means that the way we look at government now does not offer us an escape from alienation. Certainly the association exists, even if we do not emphasize it in our formal theories; we believe almost as a matter of course that we are better off if we have a "strong" President and that he can perform more effectively if he has a "mandate" (in the form of a huge majority vote) from the people, which enables him to exert his "authority."

It might have been useful to concentrate upon power instead of hierarchy; one new book calls for a dissolution of power and an end to its central position in our approaches to politics.[1] It also might have worked to focus upon authority—always important in studies of social behavior—and one author observes that it is time we recognized authority as something "extraneous to democracy."[2] Power, however, is equally meaningful in unstructured social interaction of minor concern here, and authority is closely related to modern theories of bureaucracy which cover only part of our history.[3] Hierarchy gives us a conceptual window upon a greater range of our past: it spans both feudalism and postfeudalism, modern social structures being an uncomfortable combination of both. To begin, then, we must look at the historical connections between hierarchy and alienation.

Hierarchy and Alienation:
Cause and Effect

Alienation, despite its widespread use in describing social malaise, remains unsatisfactorily defined. Most attempts to do so begin with the admission that most of us, perhaps all of us in modern societies, have never experienced *un*alienation or *non*alienation. Alienation and unalienation can be understood only with reference to each other, somewhat in the way we think of health and disease. We only know what it is like to have a particular disease because we know what it is like not to have it; without an experiential definition of health, the symptoms of the disease would appear normal.[4] Lacking any experience of unalienation, all we can do is examine the plausibility of arguments as to both the underlying causes and immediate symptoms of alienation. If we are *all* alienated, some are unaware of their illness, while others cannot comprehend its extent. If nobody can claim to *know* exactly how to transform alienation into unalienation, it seems reasonable to dismiss the claims of those who describe their Utopian communes as unalienated. To define unalienation as a state achieved by "dropping out" of society is to glorify a separateness which must itself be alienating. The analysis here departs substantially from much of the literature on the subject. It suggests that the fundamental source of alienation is *hierarchy,* that this is not a phenomenon associated only with the modern age of industry and technology but has existed throughout our history, and that "democratic" political theory and "democratic" political systems, because they are based upon hierarchy, are inherently alienating. In this sense, there is nothing to choose between capitalist and socialist versions of "democracy."

Because of the influence of Karl Marx, or the influence of his interpreters, we have tended to associate alienation with people who work in industry, especially on assembly lines in plants "owned" by capitalist entrepreneurs and exploiters. Even though we have admitted since the 1930's that the "managerial revolution" has transferred control of corporations from owners to managers, many socialists still pronounce ownership the most important factor. To the contrary, we are beginning only now to learn, more than a century after we started to think about it, that a change from "private" to "public" ownership does nothing to alleviate alienation.[5] We are learning that the individual worker cannot comprehend what it would mean to own the plant in which he works, and that he has no desire to do so. This also holds for the pilot who flies an airliner, the soldier who fires a howitzer, and the government clerk who uses a file cabinet.[6] The problem has been and is hierarchy, if it exists in secular and postfeudal modern Western societies, its roots are in the traditional feudalism of earlier periods, in both East and West. Indeed, Western organizational designs were imported from the East in the first place. In other words, hierarchy and organization, well established long before anyone thought seriously about "democratic" government, are hence imbedded in all theories of "democratic" government. The first analytical step, then, is to explore the *supposed* sources of alienation.

Conventionally, alienation is thought to exist when the world, society, or organization does not respond to the individual member, and subjects him to forces he can neither comprehend nor influence in a meaningful way. Usually the industrial worker is thought alienated because he cannot control his immediate work processes, develop a sense of purpose, feel himself a member of an integrated industrial community, and become involved in his work as a mode of self-expression. In extreme cases, the individual only reacts in unvaried fashion to the ceaseless rhythms of technology. He becomes a *thing,* simply the extension of a machine. Chained by the wrench in his hand to the ever-present assembly line, he has no alternative if he is to be paid and to survive. The image was provided many years ago by Charlie Chaplin, in *Modern Times.* The worker is separated from his work, for he plays no part in deciding what to do or how to do it. He is separated from his product, for he has no control over what he makes or what becomes of it. He is separated from his fellows; some of them are, as he is, just extensions of machines, while others (those who "own" what he makes) are his natural enemies. He is separarated from himself, because he can view his work only as something which divides his present from his future; it is only a means to an end which he hopes to realize at some indeterminate future point. All the forces he can neither control nor influence end up controlling him and, in effect, "to keep from dying, the worker sells his life." [7]

French sociologist Jacques Ellul expands this view to take in the whole of modern technological society. He uses "technique" as his focus, and defines it as the entire range of methods human beings consciously and systematically have used to organize what they do.[8] While technique is involved in such a simple task as driving a nail with a hammer, it reaches fruition in the complex organizations of modern society. In every field of endeavor, whether the organizing of intellectual activity so as to discover and disseminate knowledge, or the designing of a government agency, we use a "rational division of labor" to spell out in detail the tasks of every individual. By the very size of the phenomena which embody it, technique produces self-perpetuating organizational monstrosities which totally dehumanize the individual. Even when we speak of adapting the machine or the organization to the individual, we forget that adaptation is inevitably reciprocal; hence the individual adapts to the organization, and it swallows him. Over time, so goes the Ellulian argument, the *means* (organization) consumes those for whom it was designed to achieve an *end*.

Ellul's counsel is almost totally one of despair, and critics have taken him to task for it.[9] His mistake, a serious one, lies in his insistence that alienation is traceable solely to the replacement, by modern organizations, of earlier traditional institutions (families, religious orders) which provided individuals with a sense of community on a scale recognizable to them. When these institutional ties were torn asunder by attacks made in the name of individual freedom, the human being was left fragmented and atomized, easy prey for the onrush of modern organization. The experts of technique were able to herd individuals together, as in industrial communities, and so create the modern monstrosities. Perhaps because he is a traditional Christian and thus assumes hierarchy desirable, Ellul takes pains to dissociate the rise of modern organization from Christianity. This leads him to minimize the evidence he presents that technique is not a modern invention. After all, the pyramids of Egypt and the Great Wall of China were assembled by complex organizations that long preceded large-scale undertakings in the West.

Some of the traditional structures to which Ellul gives so much credit may have given individuals a sense of belongingness and community, but living within the confines of a feudalistic system, they must still have been very alienated. While some organizations which dominated the life of the individual were smaller than what we are used to now, they assumed hierarchy to be sacred. Indeed, the dictionary still links hierarchy directly with religion. In feudal systems, true enough, superiors and subordinates (lords and serfs) regarded each other as *persons* and, despite the degrading nature of these social relationships, persons felt a mutual responsibility to each other (lords should help serfs in need of help).[10] These relationships, however, were hardly sufficient to define such social systems as unalienated, and it is nonsense for Ellul to so argue. Serfs knew they had no choice but to accept as permanent their personal submission to their masters, to accept without question the social norms handed down to them, and to look for salvation only in some ill-defined hereafter. For the serf, the "here-and-now" was miserable and alienating; that is why people in traditional societies today laugh when we suggest they should avoid modernization in order to keep from becoming alienated.

The distinguishing characteristic of modern postfeudal organization, of course, is that relationships between superiors and subordinates are *impersonal*. The modern organization in a "democratic" society includes the premise that we are free and independent citizens; hence we glorify administration that is "neutral," "impartial," "dispassionate," "disinterested," and "objective." Yet it is the phrase "impersonal bureaucracy" which reflects our frustration when public agencies supposedly dedicated to helping us are separated, or alienated, from us. The fiction of freedom and independence, and the corollary objective of political equality, encourage us to believe that as *persons* we interact with each other in free and equal fashion. In organizations, we are *not* free and equal, so we describe ourselves not as persons, but as *roles;* we "act out" the norms prescribed by other roles. We interact, in other words, as *nonpersons*—a framework in which we are automatically alienated from one another and from ourselves. We are defined, and we define ourselves, as husbands, wives, students, workers, managers, or inmates. As *roles,* we find ourselves on a treadmill; our rank, status, and accomplishments are attributed to our roles, *not* to our *selves.*

To deal with husbands, wives, and managers in the same context is to emphasize that we live today amid an uneasy combination of feudalism and postfeudalism, which prevails in virtually all social organizations:

[1] The family remains basically a feudal organization, a superior-subordinate relationship of persons. In an attempt to escape the worst aspects of feudalism, we have impersonalized the family to some extent, but to regard marriage as the interaction of nonpersons, or roles, is inherently unsatisfying.[11]

[2] The Mafia emphasizes close-knit feudalistic family structures, but its leaders make postfeudalistic policy decisions to contract for the removal of individuals.[12]

[3] Professional athletes are the feudalistic property of owners, who make postfeudalistic decisions to sell, trade, or otherwise dispose of them for "the good of the organization."

[4] The corporation is, by custom and law, a fictitious and artificial person; in this setting, superiors have no *personal* responsibility for subordinates. In the effort to modify this alienating atmosphere, we attempt to humanize the organization and transform it into a community; we can see this happening when we speak of a top manager as the "old man." These warming relationships are

shattered when the superior, acting in his impersonal role, must fire the subordinate.[13] The combination of feudalism and postfeudalism is especially difficult for women who become the "bosses" of other executives. If the organization has attempted to humanize itself, it takes on the appearance of a matriarchal family, thus reversing the pattern of marriage. Whether women care to admit it or not, this becomes as disorienting to them as to men, for it suggests that women can be liberated only if they dominate men.

[5] Intellectuals pride themselves on the "collegial" or "family" relationships they enjoy as supposedly self-actualized individuals. At the same time, they raise higher walls between academic disciplines, argue that "facts" can objectively be separated from values, insist that knowledge can be made certain, and retain the right, by virtue of their "knowledge," to impose their views upon students or junior colleagues seeking tenure—thereby acting out roles indistinguishable from those in other superior-subordinate relationships.[14]

[6] The modern nation-state prides itself on being a government of laws instead of men, but the organizational structures of nation-states were initially designed by monarchs who looked upon their realms as private enterprises and upon themselves as agents of the Almighty (Louis XIV and Frederick the Great).[15] Present-day "democracies" retain much of the symbolism of the traditional past. The British monarch is crowned in church, and the "Speech From The Throne" is used to announce major policies. We look upon our President as both an impersonal *office* and a *person* who somehow stands above us. We insist he lay his hand upon the Bible as a condition of taking office, we scrutinize his attendance at religious services, and we have even changed our pledge to the flag to emphasize that as a nation-state we exist "under God."

The constant factor in our past and present, the one standing everywhere in the way, is hierarchy; it makes feudalism, postfeudalism, and any middle ground which combines them equally intolerable. Given our inclination to accept the inevitability of hierarchy in organizations, we ricochet back and forth between feudalism and postfeudalism in the search for a nonexistent compromise. Where large landowners and sharecroppers once constituted a feudal system, farm workers increasingly seek postfeudal unionization to deal with corporate farmers. Where industrial workers once lived in feudalistic "company towns," only to turn to postfeudal unionization, contemporary attempts to redesign industry will propel workers back toward feudalism unless hierarchy is eroded. More and more, university faculty members seek postfeudal unionization to offset what they perceive as the arbitrary decisions of quasi-feudal administrators, failing to note that the cycle cannot be broken within the confines of hierarchy. The formal, or officially acknowledged, interactions within any hierarchical structure are those of *ruling* and *being ruled, issuing commands* and *obeying them, repressing* and *being repressed.*

Those seeking to explain or escape alienation fail to recognize hierarchy as the historical cause of alienation, and thus miss the point. Ellul retains a wistful longing for the traditional priesthood of Christianity and for the presumed solace available in other traditional organizations, but that was a social design in which individuals directly repressed other individuals. Surely those whose place in life was decided upon by others must have been as alienated as anyone living today. Marx was dedicated to raising the class consciousness of workers to a level where the "dictatorship of the proletariat" would transform everyone else, perhaps the classic example of a *means* which, if implemented, would prevent the attainment of the end allegedly sought. The person defined solely as a worker is, even in Marxist terms, one whose identity is erased by his role. Where hierarchy is concerned, then, there is no choice between Ellul, Marx, and others. All of them accept hierarchy, and their proposed cures for alienation involve only more of the same. No "dictatorship" can help.*

---

* This analysis bypasses the long-debated question of whether Marx's successors corrupted his theories. *Organizationally* speaking, he subverted himself.

Many people still hope that "democracy" and representative government can help us escape alienation. Political theorist Sheldon Wolin, in an analysis that has attracted many students of organizational bureaucracies, frankly acknowledges that the individual, fragmented by his memberships in a number of organizations, is of necessity subjected to Leninist patterns of hierarchy. Elite cadres *must,* after all, make decisions and issue orders if anything is to be accomplished, or so Wolin concludes. It follows, he tells us, that an individual cannot make a *personal* contribution to society as a whole, cannot make a *political* contribution that is to say, through membership in organizations. This can only be done, Wolin insists, when the individual turns away from organizations and looks instead to politics, where the area of concern is the entire society instead of the narrow objectives of any organization.[16] Quite aside from Wolin's implicit assumption that an individual's work can *never* be self-fulfilling or unalienating (unless, presumably, he works in a political organization), this argument echoes the familiar theme that "democracy" offers us a way out. That claim cannot stand scrutiny.

Hierarchy and "Democracy": The Complete Marriage

Even a cursory examination reveals a basic contradiction. If we assume, as Wolin does, that *all organized social activity must be hierarchically structured,* and if *political activity is nonhierarchical,* then political activity must occur *outside* society. This makes little sense, so there is reason to believe that if we search our political theory and our political systems carefully, we will find they correspond to the norms of hierarchy. Our everyday language gives us an indication; most of us would have little difficulty agreeing on working definitions of "political bosses" and "political machines." Indeed, Robert Michels' famous "iron law of oligarchy" was the result of his studies, early in this century, of European political parties dedicated to "democracy"; he concluded that all large organizations—political parties, in this instance—must hire professionals to manage their affairs, and that the qualifications of the professionals set them apart from the mass of party members.[17] To examine the logic of conventional political activity is to discover the deeper connections of hierarchy and "democracy."

One nonpartisan advertisement widely reprinted in slick magazines during the campaigns of 1972 was purchased by the Youth Citizenship Fund of Washington, D.C. Visible beneath the closed curtains of a voting booth were a guitar and the bare feet and legs of an individual wearing blue jeans rolled up almost to the knee. The printed advice included only four words emblazoned across the bottom: *"Register your discontent. Vote."* This implied, of course, that the principal motivation for voting could best be expressed in negative terms: "Throw the rascals out." It follows that this fundamental act of citizenship, as we now define citizenship —a lonely act performed infrequently and out of sight and sound of all other human beings—is intended to discard or defeat a candidate we have learned to hate or at least thoroughly dislike. Although we often think of voting as a positive step preliminary to our version of the good life, this attractive camouflage cannot conceal its negative meaning. Indeed, the act is kept secret so that those we seek to repress cannot retaliate by repressing us. It makes no difference that a supposedly corrupt political machine may wish to respond violently to those who seek to punish *it;* the interaction is one of attempted repression on both sides.

While many citizens insist their votes are affirmative attempts to put favorite candidates in office and are not intended to demonstrate malice toward other candidates, this reasoning cannot stand. No personal act can have any real meaning other than in the here-and-now; a vote based upon vague hopes of what a candidate will do in the future is only another manifestation of alienation. If we look upon the act as an affirmative one in the here-and-now, we must define it as the voter's *surrender* to his favorite, an act that removes his identity. Voting and electoral processes, then, function only as organized systems which determine who *wins* (represses) and who *loses* (is repressed). The larger ceremonies of elections symbolize this win-lose drama.

Even minimal consensus must be avoided or destroyed if we are to hold elections because we need disagreement for the sake of elections themselves. The electoral struggle of 1972 was praised by many, including the two Presidential candidates, because of the polarized disagreements between them. No election ritual is complete until a defeated candidate makes a statement of surrender ("concession"), perhaps through a glaze of tears, family and friends on hand to share the humiliation. This ceremony often takes on more significance than the counting of votes, and not entirely because concession makes it difficult for the loser to argue later that his opponent stuffed the ballot box. To arrive at this combined moment of triumph and defeat, as in November 1972, candidates must concentrate all their energies upon attaining *victory, the only meaningful objective of politics.*

[1] The win-lose ritual demands that the candidate create enough heat and hate to convince people to "register their discontent"—and who cares if they really know why they vote? The misleading political commercial has become a staple of television, but other techniques are worse. Where some years ago, thousands were jammed into sports arenas to shout slogans on cue ("Martin, Barton, and Fish!," as Roosevelt put it in 1940 when he used three Republican legislators as targets), today's campaign managers think it better to fill a small auditorium to overflowing than to have a huge one half empty. In the mystical phenomenon of crowd politics, the candidate may "press the flesh" of hundreds, or stand on automobiles surrounded by "the people." Confetti is pumped into the air by giant paper-shredding machines, and the resulting film footage appears on television as evidence of the candidate's appeal. His shirts are prepared with easily detachable cufflinks which become souvenirs. The trick is to create the maximum excitement compatible with the candidate's survival, and any device that works is acceptable. It is even writ-

ten into law that one candidate can say virtually anything about another without running afoul of libel and slander laws.

[2] The latest in computer technology was put to widespread use in the long election year of 1972. Using the results of indirect interviews (individuals were not asked how they would vote, but answered other questions which could be transformed into personal "value profiles"), specialists sorted the answers into computer programs. These turned out personalized letters and recorded telephone calls designed to convince voters that the candidates recognized their personal interests. If the computer programmers ever become completely successful, the individual's vote will be the act of a robot.[18] *

[3] The most intensive involvement of the political candidate, especially a Presidential candidate, must go on at least an entire year before the election itself. By the time a new President takes office, even if he has been a public official, he has been out of touch with government for perhaps twelve months. Furthermore, he is exhausted and, by virtue of the arguments he has come to believe, may be full of hate or otherwise unfit to fulfill the office to which he has been elected.

Neither candidates nor voters come to this process as essentially evil people. All of us are trapped within a script that compels us to behave as we do if we are to win. Some time after the election, however, disillusion and confusion set in. We who voted for the victor wait for him to become a middleman who imposes *our* views upon fellow citizens, but we do not accept any personal responsibility for what he does. If things go wrong, we blame *him,* even if his decisions were those we urged in the first place. Meanwhile, he faces a dilemma: either he implements the promises he has come to believe in through repetition, or he attempts to find excuses for not implementing them because of their extravagance. John Ken-

---

* This is only the reflection of another contradiction in the system: a candidate and his supporters must struggle to dominate each other in an uneven battle (as in the case of the consumer whose tastes are managed through advertising).

nedy escalated the Cold War in 1961–1963, and launched "hot" ones as well, apparently because he had come to believe "we must get the country moving again" in foreign policy. Lyndon Johnson's actions after 1964 did not correspond to the campaign rhetoric of "no wider war," nor did Richard Nixon end the Vietnam War as quickly as he implied he would during the 1968 campaign. Any candidate has no choice but to make promises which will garner him votes, on its face an absurd requirement. Nor would it be any better if we adopted, as many political scientists have urged over the years, parliamentary (or British) concepts of "party responsibility" and "party discipline," wherein the voter presumably knows before he votes exactly what each party will enact into law. Many leaders of such parties find when they take office that conditions have changed and their promises no longer make sense.

The alienating character of the electoral process cannot be masked by the broader definitions of "participation" paraded before us. In the conventional wisdom of politics, participation is defined as some combination of "simple, common, and undemanding activities such as voting, discussing politics, seeking information and being interested in politics, and joining a political organization." [19] "Simple" and "undemanding" activities are likely to be unchallenging activities, *un*likely to bring any measure of self-fulfillment.* They are *alienating* activities, because they are tied to an electoral process whose only aim is the turning of some people against others and the victory of some people over others. That is why so many of us are so ambivalent about political participation and why our social conventions decree that one does not introduce the topics of religion and politics into dinner-party conversations—out of fear that guests will be forced to turn

* Just prior to the Democratic convention of 1972, the party sponsored a telethon to encourage "participation of the people"; Chairman Lawrence O'Brien and Senator Birch Bayh declared themselves dedicated to more of it. As it turned out, participation was defined only as making financial contributions to the party.

against one another. In all probability many people do not vote because they vaguely realize something is wrong with the act itself. We all intuitively realize that the political process is a dirty business in which people must behave abominably if they are to succeed. Was the lack of interest in the 1972 "Watergate affair" due to a widespread public acceptance of immorality, in which one political party used sophisticated espionage techniques against its opponent? Not at all. It was due to public awareness that persons intensely involved in politics are compelled, by the design of the system, to do such things.

Perhaps the nature of conventional political activity can be perceived more clearly by reflecting upon current efforts to introduce "democracy" into our prisons. Inmates undertake an "exercise in civic responsibility" by electing representatives to deal with prison administrators.[20] Prisoners have no choice but to "stand for election," and we can only wonder about the accusations opposing candidates hurl at each other. Those already rejected by society must not reject each other as part of their "rehabilitation." What statements of concession might losing candidates make? And, given the prison environment, might losers think seriously about killing winners? [21] *Dare prisoners openly discuss with each other, or with prison guards, for whom they will vote or have voted?* In prison, voters and candidates cross one another's path every day; hence those who vote must surely maintain total silence on the subject.

What we call political involvement, then, fits precisely into the pattern of formal social interaction prescribed by the hierarchical structure of all organizations. Political activity is no more fulfilling than any other organized activity. More to the point, "democratic" political theory has from the beginning been designed only to preserve and reinforce hierarchical organizational arrangements in society as a whole.

Organization Theory as the Father of "Democratic" Theory

Political theory and organization theory are usually treated as separate fields of study. Students of both fields come to accept the idea that theories of "democratic" government, socialist or capitalist, are the framework from which theories of organization have been derived. Yet *it is precisely the other way around:* all prominent theories of "democratic" government have been derived from the typical hierarchical patterns of organization theory—which, by the way, is about the same as social theory or cultural theory. In sharing this view, certain famous political philosophers are more in agreement with each other than many of us have been taught to believe.

Whatever Aristotle's contributions to "democratic" political thought (and he is often mentioned in that context [22]), his *a priori* commitment was to hierarchy as the pattern of organized social interaction; he even described society itself as the equivalent of a military structure. Arguing that "just as in any arm of the services one learns to command by being at first a junior officer," and that the individual citizen must "know how to obey as well as how to command," he defined the "good citizen" as one having "the knowledge and ability both to rule and be ruled." [23] He conceded that one group of citizens could not be superior in all respects to all other citizens, so "all must share in the business of ruling and being ruled." [24] His concept of *rotating* participation, wherein citizens take turns at ruling each other, included strict qualifications for citizenship. To Aristotle, many persons were not eligible to join in the rotation: some were naturally inferior (slaves, women, non-Greeks), some had no time to cultivate the talents of citizenship (farmers), and some lived a life not conducive to the virtuous requirements of citizenship (commercial business, manual labor).[25] Aristotle's proposed division of labor was clear enough: at any given moment, rulers *commanded,* everyone else *obeyed,* and most of the latter group could never look forward to joining the former. "Democracy," in other words, was intended to preserve the military-like *organization* of society, and the first duty of citizens (and the only duty of all others) was to learn the skills of obedience.

At least one of the common definitions of alienation permeated Aristotle's outline of politics and citizenship. Individuals who play no part in deciding what an organization shall do, whose only duty is to obey, are alienated from the work of the organization, including their share of the work. As the leading theoretician of the long period when democratic theory concentrated on the city-state (the emphasis shifted to the nation-state during the nineteenth century),[26] Aristotle can be considered a founding father of what we later came to know as town-meeting "democracy." Surprisingly, to most of us, this form of "democracy" is inherently alienating to the individuals involved.

In the old town meeting, those who won acquired from victory the legitimate authority to coerce those who lost. The majority ruled and all others obeyed, a separation of winners and losers which created alienation. With no elected representatives, winners directly repressed losers. In a very small community, winners and losers were friends (before voting), but things did not improve as communities became larger. Political theorists have constantly warned that a person cannot feel he is an important part of the political process if the number of voters is so large as to make his vote seem insignificant. Aristotle concluded that any state must stop granting citizenship when "it has filled up its numbers." [27] Much later, Rousseau argued that "the larger the state, the less the liberty." He directly compared the problems of a citizen in a state of 100,000 citizens to those of a citizen in a state of 10,000.[28] Among today's theorists, Robert Dahl seeks to stabilize the size of local communities so the individual can play a meaningful part; his objective lies between 50,000 and 200,000, and he would break up large cities to attain that goal.[29] Unless the individual *believes he makes a difference,* he feels alienated from what society does, even if he is among the winners. "Democracy," hierarchy, and alienation, then, were together in the town-meeting.*

With the rise of Christianity, religion and government were linked together for a long period, though the power of monarchs in England began to erode with the Magna Charta of 1215. A theoretical base for separating church and state was provided in the seventeenth century by Thomas Hobbes, who argued that the *sovereign ruler* (whether a single individual or an assembly) should be *absolute, impartial, and artificial.* The sovereign *Leviathan,* as he called it, would be an instrument through which citizens could govern themselves *indirectly.* Those on top, to use contemporary language, would *act out roles* as the managers of society. While Hobbes said nothing of elections, he specified that if the relationship between church and state were to be ended (and that was his objective), government would of necessity be an impersonal entity which remained above individuals. The rationale for an impersonal structure lay in Hobbes' view of human nature; men in their "natural" state, he believed, would engage in constant warfare against one another, hence the impersonal mechanism was needed to protect them from each other and ensure a livable peace. All men, that is to say, must interact as *nonpersons,* or *roles,* because persons only *kill* each other.

Most students of politics do not think of Hobbes as a founding father of representative government, because his assumptions about human nature were so pessimistic. Yet his recommendations on how to *organize* a secular society were extraordinarily close to what has emerged in the modern state. The members of Hobbes' sovereign *Leviathan* were to be authorized to make decisions on behalf of society, and they were to remain completely apart from other citizens. The "genius of modern representative government,"

* There is no unalienating solution to this problem of voting and size. Even in a group so small as to make each vote significant, individuals are uncomfortable when they repress each other. In that small a group, moreover, there is every reason to pursue consensus rather than majority rule.

in one observer's view,[31] may be wholly traceable to a narrow Hobbesian view of representation—the idea that society can be governed only if the impersonal decisions of those on top are obeyed. However much Hobbes' view of human nature may have differed from Aristotle's, his *Leviathan* was identical in design to Aristotle's separation of rulers and ruled, and the formal structure of all modern organizations is Hobbesian.

Among democratic theorists who became prominent just before the shift in emphasis from city-state to nation-state, Rousseau is often thought to have been the most committed to egalitarianism and direct "democracy." In contrast to Hobbes, Rousseau declared that human beings were by nature compassionate, and that correctly designed social institutions, including political governments, could enable them to realize their inherent goodness. The unifying social force for human realization was to be the "general will," and we often interpret that phrase as signifying Rousseau's liking for large-scale town-meeting "democracy." But Rousseau did not intend this at all; he did argue that citizens should come together to determine the "general will," by voting, but this was to occur only on rare occasions, perhaps to approve or substantially amend a political constitution. At all other times, Rousseau wanted *all* public business—including decisions on war and peace—handled by a representative minority.[32] His view of social organizations becomes clearer when we look at what he said about families. In words that parallel those in conventional administrative theory, he argued that "the father ought to command" and that "authority ought not to be divided equally between father and mother." If a father had to "acknowledge and maintain" his children, they could "belong" to "no one but himself." [33] Whatever his optimism about human nature, Rousseau's distinction between rulers and ruled was precisely the same as that of Aristotle and Hobbes. Ironically, Hobbes saw hierarchical structures as necessary to *prevent* individuals from behaving *as* persons, while Rousseau saw them as necessary to *enable* individuals to *become* persons.

The social invention of representative government, as well as the more contemporary approaches to "democracy," have perpetuated the norms of hierarchy. In the United States, our operational political theory is as much the work of James Madison as anyone else, and his design was close to the Hobbesian one. A Madisonian government must keep itself above the contending factions in society, lest one faction pursue its own "impulse," "passion," or "interest" at the expense of the "permanent and aggregate interests of the community." [34] The mainstream of contemporary "democratic" thought begins with an assumption that all social organizations, families included, are and should be hierarchically structured, and that governmental structures must be consistent with all the others.[35] Much contemporary theorizing appears more confusing and sophisticated than it actually is, because the theorists do not seem to realize the derivation of political theory. The result is a series of contradictions and potential dangers.

The Sad State of Contemporary "Democratic" Theory

This summary statement reflects the structural outline of modern representative government:

> What I take to be fundamental in the concept of liberal democracy is that those who are legally empowered to determine basic policies should be selected, directly or indirectly, for limited terms, and ultimately accountable to the electorate (which must include all sane adults, with certain generally acknowledged exceptions), in some fashion that entitles each of its members to an equal unit of political power, the vote. . . .[36]

Fleshed out, this is what some label the "process" or "method" theory of "democracy." Joseph Schumpeter's widely quoted sentence takes us a step further:

. . . the democratic method is that institutional arrangement for arriving at political decisions in which individuals acquire the power to decide by means of a competitive struggle for the people's vote. . . .[37]

The *method,* or technique (in Ellul's phraseology), is one of deciding *who* shall *rule.* It departs from Aristotle, Hobbes, and Rousseau by specifying that periodic elections not only *authorize* winners to make governmental decisions, but also enable citizens to hold those winners *accountable* in future elections for the decisions already made. It departs from all of them and from Madison by suggesting that virtually everyone defined as a "sane adult" should vote and that the electoral process should be a "struggle" —which our founding fathers sought to avoid. Logically, the method theory presents us with two hierarchical designs which are mutually incompatible mirror images of each other. An operational puzzle will illustrate the contradiction.

While the procedure has not met with total agreement, many judicial positions in the United States are decided by election. If a candidate seeking a judgeship announced during a campaign how he would decide a specific case if elected, many people would react in anger—and he would have to remove himself from that case. In some instances, the elected judge who has served a number of years can be granted permanent tenure on the bench by a yes-no vote (nobody runs against him). Surely this does not imply that voters are holding him accountable for his past decisions, or does it? All of us are puzzled about whether to vote for a candidate because we think him a "good" man and trust him to make the correct decisions, or because we agree with the sum total of his campaign promises, or because we seek a specific decision on a single issue. Only the first type of vote, however, fits a meaningful definition of representative government. When we vote for other reasons, we attempt, however imperfectly, to transform the representative into an automaton who does our bidding. This poses a harsh dilemma for "democratic" theories, based as they are upon hierarchy.

The very concept of hierarchy requires that we know for certain *who is in command,* but to assign this task either exclusively to voters or exclusively to representatives is to remove one or the other from decision processes. Aristotle, Hobbes, Rousseau, and Madison made it clear that those designated as rulers or sovereigns were to make the decisions. But we are uncomfortable with the idea that those who make decisions should remain distant and apart from us while in office, so it has become popular to search for more and more ways to make our representatives *accountable,* to make sure they issue commands only when citizens specifically instruct them to do so. Conventional political wisdom remains trapped in this dilemma, for neither extreme is satisfactory. Citizens who have no avenues of influence except an occasional, and perhaps meaningless, vote can thereby feel themselves only helpless and alienated, and representatives whose only task is to obey citizens can be only dehumanized and alienated. Countless theorists have attempted to escape the dilemma by outlining "group," "pluralist," and "power elite" concepts which argue either for or against various means by which individuals outside government *are* or *should be* able to influence public decisions. This introduces a confusion which can be illustrated by referring to the modern history of the city in which this book was written.

After World War II, Pittsburgh was in need of a face-lifting. It was justly renowned as a dirty, smoggy, run-down city, with a downtown area that had not been refurbished for many years. Anyone who lived in Pittsburgh then remembers how frequently the pall of smoke kept the city in total darkness around the clock, and both business organizations and individual citizens were fleeing in substantial numbers. The leaders of all organized interest groups recognized that overcoming a crisis of such magnitude would require new forms of interaction. Chief among these leaders were Richard Mellon, head of the Mellon family's widespread operations, and David Lawrence, the city's Democratic leader (later a multi-term mayor). The outcome was the Allegheny Conference on Community Development, initiated by Richard Mellon, which worked closely with the local Democratic machine, the state's Republican governor, university leaders, and many corporations based in the city. Labor unions were pulled in by assurances that jobs would not be eliminated. Thus began a building and renovation program ("Pittsburgh Renaissance") which only now has reached something of a pause, after a quarter-century of effort. There can be little doubt that many things in Pittsburgh are much better than before the renaissance, even though it focused on the central business district and did not substantially improve the quality of life in neighborhoods populated by racial and ethnic minorities.[38]

The Pittsburgh Renaissance began with a conventional assumption that the major interest groups in the city had recognizable leaders who represented them. A "group" theorist of politics, such as David Truman, would conclude that if the "rules of the game" in Pittsburgh were fair enough to enable citizens to form new groups and gain a hearing for their ideas, the ultimate decisions would be legitimate. As a political scientist, Truman would prefer that the authority to make binding decisions remain with elected political leadership. A "pluralist," such as Robert Dahl, would conclude the same thing, provided individual citizens had sufficient access to the leaders of their groups to make their voices heard (Dahl has standards he calls "norms of polyarchy," his term for a successfully functioning democracy). Like Truman, he would want final decisions made by elected leaders. A "power elite" theorist, such as C. Wright Mills or Floyd Hunter, would look upon Pittsburgh as a classic case of a local elite group making its own decisions concerning the future of the city, irrespective of what the general population might wish to do. In this view, the members of the elite do not compete against each other (labor versus business, Democrat versus Republican) or serve as checks and balances, but form a homogeneous group in which positions easily are exchanged (as when government, business, and military leaders trade jobs with each other).[39]

Those who conclude that modern "democracy" works rather well

(Truman, Dahl) admit to confusion when they cannot discover for sure *who rules*. If a public official makes a decision just as a lobbyist suggests it, then the lobbyist effectively replaces the official. If the official ignores all suggestions, he is on top of the hierarchy, but everyone else is shut out. Those who condemn the power elite (Mills, Hunter) argue that to permit a Richard Mellon to make significant decisions under the guise of "civic leader" is to make a sham of government. Depending upon which book you read, this confusing debate among intellectuals can be traced as far back as Arthur Bentley's *Process of Government* (1908), but the need to protect the boundaries of academic disciplines has led political scientists to misread Bentley.[40] In practical terms, the "power elite" theorists have gained the upper hand. This is because all parties to the debate agree on hierarchy, so they admit it is desirable to specify who will make the decisions that everybody else must accept. Since it would seem illegitimate to designate those *outside* government as "on top," we turn toward making elected leaders *more perfectly representative:*

- Because voting is the only formal act of political involvement, we make every attempt to extend it as widely as possible. We remove poll taxes, property restrictions, and literacy tests; we police voter registration drives; and we redefine adulthood to include those we otherwise define as "kids," [41] as we approach a time when someone is sure to propose that voting be made compulsory.
- We actively pursue the "one-man, one-vote" formula, trying to make certain every legislative district includes precisely the same number of citizens.[42]
- We develop standards by which to judge every elected body— and every organization, for that matter—as to whether it contains the "right" proportion of males, females, and every other religious, ethnic, racial, and occupational category imaginable. This drive for the equivalent of quota systems, already the subject of national debate, raises anew the suggestions made years ago by the Guild Socialists.

In the pursuit of perfect representation, we fail to realize the implications of our actions. If only a woman legislator can represent women, and if her vote precisely reflects *their* interests, it follows that the legislator herself becomes merely an instrument of other women and is, in effect, removed from the decision process. Harvey Mansfield, Jr., succinctly outlines the result of achieving perfect representation:

> . . . in the rhetoric of modern politics, it is impermissible to blame the people for the bad government they may originate, and yet they can be excused only by admitting the necessity of perfecting their representation to the point where no one but the people can be blamed.[43]

There is irony in this trend, championed by those loosely definable as "liberals" or otherwise on the "left," for it marks a complete reversal in their thinking. Beginning in the 1930's, they have spent most of their time arguing for a strong executive branch; for almost two decades, they repulsed every attempt by conservatives to limit executive power. Now, disenchanted by what they perceive as organizational monstrosities (the "military-industrial complex"), they have shifted overnight to an antiexecutive stance which relies upon the idea of an all-powerful legislature, *provided* it is a perfect mirror of the population. Quite aside from the obvious problems of any quota system (it is inherently alienating, for it insists that all of us have totally separate identities we cannot define anyway, since we do not know whether a black woman is primarily black or primarily woman), it casts aside the long record of theory and practice which suggests that overreliance upon electoral processes is not likely to improve things. A part of this record is worth enumerating:

● Even where Rousseau thought it possible to determine a "general will" by vote of the entire population, he simply assumed the losing minority would agree that its initial opinions had been "mistaken," and would adopt the majority view as the "right" version of the general will. This could lead not only to a rush to "get on the bandwagon," but to citizens publicly confessing their mistakes to avoid being punished for them.[44] This is the surest road to the tyranny of a majority, for it assumes the minority is wrong. Worse yet, since citizens could not determine what was right and what was wrong until *after* the votes were counted, they would be under considerable psychological strain when they voted. This combination of pseudoegalitarian and hierarchical theorizing made Rousseau's ideas an intellectual source of the excesses of the French revolution.

• The founding fathers of the United States recognized the repressive logic of mass-voting processes and, as individuals who were both first-rate theoreticians and skilled men of action, they attempted to design elaborate safeguards. The rules they wrote for the *indirect* election of Senators and Presidents reflected their fear of all-out political activism. It later became fashionable to label the writers of our Constitution as elitists determined to keep government in the hands of the few, and it cannot be doubted they were aristocrats. But they did not exempt themselves from the logic of repression; it was important to them that members of the Electoral College, the selected elitists who would exercise their judgment in choosing a President, be prevented from meeting together to cast their votes. The result of any such meeting would only be "tumult and disorder," "heats and ferments"; hence Electoral College members even today must cast their votes without leaving their home states (though their votes now are meaningless).[45]

• Whatever the superficial attraction of wider voting, theorists have worried about the close correlation in modern European history between high voter turnouts and the rise of totalitarianism. Social research has revealed that lower-class citizens are "authoritarian-minded," and therefore easily persuaded by extremists who seek to establish dictatorships; so theorists have concluded it is even desirable to encourage citizens to stay away from voting booths. They have added that low voter turnouts, or political apathy, probably reflect the widespread contentment of citizens anyway:

> . . . a large public which is not constantly excited and interested in political questions is probably healthy in any democracy for this reason: interest (and voting) go with partisanship and it is virtually impossible to increase one without the other. The heavier the vote, the less likely are the voters to be the rational citizens of classical theory.[46]

This line of argument is less persuasive than that of the founding fathers, for it implies that elites are rational while others are not. The problems of mass voting and mob hysteria play no favorites, however, and one can see as much extremism in meetings of university faculty senates as anywhere else. It is not by accident, moreover, that the important work of legislatures is done by small committees, not in the traditional design of the long debate with every legislator present on the floor.

Given this record, others propose changes that would have precisely the opposite effect. It has been suggested that each President be limited to one six-year term so he may function as a "statesman" who is "above politics" because he will have no worries about reelection; and we constantly consider proposals to put severe limits on campaign spending. But to adopt the one-term Presidency would imply that Presidents should not be accountable, or that the electoral struggle is demeaning and dangerous, or both. Similarly, to limit campaign spending would imply that candidates should say less than they do now about what they would do if elected. Both suggestions might help us avoid the extremes of politics, and they are put forward in recognition of those extremes, but the outcome would be an increased distance between officials and citizens.

So long as the underlying assumptions of hierarchy go unchallenged, theories of "democracy" and all proposals for improving "democratic" systems will remain trapped in the hierarchical dilemma. To head in the direction of wider and wider voting, of perfect representation, of quota systems, and all the rest is to search for an improvement which in the long run can only remove those we elect from the process of making decisions. Ultimately, we might realize that in a direct "democracy," we would have to repress one another directly, without the presence of representatives as middlemen. We are even in danger of forgetting something we learned years ago: the reform of the "short ballot" made headway because individuals could not be expected to cast votes on every issue or every office. Other reforms, conversely, would make our elected officials more distant and authoritarian. Principally because so many theorists of politics do not realize that "democracy" is derived from a social theory of hierarchy, and that voting itself is an act of alienation, they constantly ask us to alienate ourselves still more. Those revisionist theories of politics now gaining wide attention enshrine the belief that nothing can be done except through hierarchical interaction; they are designed, however unintentionally, to increase alienation. Three such approaches typify the problem:

Formal Juridical Democracy. Theodore Lowi's stated objective is to restore government to its Madisonian position "above" contending factions in society. Policy, Lowi argues, should be spelled out in detail in legislation, thus making most administration completely automatic.[47] Congress would be prompted to act by the demands pressed upon it by large-scale social movements having charismatic leaders ("emotional middlemen") capable of transforming their memberships into followings by communicating "with special intensity" the symbolism that all followers must share if such movements are to succeed. This happened in the civil rights movement of the early 1960's, Lowi concludes, until the war on poverty stripped the movement of revolutionary moral force by fragmenting it into city-by-city bargaining processes.

Lowi's concept assumes that Congress, confronted by a mass movement, should quickly enact whatever its leaders demand. But Congress, and government overall, could prove that it stood "above" the contending groups only by *rejecting* or *modifying* such demands; even to bargain with movement leaders would simply duplicate a pluralist system Lowi deplores. He starts out, in other words, by arguing from a Hobbes-Madison perspective (government must be above us), then argues that government should do whatever is demanded by social movements. His rubber-stamp model has the net effect of removing elected government. Why bother with representatives if social movements make the decisions? [48] Stripped of pretense, his concept offers us a military model of new left tyranny, followers of charismatic leaders assigned the single task of marching in ranks without asking questions. Enamored of Martin Luther King, Jr., and Robert Kennedy, he forgets Adolf Hitler.

Public Choice Democracy. Economic models seem attractive because they feature competition and individual preferences. Two versions of "public choice" contradict each other (as Lowi contradicts himself), even as their advocates profess to agree. The first follows Lowi by arguing for clear decisions at the top, but for a different method of making them. William Niskanen, himself a member of the President's Office of Management and Budget (OMB, formerly the Bureau of the Budget) looks upon the "monopoly bureaus" of public life as evils to be overcome by introducing competition—though he seems to exempt police forces and armies. At the national level, he would have agencies devise competing and overlapping programs, the President and Congress choosing among competitors. This, he argues, would release the President from his imprisonment as a "captive of the bureaucracy." [49]

In Gordon Tullock's version, everybody would be linked to central computers. Sitting in the living room, the constituent would punch a button on the television set, or dial a number on the telephone, to register a "yea" or "nay" on every issue before Congress. The individual might, if he chose, deliver his proxy to his Congressman on some issues and retain his own vote on others. [50]

By one calculation, all of us could punch buttons twenty-two times daily, 365 days per year.[51] Hundreds or thousands of miles away, the legislator would read his mandate in the maze of computer print-outs on his desk, then cast his vote. Tullock adds that citizens should be able to purchase directly the types and amounts of public services they want. The economic marketplace is the obvious model; public functions could be turned over to competing private enterprises, and individuals could pay fewer taxes and select their own schools, postal systems, and whatever—an idea attractive to both conservatives and liberals.[52] These prescriptions stumble into the same old contradictions: if the first version removes citizens from the chain of command, the second removes representatives.[53]

Participatory Democracy. A number of proposals are tied to this phrase, most of them arguing for decentralized autonomous political and administrative decision centers, and for involving individuals outside government in making specific decisions.[54] This approach, exemplified by the slogan "neighborhood control," might retransform federal systems into confederations, or might lead to a revived Jeffersonian politics that would parallel the attempts of Ralph Nader and others to break up large corporations. Neither decentralization nor the involvement of amateurs directly challenges the concept of hierarchy, and it is usually assumed that to become more participatory is to bring in those now on the *outside* while throwing out those now *inside*. Officially, the president of General Motors is an "amateur" in government, but most advocates of participatory democracy do not envision a wider role for him in public policy-making.

Carole Pateman's analysis of "classical" theories of democracy leads her to distinguish between theories of participation and those of representative government, and to conclude that democracy can be meaningful only if it includes both.[55] To her, participatory democracy must provide opportunities for individuals to involve themselves in the decision processes of all organizations to which they belong. All organizations become, by definition, political organizations, because they contribute to an individual's knowledge of participation and enable him to practice its skills. The more people participate, the better they will become at it, the more participatory an entire society will become, and the more integrative social decisions will be. Her advocacy of democratization for all social institutions, beginning with the family, places her outside the conventional wisdom but, having been trained within it, she quickly returns to it. Except for very small organizations (the family?), where presumably there should be no chain of command or superior-subordinate relationships, she simply assumes that we have no alternative to representative government. When she recombines participation and representation, she inadvertently reinstates hierarchy, for her argument implies that elected representatives should make decisions without interference from outsiders.

What is most striking about all these proposals is the degree to which conventional political analysts remain so unaware of the underlying premise of hierarchy that they can jump back and forth between opposing models of hierarchy without realizing it—thus giving us a clear demonstration of the conventional dilemma. We are told one minute that elected representatives must stand clearly above us and make independent decisions on our behalf, and the very next minute that the same representatives must act only in response to the crisis demands of social movements or the results of national button-pushing. Any of the proposals (or a combination of them) would increase alienation by encouraging tyrannical social movements, by compelling us to repress each other every day by voting directly on every issue, by turning everything over to small isolated groups at the top, or by instituting electoral campaigning in every social organization. Reduced to their essentials, all of these theories of government offer us nothing but organized pyramids of power, even if one of them is inverted (Figure 5). Conventional wisdom remains empty of hope.

"Democracy" as Extreme Alienation

This chapter began with the assertion that the fundamental cause of alienation is our belief in the inevitability of hierarchy as the only possible *modus operandi* for all social organizations, from the nuclear family to the nation-state. Yet it is hopeful to discover that hierarchy (along with alienation) has been constant throughout recorded history; the problem cannot be attributed solely to the industrial era. Since there may indeed be no Golden Age of the past to which we can turn for guidance (the view of Iranian social philosopher F. M. Esfandiary), there is no reason to romanticize that past.[56] The argument in the previous chapter, conversely, is that an alternative approach is emerging, and quickly, in the organizational world, and in the broadest definition of world; women seeking to humanize marriages are a part of the approach. If this is the case, and it is so argued here, there is no reason to assume that we must get rid of modern technology if we are to humanize or unalienate ourselves. This does not mean that technology and large organizations can continue to grow unchecked (the critical problem of growth is taken up in Chapter 3). What is happening is based upon a justified optimism that it is possible to transform *all* organized social interactions. Political "democracy," as we conventionally define it, poses a special problem, for its peculiar historical development has made it the principal vehicle through which we continually *increase* alienation.

"Democracy" was grafted onto, or superimposed upon, the social hierarchies which existed when any given community or nation-state chose to "democratize" itself. The rise of modern nationalism, moreover, caused all of us in the West to view political government as *the* important social hierarchy which stands above all other hierarchies and issues them commands in the name of the public interest. We commonly believe that the most important task of a new President is to take "firm control of the bureaucracy" and make it distinctively "his," and we wince at the thought that govern-

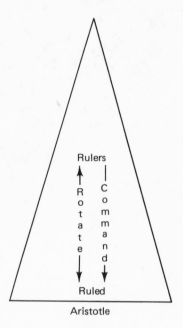

Rulers

Rotate | Command

Ruled

Aristotle

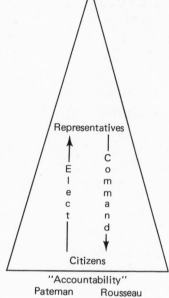

Representatives

Elect | Command

Citizens

"Accountability"
Pateman   Rousseau

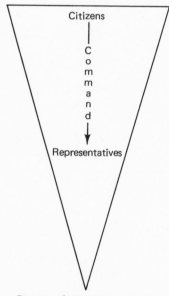

Citizens

Command

Representatives

Rousseau (misinterpretation)
Lowi (sometimes)
"Public Choice" (Tullock)

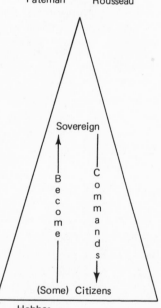

Sovereign

Become | Commands

(Some) Citizens

Hobbes
Madison
Lowi (sometimes)
"Public Choice" (Niskanen)

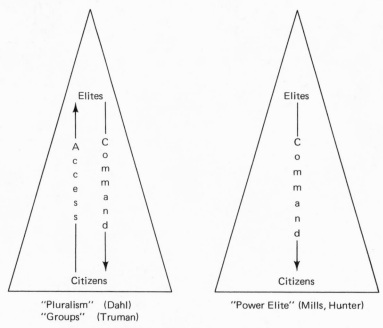

Figure 5: Models of "Democratic" Government

ment might be at the mercy of some *other* hierarchy. This leads us to insist, almost without realizing it, that the organization we call government be the *most* hierarchical of all organizations. Robert Dahl's views on worker self-management drive this point home.

Pursuing the idea that the most powerless of our citizens should be given more opportunity to influence the decisions of the organizations which dominate their lives, Dahl suggests that industrial workers might develop "their own sense of competence" if they were able to elect the boards of directors of their companies, even though he admits that this is unlikely to occur. While the deeper implications of worker self-management will be taken up in Chapter 3, the distinction Dahl makes between workers in private enterprise and those in public bureaucracies is noteworthy here. Even though he admits that public and private organizations are, in the larger sense, equally public ("General Motors is as much a public enterprise as the U.S. Post Office"), Dahl insists that this wider form of citizenship cannot under any circumstances be granted to officially public employees. In democracy, he says, "you will need administration, and administration will need hierarchy"; unless strict control of the bureaucracy is maintained from above, and by elected officials, rule will shift from "the people" to the "bureaucrats." [57] To maintain his strict construction of democracy, Dahl is compelled to contradict himself: if General Motors and the Post Office have the same effect upon the public interest, it makes little sense to advocate wider citizenship for automobile workers than for mail carriers.

As government functions expand, therefore, the new organizations created by virtue of the expansion are likely to be more internally hierarchical than the private organizations they replace. Public agencies may become so distant and impersonal as to resemble giant computers whose workings we cannot fathom but whose calculations produce decisions we must obey. Or, if we adopt Lowi's suggestions, tyrannical social movements may sweep through the streets and force legislatures to submit to them and, in turn, suppress us in accordance with instructions from the leaders of the social movements. While this turns all our arguments about the relative merits of socialism and capitalism into foolish distractions, in that both depend upon a hierarchical design, it is worth noting that *socialism, solely because of the strength of the belief in "democratic" theory, is likely to be more hierarchical and repressive in operation than is capitalism, hence more alienating.* This is because individuals in a socialist society are likely to view the decisions of government as more socially legitimate than individuals in a capitalist society are likely to view the decisions of corporate executives.

This seems the most plausible explanation for the peculiar course the organizational revolution has taken up to now. Virtually all the theories and techniques connected with the humanizing of large organizations began in private businesses rather than in public bureaucracies, and have gone further there. One need only look at library shelves to realize that most books on the subject have been written by individuals whose experiences center on private businesses. Where a corporate executive, despite his hierarchical status, can feel reasonably comfortable with some internal democratization of his organization's decision processes, a public official is likely to view the same thing as subversion or dilution of the authority he possesses by virtue of the "democratic" electoral process. This seems to account for the Kansas City councilwoman's vigorous opposition to the idea that elected officials might be helped by an industrial psychologist (see Chapter 1). Both individual citizens and groups on the outside and administrators and employees on the inside find it more difficult to influence what occurs in public agencies than in corporations.*

By the same token, the competitive struggle of all political campaigns, especially for the Presidency, becomes so unspeakably desperate as to dwarf by comparison the internal "politicking" and maneuvering for corporate promotions. To become a highly successful politician, one must develop an unquenchable lust for power, and learn to be ruthless in the pursuit of it. The stakes seem so high, and defeat so great a loss, that politicians feel they have no alternative. It will not be easy for any of us to confront head-on the probability that all this is traceable to something we have learned from childhood to accept as the very best thing we have going for us—"democracy." We must begin to grasp the historic connections between "democracy," repression, and alienation and the theory of social organization which spawned all of them. We have avoided searching for new meanings for democracy, for new ways of looking at it, because we have been afraid even to suggest to ourselves that what we have may not be the best. Yet it is time, as Arnold Toynbee reminds us, to admit that all "democracies" we know about have been tyrannical, and we must decide whether "direct" and "representative" forms of "democracy" are

---

* This is not to be taken as an argument that all is well with capitalist systems. Remaining chapters should make this point clear. Any trend toward conventional socialism, however, doesn't help at all.

the only possible alternatives.[58] In effect, a social theory of organizational hierarchy created a Frankenstein monster in the form of "democratic" government, which a different social theory must now seek to transform. This can be done more easily than might appear at first glance, but the quest for transformation must be put off until another chapter.

Hierarchy, unfortunately, is only half the problem; the other half is a concept we glorify even more—competition. Because we believe so deeply in the benefits we *think* we gain from economic competition, the concept has permeated our entire social fabric. Not only do we praise competition as the best way to select our leaders, but we base much of our social thinking upon the economic concept of "exit" instead of a more participatively political idea of "voice." We define *choice,* in social terms, as the right of the citizen to move ("exit") from one community to another (a notion which underlies the work of "public choice" thinkers), but we put less effort into ensuring that the voices of citizens are listened to where they are *now.* This is the meaning of bumper stickers which proclaim, "America—Love It or Leave It!" But the idea of "exit" may be ineffective in both politics and economics; the citizen or customer who cares most about quality is likely to be the most effective agent of "voice," but the same individual feels compelled to "exit" when nobody listens.[59] If one major problem of the moment is the resistance of conventional political thought to the idea that voting and elections have little to do with meaningful democracy, another problem is that conventional economic thinking, in the form of public choice, seeks to invade *all* public activity on grounds that the example of economic competition is an ideal one. As if we did not compete enough with each other already, we are told we must become even more competitive for the sake of greater efficiency. This is why we must examine the logic of competition on its home territory—the economic marketplace.

3 *Saturday Review* published in January 1972 six articles (five by economists, one by an economic journalist) exploring the "growing unreality and dehumanization—some call it irrelevance—of economic theory and analysis." One author concluded that economists were "unlikely to have anything very useful to add as theorists" until they recovered from a "two-century-old romance with free competition." [1] On January 24, the Federal Trade Commission (FTC) accused Kellogg, General Mills, General Foods, and the Quaker Oats Company of using anticompetitive practices to set "artificially inflated prices." In proposing to divest the companies of some or all cereal-making facilities, the FTC predicted that prices would drop 20 or 25 per cent in a "competitively structured market." Consumer advocate Ralph Nader praised the action as "one of the most important developments in antitrust enforcement in the last decade." [2] The FTC and Nader continue the "romance with free competition" that is the focus of this chapter.

Nobody except the four companies themselves, who denied the existence of monopoly or the commission of illegal acts, questioned the assertion it would be beneficial to increase cereal competition. The assumptions that competition produces benefits for all of us and that our economic system cannot function without it are so widely accepted that even those who worry most about our worship of the Gross National Product overlook the possibility that the logic of any competitive economic system (socialist or capitalist) compels the producers within it to behave in ways

THE ABSURDITIES OF ECONOMIC COMPETITION

which achieve results precisely the opposite of those proclaimed by conventional wisdom.

Competition, hierarchy, and alienation are closely related to each other in that they reinforce each other; we can grasp through a common-sense approach how this occurs. We revere the popular image of the small businessman, the corner grocer, and the family farmer. If a close friend fits one of these categories, however, we really do not want him to face stiffer competition, for we are uncomfortable at the thought that he may wake up tomorrow and find himself out of business and branded a failure. We know he constantly faces such a threat, if only because his enterprise is very small in comparison to the total market. This leads us to hope that if many businesses fail in the near future (in a sense we *want* this to happen, because it proves competition is working), their owners will be people we never have met. At the same time, we feel a vague fear that corporations such as General Motors and General Electric are too big, in that those who work for such giants and those who buy their products cannot exercise any meaningful influence over them, hence are alienated from them. But we also realize that the very size of such organizations provides their employees with enough security so that they do not feel threatened every day. If we work in a corporation, however, we understand that its strength, its ability to stave off threats of competition, is the principal factor which permits it to humanize its internal operations. The more competitive the market, in other words, the more hierarchical corporate managers must become; and the more *impersonal* or *nonpersonal* managers and workers become, the more "efficient" they are (until they realize the depths of their alienation). The ideal of competition cannot even be defined unless someone goes out of business or is thrown out of work every day, though we know we do not want this to happen to us, to our friends, or to very many others. In this inexorable sequence, hierarchy initially creates alienation, competition reinforces both, and then alienation reinforces both itself *and* hierarchy and competition.

We accept this because we believe the benefits we gain from competition outweigh the human price we pay for them. If competition is to be challenged, therefore, it must be on *economic* grounds, not merely because it reinforces hierarchy and alienation, serious as that problem may be. This chapter argues that we achieve from competition *absolutely no benefits at all.* Where a few corporations dominate an industry (the oligopoly), the outcome is prices two to three times higher than they should be— something traceable to the *competitive waste* of companies which do not compete on the basis of price reductions but instead use massive advertising, limitless schemes of promotion, and irrationally excessive capacity and distribution systems, all designed to lure a few customers away from each other. Where we commonly believe that these problems can be overcome by "more perfect" competition, this leads only to huge *overproduction,* dangerously declining prices, widespread failures, and a social chaos overcome only by government intervention. Stripped of pretense, a theory of economic competition is the equivalent of a political theory of anarchy, but it is doubly dangerous because policies derived from it forcibly prevent sensible planning or collective decision-making (what we describe as government economic planning hardly is worthy of the term). Nor can any of these problems be overcome by shifting to a socialist form of competition, as in the Yugoslav experiment; that country faces only impending disaster if it continues its present course. Finally, a new and potentially more dramatic problem looms just ahead: if those who argue for limits to economic growth, for the sake of planetary survival, turn out to be correct, we cannot coexist any longer with economic competition.

The economic assumption of scarcity, combined with Hobbesian notions of human nature and hierarchy, has led to an economic system in which individuals and corporations must lie, cheat, and swindle if they are to succeed. The old culture of the United States may be the most extremely competitive one of all. We stress property over personal rights, technology over human needs, violence over sexuality, concentration over distribution, producer over consumer, secrecy over openness, and social forms over personal expression. This combination frustrates three human desires: (1) for community (living in cooperation with one's fellows); (2) for engagement (with social and interpersonal problems, and in an environment not composed of ego-extensions); and (3) for mutual dependence (sharing responsibility for the control of one's impulses and the directions of one's life).[3]

This has special meaning for those who seek wider involvement of consumers and workers in managing things. However laudable their objectives, they cannot achieve them within the rubric of competition. If this argument is correct, the Ralph Naders of this world are working against themselves. Everywhere we turn, the outcome is the same: economic competition cannot, under any circumstances, deliver on the promises made on its behalf. This need not mean, be it noted, that competition cannot survive in any cultural form; the villain is competition tied to survival, as it is in conventional economics.

Classic Competition and Its Contradictions

When he announced his imposition of price and wage controls, President Nixon demonstrated his commitment to competition by extolling its virtues at least fourteen times in a brief speech.[4] The classic concept of competition begins with an ideal world in which many small enterprises manufacture a given product. In this "forest of firms," each enterprise is so small, relative to the total market for the product, that neither the individual producer nor the purchaser can influence the general level of prices. However much the producer manufactures, and regardless of whether a purchaser buys or does not buy, the unseen hand of the market determines the price. Producers and consumers make an infinite number of such decisions, these constituting the market. Supply and demand move constantly back and forth, and the price level continuously adjusts to meet these shifts. Four outcomes are assumed:

1. Prices are brought into reasonable relation to costs so that profits constitute only a competitive rate of return on capital invested.
2. Benefits to labor and capital are related to their contributions to production.
3. Whatever the existing policies on taxation and social action, and the resultant distribution of income, resource-use is optimum in relation to that framework. In other words, free competition is "efficient."
4. Constant pressure to reduce costs and improve products leads to continuous innovation, which is passed on to consumers. Because there are many producers, the profits of one are not affected adversely by making innovations available to all others; hence every innovation spreads as rapidly as communications permit.[5]

In its simplest outline, the classic model is summarized by Ralph Nader's study group:

. . . Many sellers compete for the consumer's dollar, and consumers, in turn, buy the best products at the lowest prices. By "voting" with his dollars, the consumer determines the types, quantities, and prices of goods to be produced. The result is that economic resources are allocated among users to maximize consumer satisfaction. Sellers who want to survive the competitive struggle must constantly increase their efficiency and seek out product innovations. "The unrestrained interaction of competitive forces," summarized the Supreme Court as early as 1904, "will yield the best allocation of our economic resources, the lowest prices, the highest quality, and the greatest material progress.[6]

The Nader group, hardly content with *laissez-faire* competition, allows for government intervention to ensure livable wages, safe and high-quality products, and prevention of damage to the environment, among other objectives. Within the parameters of remedial legislation, however, competition remains the driving ideal; yet some obvious contradictions deserve mention. These can be outlined by exploring one of John Kenneth Galbraith's arguments and one of the Nixon Administration's major policy initiatives.

Galbraith chides his colleagues for failing to acknowledge the connection between full employment and inflation. It is clear, he argues, that full employment in a "free market" leads to an intolerable spiral of wages and prices. Galbraith advocates wage and price controls, the point of his argument, but he goes on to criticize his colleagues' unwillingness to admit that price inflation occurs not only when there is *too much* demand (more purchasing power than things to buy), but also when there is *just enough* demand.[7] It seems to follow, if Galbraith does not say so, that a free market can avoid inflation only when there is *too little* demand (less purchasing power than things to buy). Inflation, in other words, is checked *only* by excess production. Common-sense examples reinforce this conclusion.

When customers have money but goods are scarce, sellers hold the whip hand. At the end of World War II, millions of people stood ready to buy the first automobiles coming off assembly lines. Many can recall the black market bonuses that dealers extorted from customers. To use a simpler example, we might visualize ten toothbrushes in a drugstore. If only those ten brushes were available, and if ten customers each needed one, the druggist could command an exorbitant price for them. The notion of automatic equilibrium is a fantasy; prices fall only when there is an excess of supply over demand (overproduction), not before.

A few months before he installed controls, President Nixon, addressing the National Association of Manufacturers, praised the economic system's ability to "meet the demands made upon it by the American people."[8] This reflected the conventional notion that individual consumers calculate their wants without being influenced by others (including advertisers), and speech-writers familiar with orthodoxy doubtless inserted the phrase. When it came time to stimulate the economy, orthodoxy did not fit. The President declared he would seek repeal of the excise tax on automobiles and would "insist" that the average price reduction ($200) be passed on to eight million buyers of automobiles that year.[9] Treasury Secretary Connally outlined the reasoning behind the tax proposal:

. . . We did not know of any better way—the President did not know of any better way—to give back to 10 million people, who are going to buy a basic commodity produced in this country, about $200 each, for those who buy a car. I think it is going to have a tremendous impact." [10]

The objective of producing and selling ourselves more automobiles transformed the President and his Treasury Secretary into advertisers and subsidizers. Given his personal style, Secretary Connally might have said, "Folks, I have in my hand $200 for everyone who steps up to buy a new automobile, $200 guaranteed!" The action was intended to create demand through bribery, something conventional wisdom does not acknowledge. Like much advertising, moreover, the statements were misleading. Anyone who bargains with a dealer about the price of a new car and the allowance for one traded in, who wonders about the ultimate disposition of the trade-in, and who then wonders about relationships between dealers and manufacturers, knows that customers may or may not realize a $200 gain.

The economic program of 1971, widely accepted at the time,[11] demonstrated the meaning of "consumer sovereignty." We were told it was our civic duty to want an automobile and to "vote" for Chrysler, General Motors, Ford, or American. The logic is that we be persuaded to want more of everything, provided we have the purchase price or credit rating to buy. We even are told it is unpatriotic to permit the government to withhold more from paychecks than we will owe in taxes at the end of the year, it being more desirable to spend as we earn and then borrow to pay taxes. Because the political system is tied to this economic system, especially to the big companies, we must explore the logic of their behavior.

Oligopolies and Competitive Waste

One author defines oligopoly as a market system in which no more than four producers have an aggregate market share of 70 per cent.[12] Galbraith uses 60 per cent as his standard, noting that four firms dominate aluminum, copper, rubber, cigarettes, soap and detergents, liquor, glass, refrigerators, cellulose fibers, photographic equipment, cans, computers, sugar, and many other items; three firms dominate automobiles.[13] The FTC accusation singled out four cereal manufacturers. If definition is imprecise, an oligopoly is not the same as a cartel. In the former, one enterprise can by itself significantly influence the market; any price decision it makes will change things. In the cartel, definable only by the existence of explicit agreements among producers, there are more of them (perhaps 20 or 30), and the decisions of a single company cannot be significant;[14] hence the need for coordination or, as conventional economics would have it, collusion. The focus here is upon the logic of an oligopolistic market system (producers and consumers of a product).[15]

Textbooks argue that the power of oligopolies to set prices exploits the consumer and leads to inefficient use of resources. The same textbooks acknowledge implicitly that only the size of such firms enables them to be efficient in capital investment, organization, and technology, the factors which sustain growth. Conventional wisdom concludes, in other words, that inefficient oligopolies add up to overall efficiency.[16] The oligopoly is viewed as something in the process of becoming a dreaded monopoly; therefore any attempt of two such companies to merge brings forth the organized rage of the Justice Department and Ralph Nader. It is conceded virtually across the board that antitrust policy prevents the emergence of new giants while leaving untouched those already in being.[17] In operational terms, government, economists, and corporate managers tacitly agree that the number of companies in a given oligopoly should be no less than at the moment.

It follows that, however such companies compete against each other, it cannot be on the basis of price. All-out price competition would lead to the failure of one or more producers; this is ruled out by the public policy that to reduce the number of companies is to encourage monopoly. The companies, large enough to set prices, use "administrative pricing," or "price leadership," or "target pricing"—all so that each "technostructure" (Galbraith's term for the professionals who contribute to corporate decisions) can plan the corporate future. This is a mutual requirement. The supplies each buys from others must have stable prices if production costs are to be known, and output must be regulated by a "flow principle" [18] (while seldom emphasized, workers have a parallel interest in administratively stabilized prices). "Price leadership" describes a situation when one company raises or lowers prices, usually by an insignificant amount, and others follow. Sometimes others do not follow, or a President protests an increase, and prices revert to where they were until the climate improves. As for "target pricing," its administrative sequence has been on record since 1924:

1. Set a target rate of return low enough to discourage new firms from entering the market or a shift of customers to smaller producers. Design the target for a period of years, not the short term.
2. Set a rate of operation. If a company tends to operate at 80 per cent of capacity, use this as a standard.
3. Calculate a unit cost of production based upon the standard rate of operation.
4. Calculate the price which yields the target profit at the standard rate of operation.
5. Evaluate the target price relative to the market, and adopt it or modify it. If it appears that everything produced at the standard rate will be sold, use the price. If sales seem likely to be greater, adopt the price and expand capacity as quickly as possible. If sales seem likely to be less, set a lower price and reduce production costs. [19]

Profit targets are set well above competitive rates of return. Between 1947 and 1955, for example, many companies (General Motors, DuPont, and General Electric, among others) used 20 per cent as a target. They seldom fell short (19.9, 19.6, and 18.4, respectively) and usually overshot (37.0, 34.1, and 26.6, respectively), because managers used correction factors only to *increase* prices. It has been common to raise prices solely because of increases in cost of labor and materials, *even when unit production costs decrease,* a violation of the alleged Step 3 in the process.[20] The high profits finance indispensable research and development (a reason for the term "retained earnings"); the largest companies, at least until recently, have seldom had to raise new capital. This suggests that target prices and massive profits transform consumers into unacknowledged and unrewarded shareholders.

When prices are stabilized, competition shifts to advertising and promotion, irrational and excessive capacity, gimmicks or services to consumers, and meaningless product differentiation; conventional wisdom often uses the term "monopolistic competition" to disguise the latter (in theory, a product can be different enough to create its own monopoly), but the competition in cereals demonstrates the absurdities of differentiation.[21] The competition is intense, even though companies tacitly agree that none of them will fail. Each manager's competitive objective, however, is to insure the survival and growth of his firm by increasing its percentage share of the market, at whatever cost. He must maintain or expand that share if he is to retain his job, and the firm's ability to set prices high enough to cover the costs of competition makes it possible to produce competitive waste in overwhelming amounts.[22] In addition to product differentiation, other examples of waste assault us every day.

● Advertising is a $20 billion annual business, and the large companies dominate both prime-time television commercials and the massive weekend campaigns aimed at children.

- All of us are flooded with coupons which promise "six cents off," and are lured into collecting green, yellow, and blue stamps that we pretend we do not pay for. Indeed, the premium industry has become a giant of its own.[23]
- Banks in urban areas add branches at an unbelievable rate. If one opens a branch in a shopping center, all others immediately follow suit, and new depositors are promised everything from can openers to vacations.[24]
- Standard Oil of New Jersey and its Humble subsidiary recently abandoned Esso, Humble, and Enco, in favor of Exxon, a label intended to evoke "national-brand consciousness" while avoiding the "Standard Oil" title ruled out by antitrust decisions in 1911. The changeover cost $100 million (research, advertising, sign replacement), and it followed a similar changeover from Atlantic (East coast) and Richfield (West coast) to Arco.[25] The service station operator tries to eke out a marginal living on a corner occupied by three competitors (we may have enough stations for the next century), all lured into captivity by the promise of "running your own business," then sacrificed to the bitter struggle for market shares. Any operator could retire to Florida and live for years on the cost of a single television commercial of the company which franchises him.[26]
- Airline managers know that, with stabilized fares, the best way to compete for passengers is to offer them more frequent flights and more services and comforts (cocktail lounges, combos, and open space). The best way to provide space is to operate so many flights that numerous seats remain empty. This is absolutely necessary, for if one company consistently fills all its seats, it will lose passengers to the competitor who has the space and the service. Each airline, then, seeks to increase its percentage share of the market by keeping seats empty; over time, each airline manager must be sure he does not fill any more seats on the average than do his competitors—and every manager knows it. The industry is the best example we have of competitive waste, for huge

numbers of empty seats obviously mean that prices are higher than they need to be. Conventional wisdom blames a permissive Civil Aeronautics Board, but this is nonsense. The CAB sets prices lower than airlines would set them, but this has no effect on competitive waste; anyone who watches television knows airlines to be among the most lavish advertisers. When it seems that the CAB will award a new route to some airline, many of them must fight for it, if only in fear that competitors will forge ahead of them if they do not. It is not unusual for an airline to spend $750 million or more lobbying for a route it is not awarded.[27] The additional factor to note here is that the mechanics of public regulation (usually associated with monopolies such as power companies) have no effect on the competitive waste of oligopolies.

The economic and social costs of competitive waste are impossible to assess, because conventional economics has no frame of reference (theory) for assessing them. It is blandly assumed that the waste, especially advertising, increases production and efficiency by attracting enough new customers to at least offset the costs of luring them. Market economics (microeconomics) concentrates on the individual firm; using the concept of "externalities," it ignores decision consequences which do not affect it, as well as costs it can transfer to others (competitors who lose customers, and society at large).[28] The advertising agency uses the same notion to assume that it acts only to expand the individual firm's market, for it would be less satisfying to acknowledge that much of the activity is aimed at taking customers from competitors.[29] The costs are tax deductible, and all of us pay them even if we do not recognize them. Advertising, despite its extravagances, is only a small fraction of competitive waste. Irrational capacity, as with the banks and gasoline stations, forces massive construction which is charged to the costs of doing business. The airplanes of corporate America, often unneeded for the purposes listed in tax returns, are used to fly public officials all around the country.[30] There is little or no corporate incentive, except in grave emergencies, to restrain tax-deductible expenditures; a tax on excess profits, the favorite device of many economists, only makes things worse. Why bother paying the tax when the profits, transformed into still more competitive waste, might increase the market share?[31]

Communications media, especially television networks wholly financed by the tax deductions of others, are expansionist industries and perhaps the best example of the spiraling inflationary effects of competitive waste and quasi-official *taxing power*. The television networks have been able to escalate prices and salaries to any levels they choose, advertisers must pay them, and all of us forward our "taxes" to the advertisers while being grateful for "free" television. Professional sports have become the financial wards, indeed captives, of "free" television. Small wonder that athletes, knowing how money is spent but not precisely how much, seek some of it for themselves, and the labor disputes of organized sports raise interesting issues of professionalism in television journalism.[32] Similarly, wage settlements with big labor seem reasonable within the rubric of competitive waste.

The tough problem is that economic controls are ineffective so long as the costs of competitive waste go unchecked.* As in the airline example, controlling prices, but not costs, amounts to worker exploitation—and big labor justifiably rebels. Yet all such settlements force increases everywhere else in the economy. The only remedy we seek is to reduce campaign costs by keeping political candidates off television, but we do not ask why the costs are so high. Given a different framework for economic analysis, we might unearth a massively overinflated subeconomy of tax-free competitive waste, more threatening to our existence than the tax loopholes we often deplore.

* When Nixon's controls were followed by some economic expansion, profits began to climb. Profits, however, were the only evidence available to price controllers; hence corporations began all sorts of spending programs to hold down profits. New airplanes were bought, expense accounts liberalized, advertising expanded, etc. *Newsweek* (October 16, 1972).

About all we know, and we have known it for a long time, is that costs of distribution (including advertising and promotion) greatly exceed production costs. Using conservative calculations, Arthur Bentley estimated a half-century ago that we could multiply output two or three times if we used the same wealth and effort in different ways. As he put it so plaintively.

How is it, we are compelled to ask, that men in one organized society, engaged in making goods for each other and using each others' goods, have come to such a pass that it costs them more to induce each other to buy the goods once made than it costs to make and deliver the goods themselves? Is it inevitable that they should show such stiff resistance to each other in the one matter that most deeply concerns them all, namely, getting from each other their daily and weekly and yearly supplies of necessities and pleasures? [33]

None of this is new, but we have not gone much beyond wailing about the middlemen (wholesalers and others) we depict as villains.

A few economists outline the social costs attendant on our economic system. E. J. Mishan in particular emphasizes the "spillover effects" which destroy the amenities of civilized living. Among these are urban blight and congestion, ravages to the environment, psychic stress and strain, and general neurosis.[34] We feel a vague discomfort with economic theories which assume, first, that even small children know what they want and therefore that the purpose of television is general enlightenment augmented by information on how an advertiser's product matches their predetermined wants; and, second, that any psychological damage the same children suffer from prolonged exposure to television programming and advertising is, by definition, an externality for a sponsor who remains unconcerned. The larger pathology traceable to the total system is all around us, and Philip E. Slater outlines one of its symptoms:

. . . Our society is presently founded on overstimulation—on the generation of needs and desires which cannot directly be gratified, but which ensure a great deal of striving and buying in an effort to gratify them. Much if not most of this stimulation is sexual—erotic delights are implicitly attached to almost every product that can be bought in America today, at least by adults . . . The act of buying has become so sexualized in our society that packaging has become a major industry; we must even wrap a small package before carrying it from the store. . . . Carrying naked purchases down the street in broad daylight seems indecent to Americans (Europeans still do it but are becoming increasingly uneasy as advertising in Europe becomes more sexualized.) After all, if we are induced to buy something because of the erotic delights that are covertly promised with it, then buying becomes a sexual act. Indeed we are approaching the point where it absorbs more sexual interest than sex itself; when this happens people will be more comfortable walking in the street nude than with an unwrapped purchase.[35]

The obvious gap in economic theory is between microeconomics and macroeconomics (national level). If the former concentrates on the firm and its market, the latter hardly looks at anything but national indices of growth. When it does, it implies that large companies should not have the unrestrained authority to make the decisions their very size enables them to make; this leads economists to support more competition. Some liberal macroeconomists (Paul Samuelson) dislike oligopolies but do not insist upon all-out antitrust action to break them up, apparently because of uncertain side effects. Milton Friedman thinks the problems are overstated; all we need is evenhanded antitrust enforcement against both business and labor, and less government interference with the free market, since, after all, relationships between General Motors and consumers are the same as those between a corner grocer and his neighborhood customers. Others have searched, and search now, for closer public control of the corporate giants.

Gardiner Means' idea a decade ago was to label the big companies as "collective enterprises," then to set up a form of public supervision to restrain their profits; he saw this as something different from straightforward price control or typical public regulation, even though he sought the same results.[36] Galbraith, long a crusader for the political redirection of economic effort toward improvement in the quality of life, seeks to bring educational and scientific communities more directly into the political process, presumably in the hope that they might overturn the decisions of existing technostructures—including those of the military-industrial complex.[37] These analyses fall short; they propose no solution to the inevitable waste of competition.[38]

The loudest advocacy comes from those who seek dramatic antitrust effort to dissolve the giants. Ralph Nader would break up most corporations having more than $2 billion in assets, ban mergers among the five hundred largest industrial concerns unless accompanied by equivalent divestitures, and quintuple the Justice Department's antitrust budget. He asks that meetings between corporate managers and public officials be matters of public record; managers failing to report them would be guilty of a federal offense, officials (including Presidents) knowingly failing to confirm them would be subject to removal from office.[39] This would require impeachment and trial of any President who did not make a public record of *every* conversation with *any* businessman. Nader, of course, would restore his version of responsibility to corporate decision-making; any time a corporation would be found guilty of a law violation, the individuals who made the illegal decision would be jailed.[40] This advocacy of Jeffersonian industrialism has a superficially attractive intellectual base. Beyond a certain point, some economists argue, bigness is no advantage, and further increases in size provide no further economies of scale (the larger the firm, the less expensive the unit production cost). The point can be determined through analysis of any industrial process, and plants should not be permitted to expand beyond that point.[41] Thus the unit of technological efficiency becomes the plant, not the firm, and each plant becomes its own firm. Given this rule of thumb, antitrust enforcement could break up multiplant firms.

All the critics, beginning with Bentley and including even Mishan, agree that whatever the undesirable consequences of the behavior of large corporations (certainly the chief ravagers of the environment), there is nothing wrong with the logic of competition. If Galbraith assumes that oligopolies are more or less inevitable, others indorse *some* increase in competition and others seek "more perfect" competition. Cutting across this issue is the question of how much direct public regulation is desirable—one yet to be handled effectively by conventional politics and economics. Public regulatory agencies usually are attacked as captives of the industries they regulate, headed by incompetents, and deserving only of abolition.[42] Confusion sets in when Nader—echoed by the experts on regulation attracted to Brookings Institution conferences on the subject—insists that increased public regulation and free competition can go forward together. The experts, and especially Nader, argue for an "unseen hand" which seems incompatible with the overhead structures they visualize.[43]

This analysis of oligopolies suggests that corporate managers have no choice but to behave as they do, given the operational, legal, and public policy environment in which they find themselves. Even as they compete—and bitterly—for improved positions in the marketplace, they are condemned for not being competitive enough. The competitive ideal, in other words, remains untarnished as a form of perfection toward which we must strive, even if we cannot expect to reach it. Suppose, however, that perfect competition is a nonsensical ideal?

Perfect Competition and Overproduction

The behavior of a perfectly competitive market is easy to describe. Unless there is an infinitely increasing number of customers who can buy the output, overproduction and social chaos are inevitable. Because customers are *not* infinite in number, perfectly competitive producers *always* manufacture more than can be sold at fair prices, assuming raw materials are available. In a market system which includes a forest of firms—each so small relative to the market that its decisions cannot affect that market—the ground rules of microeconomics make every company's decisions inevitable.

All companies have a common interest in a higher price, but no company can set prices higher than those of its competitors.[44] Each company also wants to sell as much as it can, and it increases its own output so long as the cost of producing each new unit is less than the market price. The more units other companies sell, however, the lower the income for any one company and the more its prices (along with others) must fall. The ground rules, of course, require that each company pursue its own interest, not a common interest. Thus, even when demand is inelastic (some limit to the number of customers who can buy—the usual case), each company continues to produce because by definition its output by itself has no effect on the market. If one company, correctly estimating the market, reduces output, this only makes things worse for that company; its own income continues to fall because its price falls along with everyone else's. The equilibrium of classic economics cannot be attained, for there is no way to limit production so each producer can recover his costs. The downward spiral continues until things get so bad that the producers succeed in obtaining government assistance, in the form of government price supports, tariffs, or quotas.

The typical example is agriculture; we have plowed crops under, stored massive overproduction, paid farmers to take acreage out of production, and provided direct price supports. As this is being written, the common sequence of perfect competition has completed its cycle in the egg industry. High prices in 1969 and 1970 led farmers to stock up on hens in anticipation of high profits. The market was glutted, farmers could not sell eggs for what it cost to produce them, and government had to choose among alternative solutions—one of them the slaughter of hens.[45] Conventional analysts deplore the government-agriculture partnership which enables farmers to control the supports paid them (usually by a two-thirds vote in a commodity group) and subsidizes rich farmers who seem not to need help.[46] Perhaps we should have fewer farmers than we do, but conventional wisdom can hardly advocate preventing people from starting farms. At the same time, only the price supports and other assistance have made possible the technological improvement and agricultural productivity we now see.[47] No industry not dominated by a few large producers can survive without an intervention which has the effect of ending competition even as we think we are maintaining it. It makes little difference that there may be millions in the world who could use the output; *they are not customers unless they can pay.*

The preceding paragraphs represent only a common-sense analysis of idealized perfect competition. The only thing startling about the sequence is that economic theory assumes that it is unusual or abnormal, not even allowing for the possibility that it is inevitable. The equilibrium specified in economic theory can be realized *only* if production is restrained so as to ensure that prices do not fall to the point where producers are ruined. But the theory itself makes no allowance for this restraint, nor for the means of implementing it; the theory specifies that each producer should keep on producing so long as the cost-price relationship appears favorable to him alone. Each producer, in other words, must act as though there were no other producers in the market. Government intervention, whatever form it takes, is something *external* to economic theory, actually a violation of it, and the intervention has the effect of restraining production for the sake of everyone's survival.

The relationship between overproduction and collapse is illustrated by noting what must happen if an entire economic system is to recover from disaster. In the great depression of the 1930's, President Roosevelt's program permitted producers to plan a *gradual* increase in output, everyone agreeing that a downward spiral would resume if production outstripped the ability of customers to buy.[48] The Supreme Court's rejection of this delegation of authority was, in effect, a declaration that *production cannot be planned* —a notion that lies at the heart of conventional wisdom. The point may be repeated that the sequence of overproduction and collapse is inevitable, except for the impossible situation of infinite demand (which would lead to runaway inflation anyway).

Conventional wisdom attempts to theorize the problem away by a line of reasoning extrapolated from an old maxim known as Say's Law, named for the economist who argued in 1803 that the act of production is an expression of a producer's demand for the goods and services he acquires in return.[49] The maxim is that supply and demand always equal each other because they are two ways of saying the same thing: there is always enough supply to meet demand, and enough demand to absorb supply. The Keynesian revolution in economics made it clear that demand is not automatically sufficient, and we have a general policy of stimulating it through instruments of fiscal and monetary policy. Thus, although Galbraith seems to make sense when he observes that Say's Law has been abandoned,[50] it has not been, and so we must look at the total logic of our system.

Economic Theory as Political Anarchy

Our working economic design seems best comprehended as a modified form of political anarchy, the government's role being analogous to that of a world government which stands above competing nation-states (producers) and makes decisions which compel the nation-states to war against each other while behaving abominably toward their citizens (customers). The same government insists that no single nation-state (producer) negotiate with other states to moderate or terminate the warfare, because the only interstate behavior acceptable to the government is constantly escalating warfare. In theory, of course, we insist that pure anarchy (perfect competition) is our ideal, but we tacitly admit by our policy choices that it brings only total destruction. The precise public policy and the behavior depend upon the form of competition.

In competitive systems that would destroy themselves if left alone, government strikes a tenuous balance of tariffs, quotas, supports, production restraints, and other instruments. It is tenuous because even after policies are set, prevailing norms encourage producers to be as productive as possible, so overproduction remains the tendency of the system. This has the effect of gradually increasing the subsidy as the market price declines. In effect, public policy restrains production while inadvertently encouraging it at the same time, but in either case public funds are used to equalize demand and supply—thus making Say's Law a matter of policy.

The oligopoly is another matter, and it is significant that oligopolies evolve automatically in industries which sometimes include many companies before evolution begins (twenty to sixty auto manufacturers in the 1920's). The small number of companies in the oligopoly seems traceable to public policy. Three to five dominant companies can calculate each other's planning with some precision, and they can estimate the total market for the product. It is worth recalling that the target pricing formula explicitly limits production to what can be sold. Thus the oligopoly does for itself what public intervention does for more competitive systems. Government intervenes at a later step, to make certain that whatever oligopolies decide to make can be sold at the prices set by the companies, and for three reasons: it seems necessary to overall economic health, it avoids the large-scale disasters that accompany the failure of a large corporation, and it prevents further evolution toward monopoly. This gives us social stability, but only *after* we pay for competitive waste. Government price controls, once again, have little or no effect on these costs. We have transformed Say's Law from a descriptive law of what *does* happen to a normative premise of what *should* happen.[51] Conventional wisdom ignores this because it cannot admit that overproduction is, or can be, a problem.

If perfect competition would resemble Hobbes' description of "natural" and constant war between men, oligopoly resembles an international system of balance of power among a few powerful countries. It is not by accident that theorists of international politics often use the economic analogy to describe world behavior, or that the "best" number of countries for a power balance is five, a slight increase from the typical oligopoly.[52] This is readily explained: unlike the leaders of nation-states, who have at least the option of conferring with one another on a hot-line before declaring war, the corporate leaders of an oligopoly are prohibited from reaching any explicit agreements at all—which accounts for the behavior associated with competitive waste.

Each nation-state (producer) must maintain and expand its territory (markets), for that is the index of its power. It must seek out new colonials (customers) but, more important, it must lure colonials away from competitors. Nothing sounds better to Henry Ford II than a customer's statement, "I've been with Chevrolet for years, but now I'm with you." The arrangement is a complex one which includes dependency and counterdependency. Colonials must be persuaded that they cannot do without the occupying power, but the power cannot survive without the continued sustenance of colonials. Each colonial (market) system overlaps all the others, for each colonial (customer) is assaulted by all the competitors of many market systems. The workers who make the products of one market system are colonials of that system and all others. Any time the colonials seem resistant to blandishments, the world government (public policy) steps in and, using the reverse twist of contemporary capitalism, instructs individuals not to "save their money for a rainy day" but to perform their civic duty and buy everything they can.[53] In a sense, consumers are pinned to the ground, and products are poured into them until they can swallow no more.

Two conclusions follow, one being that producers and consumers have little choice but to behave as they do. Where producers are concerned, especially in an oligopoly, we do not face evil men who lie, cheat, and swindle all of us in a ruthless drive for profits to feed their immorality. We face individuals who have no alternative if they are to remain or succeed within a system designed by public policies which reflect a failure to analyze the logic of competition. They are understandably chagrined when they achieve corporate survival and are then criticized for it. It is understandable too that executives resent being thrown in jail for price-fixing agreements which, if we look closely, *operationalize our own definition of the public interest*.[54] We forbid competing managers to reach agreements to modify their behavior, but we ignore the obvious fact that if a single corporation were to change in response to our demands, it would destroy itself. This is not to argue that corporate behavior does not damage those within an organization who are sacrificed for its survival, damage the environment, and damage all of us in numerous ways. Damage is everywhere, but it is traceable to *competition itself*.

The longer we pursue the competitive ideal, the worse it will get. As a form of anarchy, conventional economics embodies a profound heartlessness. It cannot survive without the premise that those who fail in business are somehow too "inefficient" to be worthy of survival. Conventional analysts delight in arguing that big companies should be broken up into smaller ones so that failures, until they occur in the thousands, will go unnoticed. The logic is clear enough; failures due to overproduction, the primary cause, are likely to be distributed at random, without regard to efficiency or inefficiency. With the best of intentions, advocates of competition use a logic similar to the one which includes dropping bombs from 30,000 feet, a distance great enough to make the effects invisible to the bomber:

. . . modern weaponry makes it very easy for anyone to be a mass killer without much guilt or stress. Flying in a plane far above an impersonally defined target and pressing some buttons to turn fifty square miles into a sea of flame is less traumatic to the average middle-class American boy than inflicting a superficial bayonet wound on a single male soldier.[55]

Those destroyed by a failure not of their own doing can find no forgiveness within conventional wisdom. Meanwhile all of us implicitly understand that whatever the alleged benefits of competition, it is not something we wish upon close friends.[56]

Thus far, this analysis suggests that our total economic system is, except for the growth factor, a relatively static one which has within it oligopolies (which restrain production to what can be sold, but at the cost of competitive waste) and industries with many more producers (in which public policy restrains overproduction). A number of trends, taken together, indicate that new forms of instability lie ahead.[57] The trends, which interact with one another, include the expansion of financial institutions and investment capital (much of it from middle-class professionals who can afford to invest), widespread diversification of old companies into new products (DuPont into pharmaceuticals, and can companies into "packagers" who make plastics, glass, and paper),[58] and the proliferation of conglomerates and multi-national corporations. The trends are producing new overhead power structures which cut across many industries and even nation-states, but they are increasing competition *within* many industries at the same time. This puts extreme pressure on conventional oligopolies of four or five companies heretofore able to dominate their markets. Unable to achieve target profits as they once could, they must seek capital in money markets they used to ignore, and professional managers are no longer immune to being forced out. Antitrust enforcers are in a quandary; while they dislike the concentration of power, they have second thoughts when it increases competition by adding new companies. The trends, in other words, conform to the suggestions of many economists that competition should increase by at least a moderate amount. One recent inquiry into the automobile industry, for example, concluded that it should be redesigned to accommodate ten companies.[59]

A number of oligopolies will probably become industries having ten or twenty producers. That number is too large for each to calculate the plans of all the others; hence overproduction and large-scale disasters seem likely. Along the way, moreover, these companies will give us *both* competitive waste and overproduction. Because conglomerates tend to be multi-national as well, failures will have broad ramifications, yet they cannot be prevented unless government steps in to establish production quotas. The danger seems implicitly understood already, for we see the first recommendations that the entire stock market be converted into a public utility, or that it become a centralized mutual fund under direct management of the government itself. When economist Paul Samuelson and financier J. M. Kaplan suggest that all transactions, commissions, management fees, and decisions to buy and sell be so managed, *they must feel very frightened by increasing instability.*[60] Typically, they attack the wrong target; the stock market merely reflects the deeper problem of competition itself.

The intermediate solution, between oligopoly and perfect competition, is rejected by the United States despite historical acceptance elsewhere. Ten or twenty companies can restrain production by forming a cartel, which, in effect, is only a collective planning process. We prohibit cartels for that reason, but the prohibition is valid only because it prevents groups of producers from making unilateral decisions. We fail to realize that the planned production of a cartel is better than no planning at all (perfect competition) or the "hunch" planning of individual producers who are forbidden from talking with each other (oligopoly). What we call government planning is only the designing of policies to ensure that whatever *un*planned mixture of goods is produced by a full-employment economy, money will be on hand to buy it. Those who insist that the problems we face are due solely to our capitalist framework of private enterprise believe that some form of socialism could solve them. The logic outlined in Chapter 2 suggests otherwise, but the most recent socialist innovation—worker self-management in Yugoslavia—has attracted adherents. What can be said for it?

Yugoslavia: Only More of the Same

The Yugoslav experiment attempts to transform society by converting a conventional socialist centralized-planning apparatus into a decentralized system of autonomous, self-governing economic organizations.[61] A Workers' Council, elected by all employees for two-year terms, manages each industrial enterprise. In larger organizations, the council may have as many as 120 members, the average being about 20.[62] The council elects an executive body, but it retains authority to select the enterprise's professional director. He applies for the post in the normal manner and, together with department heads, runs things day to day. The system's underlying assumptions are those of conventional capitalist economics, in that:

. . . self-governing collectives are materially interested in maximizing their incomes and . . . the Government and Parliament are able to create an economic environment in which autonomous decision-makers behave in accordance with general social interests. Both assumptions seem to have been proved correct by the modern theory of economic policy and by experience in well-organized market economies.[63]

Antimonopoly legislation forbids any limitations on free competition in production and sales. Monopolies are assumed to be unlikely anyway, because "classical forms of collusion" cannot occur in a system characterized by "spontaneous public supervision of business conduct." [64]

The Yugoslavs decided to imitate capitalist market systems because of their "proved" success, and so all the incentives of capitalist systems were built into workers' self-management. In particular, Yugoslavia adopted the notion that workers and managers *do,* and *should,* act solely to maximize their individual material rewards. Having consciously designed a system to produce behavior identical to what goes on in capitalist countries, the Yugoslavs retain a faith that, somehow or other, people in their system will behave differently than in ours. But it seems more likely that their people will behave just as they do in ours. Indeed, this conclusion is reinforced by evidence that Yugoslav economists, committed to what they perceive as the success of market economies, have succeeded in outshouting not only the criticisms of traditional socialists committed to statist planning, but also the objections of Marxist philosophers that market incentives will alienate workers just as they have in capitalist societies.[65] And, of course, this is the Yugoslav rule; each worker's rewards are tied to the fate of the enterprise in which he works. Typically, the Yugoslav Marxist philosophers see the problem as exclusively one of capitalism amd material rewards, not one of competition and hierarchy. While some conclude that the system works reasonably well, and that "education in participation" is proving itself because the Workers' Councils increasingly devote their attention to broader public issues of concern to the enterprises they manage,[66] there is evidence to support an opposite view.

Because workers' rewards are proportional to competitive success, the notion of equal pay for equal work disappears, and wage increases become tied to productivity gains.[67] Workers who first saw the new system as enhancing job satisfaction now see wages as the only reward connected with their jobs.[68] Workers' Councils behave like capitalist companies invading each other's territories. They use artificially lowered prices to destroy small competitors and, when they have enough market power, compel purchasers to absorb more than they intended to buy.[69] The competitive system, moreover, worsens the interregional disparities in economic development that have bedeviled that country for so long. The better developed northern regions have a competitive advantage which widens the gap and tends to keep other regions permanently underdeveloped.[70] Even the professional manager, finally, follows the capitalist pattern; his role is the same as that of a capitalist manager who lives on nonlabor income.

Perhaps the Yugoslav experiment can best be understood by imagining what might happen in the United States if the automobile industry were transformed into its equivalent. Each major company (General Motors, Ford, Chrysler, American Motors) would have a council elected by all workers. It would select a company manager, and the income of all workers would be the result of whatever success their individual companies achieved. The future of the United Automobile Workers would be in doubt, just as must be the case with worker solidarity in Yugoslavia. The point is that worker management, combined with competition, creates the equivalent of small economic city-states. The Workers' Council of each enterprise has little choice but to view competing Workers' Councils (and the workers in competing plants) as enemies to be defeated in competitive battle. Furthermore, any drive to increase productivity, the assumed basis for success, must inevitably compel Workers' Councils to behave as collective entrepreneurs who exploit and repress workers.[71] This can only introduce intolerable stress in a country committed to a Marxist notion of worker unity.

After listening to Yugoslavs who have visited the United States and discussed the functioning of their system, I find it difficult to escape the conclusion that they believe they adopted the best aspects of our system (competition and representative government) while rejecting the worst (private ownership). Admittedly, countries not having long experience in electoral processes can become fascinated with them, and with the corollary notion that if only it can be made certain that those elected have the appropriate class or occupational background (essentially an outline of Guild Socialism), everything will turn out well. I have even heard one distinguished Yugoslav political philosopher insist that it is important to organize elections so as to prevent the emergence of professional politicians. This thinking may be the basis for the firm Yugoslav rule that workers must rotate their memberships on Workers' Councils to give many of them the opportunity to "rule." This is only another version of Aristotelian democracy, however, which says nothing about hierarchy. Moreover, those who designed the U.S. system did not expect the emergence of either political parties or professional politicians. The Yugoslavs have overlooked the possibility that by seeking to legitimize, through elections, the hierarchical relationships of managers to workers, *they have in effect transformed exploitation, repression, and alienation into positive values of the state.* If the Yugoslav experiment does not survive, and this analysis suggests it cannot, it will either give "worker participation" a bad name (an unfortunate possibility), or it will encourage us to face the reality that distinctions between capitalism and socialism are meaningless; the problems remain those of hierarchy and competition.

What the outline of a purely Marxist economic system would be must be left to those who profess themselves knowledgeable in Marxist economics. A recent book written from that perspective visualizes such a system as one in which most consumer goods would be free to the public in accordance with decisions reached through government planning. But its author, defending such experiments as the one in Yugoslavia, concludes there is no third alternative; in the modern industrial economy, he argues, decisions must be made either by a "decentralized market mechanism" or by a "very large bureaucracy." [72] If this accurately reflects Marxist economics, it holds out little hope, for the alternatives are those of market nonrationality and the rationality of elites which dominate the state's apparatus. When even a Marxist economist can define a system of market competition, by definition nonrational, as efficient, we have reached the epitome of foolishness, but that is where conventional socialist and capitalist economics leaves us. What nonsense to insist that we can rationalize a market by making it nonrationally competitive!

Just as the historic robber barons of capitalist monopoly were efficient, at least in theory, at restraining production and costs, exploiting workers, and maximizing profits, so the managers of, say, the Soviet bureaucracy, have been efficient in planning. Organizationally, there is little choice between monopoly capitalism and statist socialism, the only major difference being that, in the latter, political and economic systems are explicitly combined. What the Yugoslavs—and most of the rest of us, for that matter—may not have sufficiently uppermost in our minds is that we invented our competitive system primarily to ensure a constant increase in production. The principal complaint about oligopolies and incipient monopolies is that they restrain production. If competitive systems either compel overproduction or tend toward overproduction, we have used overproduction as a means of escaping the harsh realities of alienation; we accept the commands of others where we work because we assume it necessary if we are to reap our own individual economic rewards. Suppose, however, that continuously increasing production is no longer possible?

A Crisis of Growth

Perhaps a simple example can suggest why a need to limit economic growth would threaten the hierarchy and competition upon which conventional wisdom relies. In today's world, suppose for a moment that I have an automobile and you do not. While part of my enjoyment of the automobile is the knowledge that I have something you do not have (we prize our possessions more than ourselves), both of us assume that if you work hard enough, you will be able to buy a similar one. By the time you do, it is likely that I will have acquired something else you cannot afford but, even as the gap between us increases, our theories hold out the promise that you can close it. Suppose, now, we both live in some future world in which I have an automobile and you still do not have one, but in which there are official limits to the production of automobiles. For some reason you have been declared ineligible to own one, and you do not have a purchase license, even though you can afford the purchase price. Alternatively, there might not be such a licensing system, but only massively increased taxes on the purchase and use of automobiles, sufficient to ensure that only the most affluent would be able to afford them.[73] If you were thus prevented from acquiring an automobile, you would doubtless regard either a denial of the purchase license or a severe tax as repressive, but you would have no recourse.

In this situation, we doubtless would have public regulations prescribing how manufacturers must build automobiles if they are to be safe, not damage the environment, and not deplete certain resources. Moreover, prices would be regulated, perhaps by taxes. If any manufacturer wished to introduce a change, it would have to be reviewed for its effect upon safety, environment, and resource depletion. If the change was judged an improvement, we would insist that it be incorporated into all comparable automobiles, and without its originator's realizing high profits from the patent. While this is difficult to visualize now, we would have production quotas for each company (assuming more than one) and standardized automobiles. Under such circumstances, what sense would it make to prohibit manufacturers from exchanging information on future plans? With production quotas preventing overproduction, with standardization preventing much of the meaningless differentiation that contributes to competitive waste, and with fixed prices, would competition make any sense at all? What would companies advertise?

Today, growth seems on the verge of becoming the greatest global issue in at least a century. Debate will make it clear that no country stands to be affected more than the United States. The Secretary of the Treasury, the President's chief administrator of massively revised economic policy, found it necessary early in 1972 to use the forum of a White House Conference to reject the concept of "zero net growth." [74] Only a few weeks later, however, the same President's principal environmental adviser, realizing that his speech "might make some waves," used an out-of-town forum to call for a "national debate on the desirability of growth." [75] Those versed in the art of evaluating trial balloons were left to ponder whether one or both statements had been cleared with the White House. It is no surprise that the issue did not figure in the 1972 Presidential campaign, for it was not an issue that could be handled by a shouting match during a time of high unemployment, continued inflation, and emphasis on increasing productivity. Yet the President will have to begin dealing *this year* with the problem of limiting growth, after campaigning on the issue of how to increase it.

What seems to be underway is a search for recognition by those concerned with population, agricultural production, natural resources, and pollution, each convinced the problem he deals with is more important than the others. This effort is being overtaken, however, by the synthesizing concept that the problems must be dealt with as a totality. The frightening aspect of the synthesizing concept is its clarification of exponential growth—understandable only if one grasps the meaning of "doubling time." Any given factor can double itself many times over, but within each doubling period never approaches significant size. Suddenly, in just one or two doubling periods, the factor becomes overwhelming in its implications.[76] In 1650, for example, the world numbered a half-billion people and population was growing at an annual rate of 0.3 per cent, the doubling period being nearly 250 years. In 1970, the population of 3.6 billion had a growth rate of 2.1 per cent, thus contracting the doubling period to only 33 years; one study terms this growth "super-exponential." [77]

The way these factors interact brings to mind the estimate that if the Chinese population of today suddenly were to raise its consumption level to that of the U.S., the Chinese requirement for energy would itself exceed present world consumption by almost 25 per cent.[78] One need only extrapolate from that estimate to arrive at what China might require thirty years from now if it were modernized to the U.S. level of the moment. We already face an energy crisis; we are running out of natural gas, and the trade association for that resource buys expensive television commercials to prepare us for substantial price increases.[79] A major question, of course, is whether the world as a whole can modernize to the present U.S. level and, moreover, whether the United States can maintain indefinitely even its present level.*

Aurelio Peccei launched in 1969 a sustained attempt to deal with such questions by organizing the Club of Rome. In so doing, he argued that global planning must take into account the entire

---

* Indeed, the immediate issue may be whether the planet can survive the heat released by our ever-increasing consumption of energy.

range of social, technological, psychological, and economic factors.[80] He and his associates secured enough money to continue studies begun at the Massachusetts Institute of Technology, and the 1972 release of *The Limits to Growth* occasioned a conference at the Smithsonian Institution.[81] The recommendations of that volume, and others, suggest the gradual emergence of a coherent pattern.

The Limits to Growth advocates a future where capital plant and population are constant, input-output rates are kept to a minimum, and levels of capital and population, and the ratio of the two, are set in accordance with societal values.[82] This would allow gradual changes as technology opened up options. The originator of the MIT studies speculates about reducing natural resource usage by 75 per cent, pollution generation by 50 per cent, capital investment generation by 40 per cent, food production by 20 per cent, and birthrates by 20 per cent.[83] One environmentalist, less concerned about population, would rely upon increased usage of natural materials, reductions in the use of nonrenewable resources, and a new division of labor for the globe.[84] A political scientist warns of forthcoming perils if nation-state economic competition continues unchecked.[85] *The Ecologist,* a British periodical, early in 1972 published "A Blueprint for Survival" which included this summary:

The principal defect of the industrial way of life with its ethos of expansion is that it is not sustainable. Its termination within the lifetime of someone born today is inevitable—unless it continues to be sustained for a while longer by an entrenched minority at the cost of imposing great suffering on the rest of mankind. We can be certain, however, that sooner or later it will end (only the precise time and circumstances are in doubt), and that it will do so in one of two ways: either against our will, in a succession of famines, epidemics, social crises and wars; or because we want it to—because we wish to create a society which will not impose hardship and cruelty upon our children—in a succession of thoughtful, humane and measured changes. We believe that a growing number of people are aware of this choice, and are more interested in our proposals for creating a sustainable society than in yet another recitation of the reasons why this should not be done.[86]

While it is not critical to the arguments in this chapter and the preceding one to decide whether one or more dire predictions are accurate, some of the arguments seem persuasive. It is more important to point out that if we, especially in the industrialized countries, decide that limits to growth are necessary, we will discover immediately that the conventional wisdom of politics and economics cannot survive if the limits are substantial at all. If hierarchy and competition are to endure for years or generations to come, it can be only in a world in which growth is used to mask alienation and repression. Even if growth does not become a crisis issue, smaller crises suggest that conventional wisdom has run its course. What we thought we knew about economics cannot keep us employed and prosperous, and we cannot blame it all upon an unpopular war. Even the rationale for constantly increasing the public debt seems less persuasive now; it no longer suffices to declare simply that "we owe it to ourselves." Servicing the debt through interest payments has become a major category of public expenditure, and New York City's official credit rating progressively declines. More and more tax money flows directly into financial institutions, and they may some day be in a position to lower the credit rating for all political governments, foreclose them, and even replace them.

What seems to face us, then, is something far more significant than that usually encompassed within the phrase "organizational change," even when it is as wide-ranging as the trends outlined in the first chapter. We may be on the verge of rediscovering our history and ourselves. Something truly fundamental may be underway, and our only choice may be between resisting it to the end, out of a misguided commitment to our conventional wisdom, or setting about the task of bringing it to fruition. Like the political scientists, conventional economists have spent their time and energy debating trivial differences. Assumptions heretofore accepted without question and seldom analyzed for that reason (hierarchy) or assumptions looked upon as positive values (competition) may have to be transformed into negative values and transformed together. If we persist in attempts to salvage them, we can at best only repress and alienate ourselves; at worst, we can destroy ourselves, perhaps within the remaining lifetimes of most of us. The trends in organizations, where it all began before and where it is underway now, signal something we must begin to conceptualize in all its excitement, grandeur, and, yes, fear.

Chapters 2 and 3 argue that whatever vision of the future we must construct—and whether we describe the transcendent experience ahead of us as a revisioning of history, a transformation, a paradigm change, or something else—the conventional wisdom of politics and economics can have no part to play in that experience. Conventional wisdom will be brushed aside as we search for something that will enable us to realize the promise inherent in the organizational changes outlined in Chapter 1, something to which we can connect those changes in ways coherent enough to show us the tasks ahead. It remains to speculate briefly about why so many scholars and practitioners of politics and economics could turn out to have been so thoroughly incorrect.

The first suggestion is that we in the West, especially in the United States, have enjoyed so much success over such a long period of time that we have become *afraid* to question what we do or how we do it. A century or two is but an instant when measured against the sweep of history, yet it spans enough generations to make success meaningful and hence to instill this type of fear. It is as if we were afraid we might discover something so badly out of kilter as to frighten us out of our wits—as if we might come to see ourselves as Cinderellas having only a few moments left before the pumpkin reappears. Despite our celebrated accomplishments, from opening frontiers to conquering mountains to voyaging into outer space, we have displayed a downright fear of intellectual discovery.

A second suggestion is that this fear has motivated us to overspecialize our intellectual efforts in order to reinforce our belief that we were discovering *more* while in reality we were discover-

OUTLINING A NEW SOCIAL THEORY

ing *less*—and less, and less. Where academic disciplines are concerned, especially those that impinge directly upon the arguments in this book, the increasing specialization and division of intellectual labor have led to a spin-off process that has produced its own extraordinary damage.

As a discipline, political science emerged from philosophy and history. To establish their separate identity, political scientists concentrated on the governmental prescriptions of Plato, Aristotle, Hobbes, Rousseau, and others, without bothering to examine the assumptions underlying those prescriptions. Thus the assumptions were imbedded so deeply in political science at the time of its birth that for all practical purposes they went completely unnoticed. Because of their roles in Political Science as an organization, moreover, political scientists became alienated and repressed along with everyone else. (It is no surprise that leading intellectuals in a given discipline are known as "authorities.") Specialization encouraged political scientists to believe that looking any further into philosophy, or into sociocultural or organization theories, was unnecessary because to do so would be to go outside the field. More to the point, they convinced themselves that government must be something separate from us, if only to justify their own separate knowledge.

The study of public administration became a spin-off from political science and, as such, arrived with the political assumptions that existed when Woodrow Wilson began to write on the subject in the 1880's. This encouraged students of administration to accept political theories (and governments, of course) as *givens* not to be questioned because they were the specialties of others. Because "democratic" theory was derived from an organization theory of hierarchy, students of organizational behavior were actually cut off from their own intellectual origins. They perceived theories of organization as subordinate to "democratic" theories, and consequently they did not even study the possibilities of change in theories of organization. In a nutshell, organization theorists did not study organization theory. To this day, organization theorists suffer from a peculiar disorientation; they are forced to live with Max Weber's formulation of the classic contradiction.

Nobody ever made it clearer than Weber that as the ideal pyramidal bureaucracy (which he and everyone else assumed inevitable in social progress) became increasingly rationalized and efficient, it would imprison both its members and the citizenry at large. In the perfectly designed pyramid, that is to say, everyone within would have his specialized tasks spelled out in detail. There would be no need to deviate from instructions—indeed, it would be forbidden—and citizens would have to follow the rules to the letter precisely because they were the outputs of a perfectly designed machine. To Weber, all this was an inexorable advance which, over time, was bound to encroach both upon individual freedom and upon the elected political leaders presumably in command of the machine itself.[1] Organization theorists were put in the uncomfortable position of realizing that they must avoid reaching the "ideal" form of bureaucracy, while at the same time maintaining the "efficiency" which, by definition, could only be attained if the "ideal" were reached. This made organization theory-building an upside-down, inside-out endeavor which amounts nowadays to constructing theories of how to "evolve away from" the "ideal" type; the "ideal" may indeed be attainable, but we know we could not tolerate it. Both common sense and research evidence should have warned us, because we have become accustomed to wondering why the more any organization attempts to make itself "ideal," the more inefficient it becomes in actual operation. Uncritical acceptance of the assumption of hierarchy has prevented us from seeking deeper explanations. Most theorists still feel that they must question and resist the involvement of middle-level administrators, employees, or citizens in public decision-making—not only because it violates conventional political theory, but also because it violates the "ideal" bureaucratic model they (ironically) know to be intolerable anyway! Even in their discomfort, however, organization theorists are better off than their political and economic counterparts who remain mired in the myths of *their* models.

All this was worsened by the uncritical assumption of intellectuals in each discipline that those in other disciplines were dealing with comparable theories. Political scientists and economists assumed that the mechanical features of their two systems closely resembled each other, in that citizens exercise sovereignty over politicians and producers by voting with ballots or dollars. What went overlooked was the Hobbesian assumptions of economics, that all of us have no objectives other than to acquire as many material goods as possible at the expense of others, and none of us is presumed to even discuss our individual wants with others. No political scientist would admit to such beliefs, but the beliefs are inherent in any assumption that political and economic systems are similar. The contrast between political parties and industrial competition is an even better example.

Political parties are only temporary military structures designed to mobilize and herd people into voting booths for the sake of victory. We have known for years that we have no consistent explanation for our dedication to a two-party system, and we are mired in the contradictions it thrusts upon us. We fear the one-party system for the same reasons we fear economic monopoly: given our addiction to hierarchy, we assume that any field of endeavor dominated by a single organization will trap us within authoritarianism. But if two is the appropriate number for political competition, it should be just as appropriate for economic competition; yet we insist on having more competition than two producers can provide. We remain fearful of multi-party systems, not because more than two parties are necessarily an evil (if we were true to our conventional ideas of "democracy," we would advocate many more parties), but only because systems of many parties seem to lead to chaos. Conversely, if multi-party competition leads to chaos, then multi-producer competition also should lead to chaos. Thus people in other countries remain mystified when we argue that they cannot prove their commitment to "democracy" unless they adopt a two-party system—as when we insisted that an election in Vietnam was "undemocratic" because only one military general (instead of two) was on the ballot. If we think about it for a moment, we should realize that political parties have nothing to do with meaningful democracy.) It is easy to imagine a society having no parties at all, or only one party, yet being more democratic than any now in existence. And it takes little imagination to grasp what it would be like to have permanent "political parties" organizing the vote in prisons when it is time to elect "representatives" to deal with wardens.

If these suggestions are not accurate in every detail, they are close to the mark. Intellectuals, either because of alienation or academic good manners, have not challenged each other directly enough, often enough, or thoroughly enough. As a result, they have permitted rigorous methodology and uncommunicative jargon to conceal the real problems, thereby failing to perform the tasks intellectuals presumably perform. That is why the man in the street, if not intellectually superior to those in intellectual communities, is at least their mental equal. He has simply not been socialized to believe that such profound contradictions represent truth. The notion that intellectuals know less than he does is frightening, for it raises the possibility that the more we educate our citizens, the less they learn. We may have to learn that the "whole meaning of history" should be overturned in a "revisioning" which will upset all our ideas of evolution, primitive culture, and archaeology; we may find that the further back in history we look, the more advanced civilizations seem to have been, and that societies now recalled only in myths were ahead of ours.[2] This is a more pessimistic outlook than is argued here, but it encourages us to understand that our culture has no claim to superiority; our subsequent humility can only help us in our attempts to discover the future.

Transformation and Paradigm (Theory) Change

In *The Transformation,* George Leonard argues:

. . . the current period represents the beginning of the most thorough-going change in the quality of human existence since the creation of an agricultural surplus brought about the birth of civilized states some 5,000 years ago. I am using the term Civilization (with a capital "c") to designate that mode of social organization marked in general by political states, markets, legal sanctions, and social hierarchies, wherever in the world it occurs. . . . I take . . . "Transformation" to stand for both the process that spells the end of Civilization and the period during which the process takes place.[3]

Our entire sociocultural paradigm is changing, and the remainder of this book is an attempt to outline the changes in politics, economics, and organizations that are necessary if we are to survive. A paradigm is the "entire constellation of beliefs, values, techniques, and so on shared by the members of a given scientific community." It also is a collection of shared examples, or exemplars—solutions to problems which, analyzed at length, enable scientists to solve yet other problems.[4] These are circular definitions. A scientific community comprises individuals who share a dominant paradigm (conventional wisdom), and the paradigm is what its members share. The day-to-day occupation of "normal science" is the use of the dominant paradigm to solve problems; this activity continues until scientists realize that something is fundamentally wrong.

An early sign of distress is the appearance of "anomalies," or puzzles that the dominant theory cannot solve. As they mount in intensity, an entire scientific community experiences increasing professional insecurity and then crisis. In the search for a new theory, some scientists shift from "normal" to "extraordinary" science; those who discover a new paradigm undergo the equivalent of a religious experience, a conversion, a change in worldview:

. . . during revolutions scientists see new and different things when looking with familiar instruments in places they have looked before. It is rather as if the professional community had been suddenly transported to another planet where familiar objects are seen in a different light and are joined by unfamiliar ones as well. Of course, nothing of quite that sort does occur; there is no geographical transplantation;

outside the laboratory everyday affairs usually continue as before. Nevertheless, paradigm changes do cause scientists to see the world of their research-engagement differently. In so far as their only recourse to that world is through what they see and do, we may want to say that after a revolution scientists are responding to a different world.[5]

Where our entire political and social life is concerned, the crisis of paradigm change goes beyond the conversion of a few intellectual communities; it involves all of us, directly and immediately. The logic of our system is so systematically deranged that unacceptable behavior and bad policy outcomes are inevitable until we produce an "epic" theory:

> . . . By an act of thought, the theorist seeks to reassemble the whole political world. He aims to grasp present structures and interrelationships and to represent them in a new way. . . .
> Most of the important theories were a response to crisis; they have reflected a conviction either that political action might destroy certain civilized values and practices, or that it might be the means for deliverance from evils such as injustice or oppression . . . epic theories issue not from crises in techniques of inquiry, but from crises in the world.
> When Hobbes allowed that his readers would be "staggered" by his theory, he was not merely stating the obvious fact that his views . . . were incompatible with traditional religious and political notions, but the more profound point that unless his readers were prepared to revise or discard those notions, they would not be able to grasp the full meaning of the theory, and the theory itself could not become an effective force in the world.[6]

A paradigm or theory,* then, serves as a set of lenses through which we see our world. In living through a social theory change, it will be important to use the new lenses for reconstructing the

---

* The concept of paradigm (paradime) has been popularized to some degree by Thomas Kuhn. I emphasize the better-known and simpler term "theory," and I consider them interchangeable. It should be remembered that "theory" is a value-laden word, not restricted to conventionally "scientific" undertakings.

past as well as the future. I implied in Chapter 1 that organizations may be perceived not only as "withering away" now, but as never having existed at all in the forms attributed to them. This type of revolution may be called scientific, cultural, or intellectual (though not limited to intellectuals), and it may profoundly change the world in ways entirely different from those which follow typical political revolution.

If the prelude to theory change is crisis (problems the conventional wisdom cannot solve), and if hierarchy and competition are the causes of crisis, then the forthcoming paradigm change will be an unusual one. It must be something all of us experience both individually and together, for a theory which rejects hierarchy cannot, by definition, be imposed upon nonbelievers by those who believe in it. If we think for a moment about "believers" and "nonbelievers," and if we reflect upon the historic relationship between religion and hierarchy, then our new theory must include, almost as a first order of business, a restructuring of religious belief.

Theory Change: Religion and Ethics

We already seem to be in the midst of a religious revival which portends a spiritual revolution. Among the religions that will be cast aside or profoundly altered is nationalism, a creed that has ruined many civilizations.[7] If we have not succeeded in satisfactorily disengaging church and state, it is because we cling to religious thinking which justifies outrageous nation-state behavior ("Praise the Lord and Pass the Ammunition"). An alternative moral theory is available. To oversimplify, H. Richard Niebuhr transformed the phrase made famous by his brother Reinhold: instead of thinking of the moral individual who is corrupted by immoral society, as in the doctrine of original sin, H. Richard Niebuhr argued that the individual *cannot have a moral existence apart from society.* He asserted that the human "self is a being which comes to knowledge of itself in the presence of other selves." The fundamental social unit is not a "contract society" of "atomic individuals," but the "face-to-face community in which unlimited commitments are the rule and in which every aspect of every self's existence is conditioned by membership in the interpersonal group." [8] This departs from traditional Christianity's single-minded emphasis upon the individual by insisting that being, or existence, *is* association with others. To be alone is not to *be*.

It follows that whatever individuals value can only emerge from interaction with other individuals, for *value* can be defined only as an attribute of being-in-relation-to-being.[9] This does not mean that interpersonal interaction *always* leads to the creation of legitimate values, but that values cannot be created any other way.[10] Beings, or selves, must engage in a "creative conflict" based upon the premise that all beings in the universe are entitled to reverence, understanding, and service on the part of all the others.[11] It is not important whether this approach be termed "radical monotheism" (looking to God as the "center and source of all existence" [12]) or "socio-existential monotheism." [13] It is a way of thinking which prevents an individual, or a group, or a nation-state from assuming that Christian life is right-believing, or that Christianity is the only true religion.

This moral theory can, almost of itself, be translated into an operating social and political theory. No individual, even an officially designated decision-maker, can have values of his own which direct or command him to impose those values upon others. Values (objectives, goals, ends) can emerge only from social interaction in which the parties are unable to coerce each other. The individual brings to the interaction not values, but perceptions; values (objectives, goals, ends) can be created only through *collective* processes. Values can be carried over from one social process to another only as they are adopted by the members of that second process. The effect of this approach is to de-objectify both individuals and values, transforming both into the consensus outcomes of interpersonal and intersubjective interaction. The unit of social action can *never* be the individual, *only* the group.

By the same token, decisions never can be fully legitimate unless they take fully into account the consequences of those decisions for all beings, not just human beings, and for nature as well. Those affected by social decisions, it follows, must be members of the processes which produce those decisions (values, objectives, goals, ends). Neither priestly nor Presidential decisions can be legitimate by themselves; even the word of God is merely what interaction agrees it to be. Interaction between Christians and non-Christians cannot be superior-subordinate, and war (and competition designed to damage others) cannot be valued. None of this removes the individual from a position of importance, because the individual self is defined by its contributions to the processes of organized interaction. This universalistic view points to a potential synthesis of the Western ideal of individual integrity and the Eastern approach to the integrity of the community.[14] Both are indispensable; to abandon the repression of hierarchy without substituting a notion of *collective will* would lead only to anarchy, in which there is no escape from alienation.

Beginning with a theological outline of how knowledge, values, and objectives must be created in order to be socially legitimate emphasizes that scientific studies of social behavior always contain underlying assumptions which cannot be proved or disproved. Organized Christianity, after all, arrived upon the scene some 3,000 years after the shift to agriculture, which may be the origin of hierarchy, Christianity incorporating into its theology (assumptions) the social forms already existing.* That Niebuhr's theory is not now dominant among students of theology simply reflects the necessity to transform all lines of thinking, not merely a few. But this requires only that we agree to the transformation,

---

* Witness the fate of Onan, who ran afoul of the notion that sexual activity must be related solely to procreation, for the sake of increasing the population available to till land or herd animals. Organizationally, people were slaves to the agricultural or pastoral technology of the time.

not that we insist to each other that we require proof. To brush aside an argument of this sort, on grounds that it does not fit what we know, will not suffice, nor will it do to shout "Impossible!" when confronted with something we have not attempted. It follows that if this theological approach has direct application to politics and economics, we should be able to find its counterparts in those areas.

Theory Change: Politics

In remarkably similar words, Mary Parker Follett defined individuality a half-century ago as the "capacity for union." "I am an individual," she argued, "not so far as I am apart from, but as far as I am a part of other men." [15] In her political and organizational theorizing, she began with the same organizational relationship as does Carole Pateman: the two-person relationship of, perhaps, a family. She defined loyalty, for example, as something both persons give to the "whole," to the "situation," to the "process," to the "group idea," to the "group personnel." [16] A two-person family, therefore, cannot rely upon voting processes if it is to reach democratic decisions; this would require a third party to break ties. The old model of male domination is becoming a victim of theory change; some persons are mistakenly attempting to retain it, and we do use its equivalent in most organizations—as when we insist that even in a two-person office one must be in command of the other. The family decision process, itself a political one, can be democratic only if it follows the consensus outline given in Chapter 1 and if it leads to the creation of a *collective will;* that is, decisions are different from, and better than, each individual's initial perception of the "best" outcomes. These can be authoritative decisions, but authority belongs only to the process, not to an individual.

Follett went on to call for "experimentation" to "find out if a collective will could be created" in any organizational environment and in society as a whole. At a time when studies of organizational dynamics were in their infancy, she grasped the notion that collective will requires collective development of it. She spanned politics, administration, and psychology, in suggesting that we search endlessly for the "right number" of individuals for each group process, for arrangements to "bring out as many differences as possible and yet form a whole or group"—this to be followed by the linking of one group to another, then by the resolution of intergroup differences through new processes incorporating members of the disagreeing groups. Follett's theorizing led her to perceive all the conventional baggage of politics as incompatible with her ideal. To her, representative government, voting, political parties, and even the collective bargaining of labor and management,* offered only an opportunity for groups and individuals to express judgments already formed and hardened, while denying them a chance to create new values.[17] These notions correspond almost exactly with what is evolving in the modern organizational world, but which remains blocked by conventional wisdom. Now, more than a half-century later, we have discovered a great deal about the right number for group processes, even if we do not perceive it yet as the basis for an all-encompassing political theory, rather than for use within isolated and autonomous organizations.

Writing at about the same time, though his manuscript remained unpublished for many years, Arthur Bentley called for a "middle-class counter-revolution and reconstruction" that would avoid "destruction and violence" and be "radical not in attacking or destroying . . . but in purpose." Only the middle-class, he concluded, could synthesize the dichotomous demands of "masters" (industrialists) and "makers" (workers).[18] Like Follett, he sought to change the processes by which social decisions were reached,

* While not emphasized in this book, collective bargaining is typical of the win-lose approaches we must outgrow. It is unfortunate that universities, supposedly the centers of innovation, are adopting this approach just as it becomes obsolete.

without necessarily removing anyone from the position he or she occupied. Though Follett concentrated on large numbers of small groups linked together, while Bentley looked to larger groups, they pursued similar paradigms. Why did this type of thinking disappear for almost a half-century? Perhaps Follett fell from sight because she seemed too conservative to stir human minds.[19] She did not venture far into economics, though she abhorred competition, and she may have appeared a defender of capitalism. An alternative explanation advanced here is that all such thinking fell victim to the reactionary wave throughout the West, especially the United States, which followed the Soviet Revolution of 1917. The history of the Cincinnati experiment is illustrative.

One Wilbur C. Phillips learned about the benefits of consumer involvement from his work with the New York Milk Fund, a subsidiary of the New York Association for Improving the Condition of the Poor.[20] He admired the ability of uneducated immigrant women to learn child health practices through involvement with professionals. He and his wife then joined a newly elected socialist government in Milwaukee to establish a municipal child welfare commission. This had to be abandoned in 1914 when the socialists were ousted, Phillips along with them. He spent the next years working out a "social unit" plan and, with the help of affluent New Yorkers, established the National Social Unit Organization; his sponsors included such names as Harriman, Pinchot, Guggenheim, and Edison. Sixteen cities applied for the first "experiment," which began in Cincinnati in January 1917.

The social unit encompassed thirty-one blocks, each organized into a block council which selected a block worker; these, in turn, comprised the citizens' council for the unit. Alongside this council was an occupational council which included representatives of each functional group (individuals either working or living in the area). Concentrating first upon health services, the experiment added recreation, other social services, and some aspects of landlord-tenant relations. The experiment, despite evidence of success, fell victim to the confused politics of the postwar period.

Two things happened on the same day in 1919; Secretary of Interior Lane accepted an appointment as honorary national chairman of the social unit movement, and the mayor of Cincinnati attacked the program as a "dangerous form of socialism." Though the organization did not officially dissolve until 1921, the end actually came with that attack. While it lasted, the experiment gained wide attention, but it could not survive in the climate of the times.

The fact that wealthy backers of the Cincinnati undertaking could not be identified as Bolshevists did not save it from extinction. The "red scare" swept away programs which emphasized collectivism of any sort, even the interaction of neighbors. Indeed, not until World War II and thereafter could the concept of planning be advanced without fear of rejection on grounds that only "communists" planned. In all likelihood, the rich New Yorkers who financed the experiment did not understand that if it succeeded and expanded, concepts of private property and ownership might not survive alongside it. The point is that we may have been on the way even then to a nonviolent theory change, to a form of collectivization which did not depend upon the form of dictatorship installed in the Soviet Union. What we shut off in 1921 is emerging again.

Political scientist Henry Kariel urges intellectual colleagues today to begin "experimental probing" where they are—in "classrooms, departments, institutes, or colleges." He suggests that we all treat all social systems "as if they used greater violence and more discipline than is necessary." We must create, he proclaims, a "new reality" which accepts as democratic "nothing less than a society all of whose members are active participants in an interminable process—*and who will not mind such activity.*" To create the new reality, we must strengthen communal tendencies, support what we perceive to be characteristically feminine roles, and abandon the Western notion that individuals should perform only highly specialized functions. This is another call for universalism, which would synthesize the definitions of citizenship in industrialized and developing countries.[21] It should be added that differentiation, or specialization, or the acquiring of skills is not an evil of itself; the problem lies in combining them within a postfeudal notion of hierarchy.

Because what is happening lies outside conventional wisdom, some ideas not normally considered theories of politics are just that. Among these is Charles Reich's Consciousness III, an outline which parallels Bentley's old call for middle-class transformation. Given today's situation, Reich includes both professionals and workers. Professionals' dissatisfactions are "at least as great as those of their children," and workers, despite their improved economic conditions, remain "niggerized," as they are indeed on automobile assembly lines.[22] Reich's affinity for the "turned-off youth" of affluent parents, especially those shipped to Yale University, cannot obscure the substantive political theory he advances.* Similarly, one forthcoming book will outline an overlapping small-group design for making decisions in a university and in an urban area (Detroit). This already exists in many communities in the form of "block clubs" which, along with charrettes, we will see as an explicit part of our political system. As with the social experiment of 1917, the emphasis will be upon social services, and there are other theories which fit the pattern.[23]

While a diagrammatic outline awaits elaboration in the following chapter, the overall thrust here is that the individual citizen is directly and explicitly linked to the social decision processes which affect him, beginning in his neighborhood or local community. To remove the distinctions between political leaders, administrators, and citizens would reveal electoral processes, as we know them, as the silly charades they are. Indeed, the operationalization of a new political theory will lead us to question whether we should ever have another typical election, because we would

---

* To a considerable (if lesser) degree, however, Bentley and Reich repeat Marx's error. Any approach which even *implies* that one group (class) will transform others implies hierarchy and alienation. As with Marx, the *end,* no matter how humanistic, cannot justify the *means.* Of those cited in this section, only Follett and Kariel escape the trap, even if they do not sufficiently spell out *their* preferred means.

have reversed our notion of what is important and what is unimportant. Instead of viewing the competitive struggle for leadership (power and authority) as significant, we would perceive only *decision processes* as important, for these would be our means of determining a *collective will*. If a President, for example, could *never* make a decision on his own, but could only be a part of a wide collective process, we would become progressively less interested in the identity of the person holding that position. This is what requires us to recombine in our minds our guiding theories of organization and politics. As argued in Chapter 1, it is not the acquisition of status, power, and authority which facilitates suitable decision outcomes, but *precisely the opposite*. Just as in any organized process, the less formal authority is assigned the so-called leader, the more likely an effective decision will be.

If past and present thinking along these lines has concentrated on the distribution of social services, the problem of limiting economic growth may lead to a world in which things we now think of as economic private goods, to be purchased in the marketplace according to one's ability to buy, will be redesignated as social goods, to be distributed according to socially acceptable decisions. It follows from the automobile example outlined in the previous chapter that we will develop techniques and rules for *sharing* many resources.

Theory Change: Economics

The economic task is clarified if we recall that the present dominant theory prohibits overall planning for production. Only systems of statist socialism and monopoly capitalism have done such planning in the past and, because both are repressively hierarchical, they are not keys to the future. But it is worth recalling that the principal reason for our opposition to monopoly capitalism is restraint of production; one of the objectives of the historic robber barons of monopoly, in other words, is likely to become one of our principal social objectives in the near future. Under certain conditions, the outcomes of monopoly can be desirable.

Some economists have noted that monopoly may be necessary if we are to stabilize prices, output, and employment under conditions of elastic supply and inelastic demand (more output than customers).[24] Some operational monopolies, moreover, are not so bad. Whatever criticisms we may direct at the American Telephone and Telegraph Company, its ability to plan a comprehensive communications system produced results infinitely superior to what has happened, for example, in transportation.[25] The problems AT&T has had in New York and elsewhere do not detract from a system that could never have been designed in a competitive jungle of companies erecting multiple networks of telephone poles.[26] Admittedly, conventional wisdom uses the idea of "natural monopoly" to allow exceptions to its antimonopoly prescription. The term refers to market systems in which competition is impossible or obviously inefficient, those we usually call public utilities. These are only grudgingly accepted, for conventional economists dislike admitting that monopolies are ever needed. While urban transit systems are acknowledged to require monopoly operation, this is not true for other forms of transportation (bus, plane), at least not until financial disaster compels it (train). Furthermore, our little-emphasized experience with natural monopolies is that their costs have been falling for years, despite generally upward cost trends in all other sectors.[27] Finally, if AT&T's experience is any criterion, the conventional assumption that monopolies resist innovation may not survive intensive scrutiny. Truly efficient innovations are likely to increase profits while making it more difficult for new competitors to enter the market. Moreover, the innovations of a monopoly are more likely to improve quality than those in competitive industries, since most competitive innovations turn out to be meaningless product differentiations which may not improve quality at all (as in cereals).

Conceptually, the notion of public utilities provides a stepping-stone toward a new economic theory. The term itself means that the goods or services so provided should be made as widely available as possible, and at the lowest price. The designation carries with it the implication that other goods and services are private utilities or public *dis*utilities. Yet it should be clear by now that virtually anything produced by an oligopoly is much higher in price than it would be if the industry were treated as a natural monopoly. If automobiles were declared a public utility, they could be made available to more people at less cost (if we wanted that many automobiles).

A new approach, then, assumes at the outset that individual human needs are easily satisfied, that the resources for doing so are available, and that competition is unnecessary. The social objective is to maximize well-being with a minimum of consumption, a notion that has been defined as "Buddhist economics." Where capitalism assumes that the employer sees labor as only an item of cost to be minimized (or removed by automation), while the worker sees his labor as only a sacrifice of leisure time, a new approach sees work as something which gives human beings an opportunity to develop and utilize their faculties, and to bring forth goods and services for local needs; dependence upon imports and the need to export are uneconomic and unjustifiable for the most part.[28] If this also has the flavor of Marxian philosophy, we should bear in mind that the organizational implications (work should be enjoyable) are just as acceptable to the editors of *Fortune*,[29] and that this aspect of Marxism has not been implemented anywhere.

The conceptual shift will be away from *production* and toward *distribution* geared to the quality of both work and life. This will become inevitable in a world of limited growth. Surplus resources, especially capital, will be unimportant by definition, and so will those who control the surplus. If hoarding it for purposes of growth makes no sense, its only function will be its consumption by others, and "ethical demands for equal participation in the consumption of the surplus could not be countered by arguments that inequality is necessary for accumulation." [30] In this context, nothing makes sense except a distributive economics worked out in cooperative, collective, nonhierarchical social processes—on a global basis.

This brings to mind Bentley's old argument for standardization as one solution to the wastes of competition, something that will challenge us as individuals. We will discover that we do not express individual uniqueness by choosing white over black upholstery in a new automobile, for that only defines us by what we buy. Nor do we express our *selves* by competing to see how much we can accumulate at the expense of others, for this activity automatically alienates us. Some societies have arrived at a point where many people must pretend that everything is scarce and keep on accumulating, as the products figuratively run out of their ears. If we must limit production, cooperation inevitably will replace competition as we head toward distributive economics. Even if we increase production, we can do it at less cost in a cooperative system.

Only the removal of competition will enable individuals in organizations to discover how humanely they can behave toward one another.[31] The logic of competition is one of fear, of being driven out of business, of losing out on promotions, of being fired, of losing status. This dictates the military model of organization, and the resultant combination of hierarchy and competition only accelerates alienation. The sociocultural changes now under way are bound to fall short of transforming us unless we realize the totality of what we must do.

Theory Change: Culture and Process

What passes now for cultural revolution, for changes in life-style, and hosts of other things occurring among people in religious organizations, youth, minorities, women, and ethnic groups—to name but a few areas where people seek change—can be seen as a groping toward a new theory. At this time, we are witnessing contradictory trends. Many of those who seek change, because of their earlier socialization into the conventional wisdom, are still using the outmoded designs of the old culture, often without realizing it. While there is indeed a collision of old and new cultures, careful sorting out is needed.

The new culture understandably adopts norms opposite to those of the old, deliberately choosing personal over property rights, human needs over technology, cooperation over competition, sexuality over violence, openness over secrecy, consumer over producer, personal expression over social form—all in an attempt to satisfy human desires for community, engagement, and dependence. Where we now train young children to cooperate, share, and trust, then retrain them to compete with and be indifferent to each other, the new culture would continue the early training, as we are beginning to do in our schools, and eliminate later training for competition.[32] The new culture sees existence itself as process, and the future as something constantly in the state of *becoming*. Its adherents seek meaningful involvement in terms of that process, a creative one, but not in terms of externally imposed yardsticks of success. They question and confront one another, and they confront issues and problems. While they have a profound sense of inner direction and autonomy, they show concern for, and acceptance of, others, and they are committed to nonexploitative relationships.[33] While rejecting hierarchy, they seek to retain technology, but not in a relationship which makes it superior to humans, and they define responsibility as that of a collectivity for what it does, not as a response to the commands of others.[34] Much of this is familiar to followers of the "youth culture," but the schisms within that culture are traceable to misguided attempts to invoke change through old methods. Militants, for example, seek some new culture, but they advocate a violent seizure of control which our future world will not tolerate. Conversely, "yippies" "drop out" to "do their own thing," but this confuses anarchistic permissiveness with the more collective future we must seek. Other groups make similar errors.

Too many "Jesus freaks" and "Jesus movements" develop an

internal structure of rigid hierarchy and fundamentalism that cannot work. Blacks who are aware of economic deprivation search for success, reinforcing the old culture even as they attempt to transcend it. The sons and daughters of less affluent whites, especially industrial workers, seek to fill the gaps left by their richer associates who "drop out." Given the achievement norms with which they were raised, they threaten to replace the "greening" of America with its "blueing." [35] Some women translate "liberation" as "domination." All sorts of ethnic groups, from Italians to Poles to Hungarians to hosts of others, seek to reassert their autonomous identities, effectively removing the Melting-pot tradition which admittedly was a repressive one.[36] Spokesmen for these groups seem correct at first glance when they argue that they had no racial prejudices when they arrived in the United States, and they think it possible to ally themselves with blacks on the basis of mutual issues, interdependence, and respect.[37] It is not quite that simple.

The old culture is not the exclusive province of white Anglo-Saxon Protestants (WASP's), but of a broader grouping which must evolve toward some other future. The most diabolical and thorough forms of repression have occurred in white-versus-white situations, those which led to the international concern over genocide. The old culture has dominated the entire West, and it seems unique as the only cultural entity which has evolved constantly toward political disunity instead of unity.[38] Many of the searchers for a new theory, then, inadvertently head in old directions, and this is nowhere more true than in the "new politics." At the moment, we can only hope that all those who have engaged themselves, with so much personal dedication, in conventional political processes will understand they are working against their own visions of the future, hopefully before they are permanently alienated. *It is absolutely impossible to assist the change we seek by winning an election.* They, and all of us, must learn how to reverse the old habit of casting aside things and people that do not fit the uniform pattern. We institutionalize—in ways that remove them from our sight—the aged, psychotic, infirm, and retarded, and we define freedom as exit from distasteful situations.[39]

The argument here deliberately avoids the total emphasis on the here-and-now often associated with the search for a new theory. What we must discover is not only a vision of the present and future, but also a revisioning of the past that is consistent with both. This accounts for the use of relatively old theorizing in this chapter. Much remains to be done, for we do not know what other evidence from a long past can be of help. We may discover, for example, that the most natural forms of human organization resemble the cooperative bands of hunters which preceded the shift to agriculture thousands of years ago.[40]

The central task remains one of outlining in greater detail the organizational processes which could transform our political and economic systems. This requires that we think about expanding the trends outlined in the first chapter, with the help of the theory outlined in this chapter. If there is a key unit, short of the world itself, it is not the individual but the small-group process, which enables its members jointly to create values, objectives, goals, and ends and, through multiple series of linkages, to achieve an ever-widening consensus with other small-group processes. The sequence in achieving consensus decisions probably will resemble what has been called "creative bargaining," which is distinct from most conventional models of bargaining. These five steps are part of it:

1. Getting a sharply defined perception of the essential aspects of the conflict.
2. Developing a disturbing concern for the satisfaction of opposing interests.
3. Discovering new possible aims or interests, in which conflicting ones can be absorbed to the larger advantage of all.
4. Embodying the new aims in a practical program.
5. Expressing all ideas used throughout the process in ways which enable everyone to identify deficiencies in those ideas as they are now used.[41]

This emphasizes the *creativity* which lies at the heart of real consensus; something emerges as the desirable outcome, even though no member of the group thought about it in advance. If this is a theological paradigm in the Niebuhrian sense, it also is a theory of learning and knowledge. The group process becomes an environment in which we learn from each other and are enriched thereby. When we achieve consensus, the only legitimate outcome, we have created new knowledge of what we want to do. We cannot hesitate to attempt to design and use such processes because they violate conventional wisdom, nor can we permit those in charge (presidents, governors, legislators, organizational elites) to block that attempt because it threatens their status. Because removing them is no answer, they must be transformed. Since the dominant theories of politics and economics emphasize the central position of the nation-state—the source of the modern religion which has created so much of what bothers us now—it seems sensible to ask how those individuals involved in the policy processes of the nation-state might function in the early stages of transition to the new paradigm. If we can visualize the reshaping of national policy processes, the outline of a livable near-term future might suggest itself.

And so it is time for another leap, this one from theory-building (which might appear unrelated to the real world in which we live) directly to the day-to-day decision process which centers on the U.S. Presidency—as important a place as any to put to work a new theory.

As in the previous chapter, this argument for revising U.S. policy processes includes examples from the past as well as suggestions for the future. Because much of the historical evidence is drawn from experience with the National Security Council (the statutory arrangement for bringing together a President and his advisers in the formulation of foreign and military policy), some may conclude immediately that the evidence is inadmissible. After all, have we not pursued disastrous foreign and military policies in the recent past, and are not the processes by which those policies were determined the worst possible examples? The question cannot be avoided, for it is a reasonable one; hence the need to begin with an overview of the Presidential policy process.

The argument throughout this book is that political theories and systems of "democracy" were derived from organizational theories and systems of hierarchy, a relationship that has a peculiar effect upon how we look at high-level policy processes. We tend to emphasize the supposed need of the President to bring his personal style to bear upon the bureaucracy as a whole and upon his immediate office—as though style alone not only makes insignificant the individuals with whom he interacts but virtually eliminates even the need for a systematic process of interaction. This encourages Presidents to reorganize on the basis of style and, because a President often feels he must appear "informal" and "democratic" in the conduct of his business, the outcome is a series of abrupt changes in the way policies are made. Most organizations could not survive the cyclical demolitions and reconstructions that have

THE THEORY APPLIED: U.S. POLICY PROCESSES

characterized the modern institutionalized Presidency. And these changes may be all the more damaging because a new President comes to office committed to putting his personal imprint upon his office before he can even find the telephone. The thrust of the organizational revolution, conversely, is toward the transformation of superior-subordinate relationships into nonhierarchical small-group processes in which no single individual can impose his style upon others. If this removes personal style as the crucial factor, it also rids us of the notion that informality is praiseworthy. When we speak of "informal style," we have in mind something almost casual and unpredictable. Worse yet, we fail to realize that any such style is incredibly authoritarian: it implies that an individual manager (in this instance a President) *decides for himself* with whom he will interact before making a decision. An informal President, in other words, can be dangerous, for his decision processes cannot be known to others.

The unsatisfactory foreign and military policy-outcomes we have experienced in recent years are traceable primarily, almost solely, to the *absence of systematic policy processes*. We must learn from our experiences with the institutionalized Presidency, and devise schemes that will prevent an individual President from making unilateral decisions. To do that, we must change our images of the Presidency, and a few preliminary assertions can set the stage: (1) It is time to adopt the notion that "weak" Presidents are preferable to "strong" ones, for the weak know they cannot act alone. (2) We must get over the idea that a President should be a lonely decision-maker whose task is best expressed by the slogan "The buck stops here." (3) We must abandon the corollary notion that when a President meets with his advisers (including Cabinet members), they are all wasting time that could be better spent in their individual offices. (4) The concept of a group or collective Presidency makes some sense, though members of the group must be defined with care.[1]

One way to argue for changing the policy processes which involve a President is to predict what will happen if we do not change them. Should we continue to rely upon conventional approaches, most important decisions will be made by the U.S. Supreme Court. To be sure, many people consider that the Court has performed a needed role in the last two decades,[2] but the famous case of the Pentagon Papers shows why the trend is not desirable. When Daniel Ellsberg decided that the Department of Defense's internal study of the Vietnam War should become public knowledge, *The New York Times* and *The Washington Post,* not to mention Senator Gravel of Alaska, concurred. The result was a confrontation of hierarchically structured political systems— perceived in this way by at least one prominent member of *The Times* staff. James Reston, discussing the possible fate of the reporters who analyzed the Pentagon documents and produced the stories published in his newspaper, argues that reporters are in precisely the same position as U.S. ambassadors assigned to other countries. It is an ambassador's job, Reston observes, to collect whatever information he can, then forward it to his superiors in Washington. *They* decide what to do with the information; the ambassador is only an instrument of the government and, as such, cannot have any *personal* responsibility for whatever use is made of the information he collects. Similarly, Reston continues, the reporters were merely agents of *The Times; their* superiors decided what should and should not be published. Thus, the reporters *could not be held responsible* for the decision to publish.[3]

Reston's argument is clear enough, and it typifies the conventional hierarchical approach; since the individual is only an instrument of the organization, he is alienated when he does merely what he is told. It follows that an individual *can* be responsible for his actions only when they run counter to the decisions of the hierarchy which employs him. Ellsberg, in other words, was responsible for acting contrary to the regulations applicable to the RAND Corporation, but he would not have been responsible for complying with them. This logic will not suffice for the future, of course; not only does it perpetuate the alienation of individuals who perform in accordance with the roles assigned them, but it can lead to legitimation of actions by war criminals who merely "follow orders." There is a deeper logic at work here—and it is even worse.

If we assume for the moment that neither Ellsberg nor the newspaper reporters will be convicted and jailed, then the decision to free them will amount to an official ratification of their actions by our society. If the cases go to the Supreme Court, and if that is the outcome, then a closed elite group will have transformed Ellsberg and the reporters into nonpersons, or roles, by declaring that what they did was what everybody involved (*Times, Post,* RAND, and the government) should have done in the first place. This means—using the logic of hierarchy and alienation—that a person can express personal responsibility and worth only by violating the instructions given him and that, if the violation is to be meaningful enough to enable him to retain that responsibility, the organization must respond by punishing him. Things will inexorably become more uncomfortable if these types of decisions, which have so much to do with defining us as persons, are made by a Supreme Court which takes on the role of a distant Hobbesian sovereign.

The idea of the Supreme Court as a *political* actor is not new. In 1937, Franklin Roosevelt sought to transform a conservative Court because it stood in the way of his economic reforms. Harry Truman, convinced that uninterrupted steel production was vital to the Korean War, nevertheless concluded that he should not defy the Court and hold on to the steel mills he had seized. Dwight Eisenhower, not generally thought to favor instant desegregation, federalized the National Guard in Little Rock to ensure that the Court's orders would be followed. Richard Nixon, despite his dedication to slowing down a liberal Court, fits the now-established pattern which sees the Court as a political issue precisely because its decisions are very nearly the last word.[4] Unless we revise the way we make decisions, the Supreme Court *is* our future—hardly an optimistic thought.

All this is accelerated by our view of the separation of powers theory as something which grants authority for unilateral decisions to a number of distinct sovereignties. Among these are not only the executive and legislative branches at the national level, but all the other actors in our federal system (states, counties, municipalities, and school districts). When any one of them exercises that authority without including in its decision process all those affected by the decision outcome, the result is likely to be a court test of the decision. To some extent this has been so from the beginning: Alexis de Tocqueville observed early in the nineteenth century that "scarcely any political question arises in the United States that is not resolved, sooner or later, into a judicial question." [5] What seems new is the tendency for any decision of any subsystem to be so defined (as a political question), and thus find its way into the courts. Where I live, even a school athletic council's decision on how to award monograms for participation in varsity sports has been tested in court.

We seem on the verge of a sudden expansion of our judicial systems into full-fledged managerial organizations. As the Chief Justice of the Supreme Court puts it, "Court systems are complex institutions" which should "become . . . organizations with identifiable systems necessary to their objectives." [6] The Institute for Court Management is turning out "executive officers" who will manage "nonjudicial functions" associated with our courts. Predictably, the courts will soon have available all sorts of professionals, sociologists, and systems analysts to provide predecision analyses of alternatives for judges faced with tough social and political decisions.* However popular some Supreme Court decisions may be, we will not like this arrangement when it becomes more apparent than it is now. If the courts are becoming avenues to participation because other avenues are blocked, we must search for

---

* Not to mention the high probability that we soon will have a pre–Supreme Court to decide which cases the Court will hear. Ostensibly designed to ease the Court's workload, this arrangement (within a hierarchical paradigm) will make the pre-Court the most important one. *That* will be a mess!

better alternatives, since participation and an all-encompassing judicial structure are mutually exclusive concepts. This search begins with the U.S. Presidency.

The National Security Council as a Point of Departure

Statutorily established in 1947 as a formal linkage of the President with his principal foreign policy advisers, the National Security Council (NSC) has functioned throughout most of its lifetime as an interactive process which conforms in significant ways to the models in Chapter 1 and the theory in the previous chapter. True, those in academic straitjackets may not have seen it as such. Students of public administration rarely explore foreign policy decision-making; they focus on domestic agencies, and even there seldom deal with what goes on between Cabinet officers and Presidents. Students of international politics come from a scholarly tradition which looks askance at the inner workings of bureaucracies, though they may occasionally pay attention to individual agencies such as the State and Defense Departments. Still others concern themselves with the "style" of individual Presidents, and thus are blinded to important continuities which may emerge. Anyone who looks carefully at the NSC will find that its history covers four periods which do not match the terms of the five Presidents who have been in office since its inception. One of the four periods belongs to Truman, one to Truman and Eisenhower, one to Kennedy and Johnson, and the fourth to Nixon.

Early Truman, 1947–1950. The NSC was established by the legislation which created the Department of Defense, and was a victory for those who believed that Roosevelt had operated too independently of his advisers. The widely held impression, derived from Harry Truman's memoirs, is that Truman disliked anything which resembled a "super-Cabinet" or which implied group responsibility, hence that he either stayed away from NSC meetings or did not speak up when he was in attendance.[7] The unimportance of the NSC in his early years, however, seems more traceable to the personal tragedies of two successive Secretaries of Defense, James Forrestal and Louis Johnson.

We know now that mental illness affected Forrestal's performance long before he left office to enter a hospital. Before his illness was diagnosed, he exhibited contempt for the President, and Truman and other advisers believed Forrestal was subverting the President's decisions.[8] Under the circumstances, there was little hope that Truman and his colleagues could discuss face to face the policy choices available to them. (The Secretaries of State and Defense, the Director of the Central Intelligence Agency, and the Chairman of the Joint Chiefs of Staff always have been the principal, if not the only, NSC participants.) If Dean Acheson is a credible witness, the same was true of Louis Johnson. He and Acheson could not work together. Johnson even ordered his subordinates to clear personally with him all communications with the State Department.[9] While this once seemed only a personality clash which discouraged Truman from bringing them together, Acheson later concluded that Johnson's erratic behavior must have been caused by the mental illness which led subsequently to brain surgery and death.[10]

The Forrestal-Johnson periods demonstrate the need for mechanisms to *head off* or *prevent* breakdowns in important policy processes. Presidents and their advisers, in other words, must become aware of their competence (or incompetence) in the skills of interpersonal interaction, and many could use professional assistance. This is an appropriate task for an OD consultant, even if public officials (like the councilwoman from Kansas City in Chapter 1) might view it as a threat. Unfortunately, we punish a person (Senator Eagleton) who admits that he needs help and secures it. Conventional models of administration encourage a President to cancel meetings rather than face the problems of a Forrestal and a Johnson; so long as they *appear* to be successfully managing their departments, the breakdown of an NSC process seems relatively insignificant. Once the process is forgotten, however, the problem becomes insoluble. What subordinates of Forrestal or Johnson could have been expected to tell the President that the Secretary of Defense needed professional help? Admittedly, another significant question is put aside here—one we have wrestled with for years in the United States, most recently during Eisenhower's recuperation from a stroke: what would we do if a consulting psychologist concluded that a President could not function in interpersonal interaction? * It is more important to this argument to note how the NSC process changed, and abruptly, in 1950.

Truman and Eisenhower, 1950–1960. While the Korean War helped to solidify the NSC, the emergence of Acheson, George Marshall, and Robert Lovett as the President's key advisers was more significant. They worked well together and with Truman and, until he left office, he presided at scheduled weekly NSC meetings. As Acheson put it:

> . . . Although many presidents have been lawyers, none of them—notably his immediate predecessor—utilized in administration the law's most fundamental procedure. For centuries courts have required all parties in interest to be present before the court at the same time with the right to be heard and to hear one another. President Truman introduced this procedure into executive administration. To it he added an equally ancient, and in administration equally novel, practice of law: the decision was immediately reduced to writing.
>
> The vehicle for these innovations was the National Security Council. . . . *It was kept small . . . a practice . . . that made free and frank debate possible.* Those present came prepared to present their views themselves, and had previously filed memoranda. (Emphasis added.) [11]

* Actually, the question is less one set aside than one which vanishes in a nonhierarchical world. The President would have no greater significance than his colleagues, nor could a psychologist make unilateral determinations.

From Lovett's perspective, NSC meetings were lively affairs which enabled the President to "look down the full length of the hard road and not simply the first few steps of it." Moreover:

> I recall with some sense of discomfort, because I usually was not as persuasive as I would like to have been, the debates in which I engaged with the Secretary of State at that time. They were hearty and covered the subject rather fully.[12]

The NSC substructure became a definable transorganizational process. The principal component was the "senior staff," the assistant secretaries who met twice each week to pave the way for NSC summit meetings. Their additional assignments to the NSC structure encouraged them to develop broader perspectives. From this came the first systematic development of country and regional policy directives.

Eisenhower came to office publicly committed to changing the NSC, but he used it just as Truman had used it after 1950.[13] Ike replaced the civil service executive secretary of the NSC with his own special assistant, but the three officials who held that job under Eisenhower (Robert Cutler, Dillon Anderson, and Gordon Gray) remained neutral in policy debates. The senior staff was renamed the Planning Board, its members now holding officially overlapping assignments as both Presidential appointees and subordinates of their Cabinet superiors. Eisenhower specifically instructed those invited as advisers to speak up even when they had not cleared their views with their superiors. He also organized the Operations Coordinating Board (OCB) as a postdecision counterpart to the predecision Planning Board, the idea being that the OCB would supervise the implementation of NSC decisions. The OCB never worked well; among other reasons, it was chaired by the Under Secretary of State, and, as argued in Chapter 1 (transorganizational processes), other departments could not be expected to subordinate themselves to the State Department.

Eisenhower's NSC remains clouded by the imagery that his Administration and its critics used in arguments against each other. On the Administration side, Robert Cutler's metaphors became favorite targets. One of them was "policy hill," his description of the sequence in which policy papers worked their way through the planning cycle, were approved by the President, then were dispatched down the "operational" side.[14] Critics fastened on this apparent separation of policy and operations, even though NSC members doubled as advisers and implementers.[15] Cutler had once been an Army general, and his references to the "Old Soldier's" (Eisenhower's) desire for careful staff work invited attack from those who disliked being reminded of Ike's military service. Finally, Cutler's comparison of the NSC to a corporate board of directors aroused criticism from those who resented Eisenhower's affinity for businessmen and business methods. The conventional picture of the Eisenhower years is that of an inactive President who wanted only one-page memoranda of the agreed views of his subordinates and who was insulated from advisers by an all-powerful "Chief of Staff" and a dominant Secretary of State. This image is nonsense.

Sherman Adams, the so-called Chief of Staff, had nothing to do with foreign policy, whatever his status in domestic policy-making. No careful analyst could study the Eisenhower years without noting that the President attended virtually every NSC meeting (except when he was ill), participated actively in long policy·debates, reviewed in detail every significant written decision (often rewriting them as he did so), and involved himself completely in all NSC matters. On innumerable occasions, the NSC met not to ratify agreements reached by subordinates, but to resolve the splits between them; documents often came to the NSC with six to twelve points of disagreement to be settled, and it sometimes took six meetings to work them out.[16] Those involved came to view the *process* as more significant than the documents it produced, for it "forced a large number of officials—both high and low— . . . to interact and collaborate with each other." They went through intensive exercises in which they had to analyze world trends, explicitly confront questions of means and ends, identify problems, and consider the advantages and disadvantages of solutions . . . face to face with one another and with one another's perspectives . . . if it did not always have harmonious results it at least clarified areas of agreement and disagreement and forced out the rationale behind them . . . perhaps the most important thing they did was educate themselves.[17]

For those who teach such subjects in universities, this description corresponds to what are called "simulations," in which students act as though they were official decision-makers facing some public problem. In the NSC, the actual decision-makers dealt with policies for certain areas of the world at times other than those of immediate crisis. It may be noted how such terms as "intensive," "explicitly confront," "face to face," and "agreement and disagreement" conform to the objectives of persons who seek to expand nonhierarchical decision processes. The NSC of the 1950's, then, functioned as a low-intensity "sensitivity" group which focused on issues, but with a significant addition not usually incorporated within ordinary group processes.

The outputs of the NSC sessions were *written* papers, and in many cases words, sentences, and paragraphs were debated and resolved, *collectively,* during the sessions. This same "hassling," moreover, occurred at lower levels as the papers worked their way to the NSC principals. The process seemed to some observers an endless tangle of paperwork, but it was a systematic approach to the output of *collectively written* policy documents, and it enabled two successive Presidents and their advisers to function in a continuing seminar on foreign policy. This continuity did not extend into the 1960's because John Kennedy and his colleagues brought with them a wholly different view of how to administer the Presidency.

Kennedy-Johnson, 1961–1968. One observer in the Kennedy years labeled the NSC as only another useless committee.[18] Kennedy himself had at hand the materials produced by Senator Henry Jackson's Senate Subcommittee, which had spent much time in 1959 and 1960 exploring a process its Democratic majority already had decided to attack (to win an election, one must create issues). An especially influential 1960 report remains a classic of conventional analysis; while all its defects cannot be chronicled here, a few of its sentences speak for themselves:

> The main source of policy innovations is the contribution of an individual. He may be found outside, or anywhere within, the government. . . . Given imaginative proposals from such individuals, interagency committees like the Planning Board can be helpful in criticizing and commenting. But if, in the interest of "agreed solutions," such committees blur the edges and destroy the coherence of these proposals, they do the President a disservice. . . .
>
> But one point is fundamental: policy *papers* and actual *policy* are not necessarily the same. . . . NSC papers are policy only if they result in *action*. They are policy only if they cause the government to adopt one course of conduct and to reject another with one group of advocates "winning" and the other "losing."
>
> It appears that many of the papers now emerging from the Council do not meet the test of policy in this sense.[19]

Few documents have ever expressed the conventional wisdom with such clarity. Ideas can be generated *only* by individuals, *never* by groups. Everything must be reduced to a question of who wins (represses) and who loses (is repressed). If every party to a decision is in agreement with it, the decision, by definition, must be incorrect, for consensus is an evil to be avoided at all costs. This, in a nutshell, is the theory of the Presidency which holds that meetings which include a President and his advisers are meetings between enemies.[20] This was the framework Kennedy brought with him, and it remains a classic example of faulty analysis. The critics ignored the closed side of the Eisenhower Presidency (domestic policy) while attacking the more open side (foreign policy).

Convinced that the NSC had diluted Presidential control of foreign policy and determined to make the White House dominant,[21]

Kennedy also committed himself to the contradictory objective of having the State Department firmly in charge of foreign policy.[22] From those incompatible perspectives, the NSC seemed to impose "needless paperwork and machinery between the President and his principal advisers."[23] The OCB, the creature of an Eisenhower Executive Order, was abolished (not a loss)[24] and, while the NSC remained officially in existence, the machinery simply wasn't used.

The Cabinet officer assigned a problem was expected to analyze it, arrange for coordination, and present recommendations to the President.[25] NSC meetings sometimes were held, but only to make minor decisions or to pretend to make important ones that had already been made.[26] While some decisions were put in writing, there was no clearly assigned responsibility for doing so; in some instances, only the responsible officer kept a record.[27] The written files of the NSC, far from being used as an institutional memory, gathered dust.[28] The Special Assistant (first McGeorge Bundy, then Walt Rostow) became an activist policy-maker. Even though this was not Kennedy's original intention, in the absence of systematic process it had to occur. Since meetings and agendas were not carefully prepared, the President had to talk to somebody, and the White House staff was nearby. His informality gave Kennedy's assistants an access not available to Cabinet officers. When this increased tensions between assistants and Cabinet officers, Kennedy sought to "minimize conflict" and "restore unity" by increasing the number of "bilateral" meetings with Cabinet members.[29]

Stated simply, there was no logic in the Kennedy system. The Administration, supposedly dedicated to exploring alternatives so the President could decide between winners and losers, turned each task over to an individual Cabinet officer, who handed the President a single recommendation reflecting, of all things, either the Cabinet member's *own* viewpoint or an *agreed* position. NSC meetings were derided as sham, and the President and his assistants decided that *ex parte* meetings would help. To understand how they arrived at such a hopeless position, one must consider its intellectual wellsprings.

Kennedy was influenced by the scholars who had been fascinated with Franklin Roosevelt's success as an administrator in the early years of his tenure (the only ones Arthur Schlesinger ever explored in detail). As Presidential observer Richard Neustadt put it, "the essence of Roosevelt's technique was competition." The technique was described as "check and balance," "espionage," "informal," "unorthodox," "confusion and exasperation on the operating level," "overlapping," "divided authority," "clashing temperaments," and "competitive personalities." [30] Roosevelt preserved his ability to decide things by putting several Cabinet officers and aides to work on the same problems, often not telling them that others had been assigned the same task. The inevitable collisions between them made it certain they would come to him. The advisers learned they must fight to survive—and fight they did, often in public.

There are at least three reasons why this approach can no longer work:

[1] The bureaucracy that Roosevelt took over was minuscule in comparison with the giant structure that emerged even by the end of his first term. This meant that extreme informality could not work. Organizational processes had expanded beyond the point where they could be managed "off the top of the head."

[2] In the early Roosevelt years, the President was not personally responsible for the budgets of all government departments. Once he became responsible for national economic policy, this could no longer obtain.

[3] Open competition between Cabinet officers and aides, however much Roosevelt's admirers may praise it, has become anathema to all Presidents. Today, all important statements by Presidential advisers must be cleared with the White House, and should journalists report discord between advisers (as between Henry Kissinger and Secretary of State William Rogers, for exam-

ple), the advisers appear before television cameras to demonstrate their harmony.

Truman and Eisenhower, perhaps without realizing it, discovered how to preserve the few advantages of the Roosevelt system. Their NSC combined *conflict* between advisers with a *systematic process* for *resolving conflict;* the machinery, in other words, retained conflict as a positive and creative value. But instead of relying upon formal conflict and resolution, Kennedy searched for what might be called informal unity. The results, from the perspective of this book, were disastrous, and they deserve some additional analysis.

The Cabinet officer who feels he should have been invited to an important, but informal, Presidential meeting is not likely to complain openly about it unless he is prepared to resign. (In the Kennedy years, Secretary of State Rusk felt shut out by White House assistants, something which he quietly made known but which might not have been publicized save for Kennedy's death.) [31] A Cabinet officer is unlikely to submit an innovative proposal if the President hasn't asked for one, for even the suggestion may be perceived as a criticism of existing policy. (Henry Stimson, who certainly had no further ambitions, hesitated to make suggestions to Roosevelt for fear that he would appear disloyal.) [32] A high official may hold back his opinions if he believes the President already has decided an issue. (It is difficult to read the accounts of Kennedy's meetings before the Bay of Pigs invasion of 1961 without concluding that those present felt Kennedy was committed to it.) [33] A Cabinet officer officially responsible for policy is unlikely to be criticized by colleagues even if they disagree with him. (When Secretary of Defense McNamara underestimated the costs of the Vietnam War by 100 per cent, a $10 billion error in one year, the Budget Bureau and the Council of Economic Advisers defended those estimates against Congressional attack, but later complained off the record that they had to use the estimates even though they thought them inaccurate.) [34] Finally, a President who clearly assigns responsibility for any given policy area to a single official has the choice of accepting or rejecting the adviser's recommendation, and to reject it is to indicate lack of confidence in that adviser.

Lyndon Johnson made only insignificant changes in what he inherited. The issue of interdepartmental coordination was turned over to General Maxwell Taylor after he had completed his tour as ambassador in South Vietnam, and the outcome was something called the Senior Interdepartmental Group (SIG). Headed by the Under Secretary of State, and allegedly designed to reinforce the authority of the Secretary of State,[35] the SIG proved to be a meaningless device. It was not directly connected with the NSC at all, except for the vague provision that the Under Secretary's decisions could be appealed to higher authority. For reasons outlined in Chapter 1, the SIG could involve itself only in minor issues. Meanwhile, Johnson, restless because even the Vietnam War did not produce enough foreign policy discussions to occupy his time, took to reassembling the NSC on alternate Thursdays (the Vietnam War was handled by "Tuesday luncheons").[36] Neither the old NSC machinery nor the SIG, however, was put to work to prepare systematically for any of these meetings, so the President's sessions became disconnected from the rest of government.[37] All in all, the demolition of the NSC structure in 1961 was one of the notable disasters of the last century, traceable more to the sorry state of our thinking about politics and administration than to the inherent clumsiness of a few individuals. Indeed, some of those who wiped out the machinery in 1961 were quoted (anonymously) later as observing that "we aimed at Eisenhower and hit Kennedy," and "we did away with the old and didn't put anything in its place." [38] Convinced that anything bearing the Eisenhower label must be torn down, they could not see that what they destroyed had actually been erected by Truman.

Nixon, 1969–1972. The 1969 restructuring of the NSC made it, and the White House staff, more elaborate than ever. New subcommittees were added, especially one which enabled the Office of Management and Budget (OMB) and the Council of Economic Advisers to inspect all proposals for military expenditures; while this group is in existence, it is unlikely that budget estimates can be so grievously miscalculated again. For the first time, a President in office publicly emphasized the need for "full debate" and "fair hearing" for all agencies *before* decisions were made, and he committed himself to the circulation of written decisions.[39] These public statements, which did not fully reflect the reality of the Nixon NSC system, made the process appear about the same as it was under Truman and Eisenhower. The Nixon system borrowed from Kennedy-Johnson, however, in retaining the Presidential assistant, Henry Kissinger, as an important source of analysis and recommendation. Indeed, Kissinger became an all-purpose, all-powerful foreign policy deputy, acting both as the custodian of the formal machinery and as the personal confidant and secret diplomatic agent of the President. He was a combination of FDR's Harry Hopkins, Dwight Eisenhower's Robert Cutler, and Kennedy's McGeorge Bundy, not to mention Woodrow Wilson's Colonel House.[40]

The quality of the analysis produced within the Nixon system seemed higher than ever before, for this was the first time a first-rate foreign policy thinker (Kissinger) was at the center of a collective effort to bring to bear whatever wisdom existed in agencies involved in foreign policy. All of them seemed to have a chance to provide whatever input they desired, and in a climate of conspicuous fairness. Alternative policies were dealt with not as departmental proposals, but as options identified only with the *process* which included the President and his advisers, thus minimizing the commitment of individual advisers to their own proposals.[41] Compared to the Truman-Eisenhower period, however, Nixon's NSC did not meet frequently as a group. Where weekly meetings were virtually a norm during that earlier period, Nixon's NSC met only sixty-three times in its first two and a quarter years.[42] At the time of the Cambodian invasion of 1970, when

Nixon retired to his office outside the White House to prepare a speech on his decision, his advisers did not see a copy beforehand; reportedly they disagreed with some of its details. From this, and from his decision to mine North Vietnamese harbors, one gets the impression that Nixon met with his NSC only after he had decided upon a course of action.[43]

If Nixon's accomplishments in foreign policy surpassed Kennedy's or Johnson's, and they seemed to, this record was the result more of the *process* reinstated in 1969 than of the talents of specific individuals. We may have, in the contrast between the 1960's and 1970's, a classic example of the relative importance of organizational processes and individual Presidential styles. The absence of processes could not be overcome by two Presidents (Kennedy and Johnson) noted for their personal tendencies to discuss policy options with any number of people, while a President with a tendency to speak with very few people and act out the role of a loner (Nixon) was saved from the worst outcomes of such behavior by the structure he reinstated. Were the argument to stop here, it might seem only a plea to stick with the Truman-Eisenhower system of the 1950's while launching a debate over whether the role of a Henry Kissinger should revert to its essentially neutral, or secretarial, stance of the earlier period. But that would not do at all; the argument here is that *some* of our experience with the NSC—and it is an unusual apparatus in U.S. history—conforms in *some* ways, certainly not *all* ways, to the transitional theory we must seek.

The Threat of Conventional Wisdom

Acheson, Lovett, members of the Eisenhower Administration, and Nixon have praised interaction, conflict, and systematic processes, but they also have reinforced the notion of the lonely President who must remain solely responsible for foreign policy. (Acheson's judicial analogy gives us a Hobbesian court with a single judge and no jury.) Conventional analyses argue for a centralized White House staff standing above the Cabinet, managed perhaps by a Vice-President for Foreign Affairs, or a First Secretary of the Government, or a Super Secretary in command of both the State and Defense Departments, or a strong Secretary of State who stands above Cabinet colleagues.[44] All these proposals remain trapped within contradictions which parallel those of conventional political wisdom. To depend upon White House centralization is virtually to remove the Secretary of State from the policy process, while to rely upon a strong Secretary tends to remove even the President. Because of a suspicion that Nixon overcentralized things and relied too much upon Kissinger, the intellectual pendulum swings once again toward State Department rejuvenation; yet the events of 1972 highlighted the absurdities of proposals to strengthen the hand of the Secretary of State.

There was widespread resentment in Congress and throughout the United States that a President could unilaterally decide to step up the bombing of North Vietnam and lay mines in harbors frequented by Soviet ships. The same Congress, moreover, was deeply frustrated in its search for solutions in at least two ways. First, using the doctrine of executive privilege, Nixon prevented Kissinger from testifying before Congressional committees because, so he claimed, that would destroy the confidentiality of his personal advisers. This made it attractive to some analysts to argue for reliance upon a strong Secretary of State available to Congress. Yet neither Congress nor the public at large would be happy if the Secretary had more to do with foreign policy than the President himself.[45] Second, Congress' own commitment to conventional wisdom prevented it from making any proposals for change other than those designed to limit the President's powers as Commander in Chief. A Senate-passed bill would permit Congress to reverse a Presidential decision to take armed action within thirty days after he had decided to do so. This proposal was based on the conventional premise that the President, in the language of the Supreme Court, must retain "exclusive power . . .

as the sole organ of the federal government in the field of international relations." [46] This logic cries out for analysis.

The legislation assumed that an initial decision can and should be made by a President because he bears sole responsibility for foreign policy and military deployment decisions. So far, so good —logically anyway, even if the logic is hierarchical. If Congress, however, can overrule the decision, then Congress becomes solely responsible for the outcome, and, once a major decision was reversed, a President would be of no further use in foreign affairs (as happened with Woodrow Wilson). And so the old dilemma reappears: Congressmen seeking to influence the policy process find themselves proposing that Presidents be removed from the process, without even realizing they are doing so. To turn the situation around is to make the absurdities even more evident. Suppose Congress declared war but the President did not agree? Presumably, as Commander in Chief, he could refuse to deploy the military forces; Presidents have decided on many occasions not to equip the armed forces as directed in military appropriations passed by Congress. It seems to follow that our Constitution can and *should* be interpreted as relying less upon the doctrine of separate powers than upon an indispensable *consensus,* or *collective will,* of Congress and President—if foreign policy is to be workable. It is almost as though the founding fathers made a serious attempt to avoid a chain-of-command hierarchy but their descendants remain so committed to hierarchy as to constantly turn to it. In our attempts to further clarify our Constitution, we have sought to clarify the chain of command instead of fleshing out institutional mechanisms for achieving consensus. This suggests we must design policy processes that enable us to develop a *collective will, perhaps to admit that we have been contravening our own Constitution all along.* How might we do this?

Building upon NSC Experience

A revised theory begins with the notion that a Presidential policy process, even if collectively interactive as in the 1950's, falls short if it includes only individuals and organizations within the executive branch of government. The theory assumes that the President will remain, at least for the foreseeable future, a major participant in the foreign policy process, but does not assume that he should or can bear sole responsibility for decisions reached in the process. Others should share that responsibility, and some of them should come from outside the executive branch. The obvious place to begin is with Congress, and to suggest that it be *systematically* linked to the NSC policy process. The instantaneous reaction to this proposal, especially from those close to the Senate Foreign Relations Committee, is that it would compromise the "separation of powers" doctrine.[47] Yet the theory is not a new one.

In February 1947, the British announced they would reduce their commitments in the Middle East, thus making it imperative that the United States decide what to do about Greece and Turkey. The first high-level meeting included only Truman and his immediate advisers, for at this time the NSC did not yet exist. Truman's reaction was to invite Congressional leaders to the White House for exploratory discussions. The leaders of both parties attended, except Senator Robert Taft; but at Arthur Vandenberg's suggestion Taft was invited to later meetings. The first meeting began in bumbling fashion, but an important consensus was reached. All present agreed the President should hold another meeting before he formulated his final proposals, it being understood Congress would support the proposals provided he sent a formal message and made a special public broadcast. Between then and March 12, when the President appeared in person before Congress, there was extensive interaction among all government agencies and Congressional staff members. When a meeting with Congressional leaders was held on March 10, Truman and Vandenberg jointly announced Truman's forthcoming appearance.

Vandenberg then held a long meeting with his Republican colleagues, designed to pave the way. By the time the President spoke, the entire affair had been extraordinarily well prepared, and it led directly to the Truman Doctrine and the Marshall Plan. Between March and June, when Marshall made his speech, he met regularly with Congressional leaders to work out details. Hence both Truman's and Marshall's announcements came after collective agreements had been reached. All this occurred not only before the advent of the NSC, but even before the establishment of the State Department's policy planning staff.[48]

Conventional analysis of this interaction traces it to Truman's weakness as a caretaker President whom Republicans expected to replace in 1948. From this perspective, Truman "paid" for the collaboration, for he felt compelled to grant every request Vandenberg put forth.[49] Vandenberg met every week with Secretary Marshall, and many of the internal activities of the State Department were directly tied to Vandenberg's requests. By implication, a strong and powerful President could have managed everything better. Yet whatever the price Truman paid in 1947, it contributed to his 1948 reelection. After reelection, however, he felt strong enough to go it alone, and the results were much worse.

When the Korean War was launched in June 1950, Truman informed Congressional leaders of his initial decision not to send troops. He sent no message to Congress until July 19, and he made his first radio address the same night, well after deciding to send troops. No comprehensive report on strategy was made until December. Both Truman and the Democratic party paid dearly for his failure to involve Congress.[50] Similarly, Truman sent U.S. troops to Europe in 1951, insisting that his powers as Commander in Chief gave him the right to deploy troops without Congressional consent. Ultimate consensus was achieved only at the expense of the President's prestige.[51] While three instances do not constitute proof, Truman's most successful achievements came when everyone (including himself) assumed he was powerless to act on his own; this accords with the maxim that effectiveness is inversely proportional to authority.[52]

There is little to be gained from an exhaustive rehash of the interaction between Presidents and Congresses in the years since the institutionalization of the NSC process. The trend has been toward an increasing separation of President and Congress and the more or less systematic exclusion of Congress from involvement in the making of specific decisions.[53] Whatever the interaction, it has not involved even the implied sharing of responsibility which characterized the atmosphere of 1947.* It is more significant, therefore, to suggest improvements in what we have now.

We should *explicitly* link certain Congressmen and their staffs to the NSC policy process; these might be defined as the leading Democrat and Republican from each of the foreign and military affairs committees. The possibility of doing this has steadily receded because of the increasing estrangement between any President, regardless of party, and those Congressmen most involved in foreign policy; but we must reverse the trend. After all, conservative President Nixon, bent upon setting the United States on a course intended to bring "peace for a generation," found it reasonable to engage in interaction with the Chinese and the Soviets more intensive than any of us would have thought possible a few years ago. We seem on the verge of a more institutionalized transnationalism than traditional analysts appear willing to accept, one which includes both presumed friends and enemies. Just as in the case of the transorganizational processes outlined in Chapter 1, subordinates within the U.S. organizational pyramid (Congressmen and everyone else) have less access to a Presidential policy process than do the leaders of the Soviet Union and China. Henry Kissinger himself reminds us of the importance of including friendly

* Given the way we conventionally look at administrative structures, especially when spelled out in statutes, the establishment of the NSC probably encouraged Presidents to exclude from its deliberations those not "officially" assigned.

countries within our decision processes before reaching decisions which affect them,[54] and this has now been extended to cover enemies as well. While Congressmen do not yet see it this way, the issue is actually one of equal rights for *them*.

The estrangement between Presidents and Congressional foreign policy leaders is already too well established for comfort, and it would take some time for all the participants to get used to having Senator J. William Fulbright sit in on NSC meetings. Yet a principal factor in the estrangement has been the systematic Presidential exclusion of Congress. Individuals who feel excluded are likely to oppose decision outcomes for that reason alone, even when they might come to the same decisions if involved in the process of making them. This is not to argue that Fulbright would have agreed with each foreign policy decision of the last decade had he been party to the deliberations preceding it. Nor is it to insist that every decision would have been improved had he been a part of the policy process, even if this new paradigm assumes that decisions are likely to be better if *not* everyone sitting at the table is formally subordinate to the chairman (the President).

The linkages urged here are natural ones, and only conventional wisdom stands in their way. In 1970 the Senate Foreign Relations Committee began sending its staff members, some of them former members of the Foreign Service, on overseas inspection trips. Their cables from abroad were forwarded to the State Department and the White House staff, thus bringing the executive branch within the ambit of information processes of the legislative branch.[55] Ambassadorial cables from abroad could be entrusted to appropriate Congressmen, thereby expanding explicit linkages in the opposite direction. To involve staff members of the same Congressional committee directly in NSC staff work preceding summit meetings of the President, his advisers, and the Congressmen would seem only another logical extension.

No sensible distinction can be made between participants drawn from the executive and legislative branches of government and participants drawn from elsewhere. We saw nothing unusual in

Kennedy's inclusion of outsiders in deliberations on the Cuban missile crisis. And, for that matter, the Council on Foreign Relations has regarded itself as a part of the foreign policy process for years.[56] Once we can make it clear to ourselves that distinctions between political and nonpolitical actors are meaningless, we will see the futility of attempting to narrowly define "authority" and "responsibility." There are now and there increasingly will be innumerable foreign policy issues which, to be sensibly decided, require the involvement of individuals and organizations looked upon as outsiders. One issue of the Vietnam War is an example of what might have been done.

When U.S. troop commitments to Vietnam became very high, President Johnson and his advisers decided not to mobilize National Guard and Reserve forces, but to rely upon an army made up of drafted young men, especially young men unlikely to attend college. This instantly transferred to a small segment of the citizenry virtually the entire personal risk associated with the war. The decision also had the effect of alienating those not drafted, many of them college youth who knew they were studying only because others were dying overseas. Whether one is for or against the Vietnam War, one can see that decisional outcomes would have been vastly improved had those most affected by such decisions (in this case, those drafted and those not drafted) been party to decision processes. From the prowar perspective, a more equitable sharing of the burden could have been worked out; from the antiwar perspective, decision-makers would have known in advance that the political and social costs of such a decision could not be tolerated over time.

Operationalizing this approach to making significant decisions could be extremely difficult or relatively easy. We must find out, for it will not do to argue that it is impossible or that policy-makers legitimately can decide on their own who marches off to die and who does not. This is not only unfair to the individuals selected; it is just as unfair to the decision-makers, who, after all, pay an equivalent psychological cost. There can be no substitute for a collective approach which, at the minimum, includes those affected by decision outcomes. It is necessary, then, to suggest an organizational outline for linking all of us together in social decision processes. This can be done most coherently with domestic policy processes.

The Expanded Outline: Domestic Policy

In 1956 an observer suggested that future Presidents would need "functional sub-Cabinets" to help them deal with policy areas in a systematic way.[57] President Nixon took an explicit step in this direction by establishing in 1970 a Domestic Council, describing it as the counterpart of the NSC.[58] This came shortly after he had directed major federal agencies (Labor; Health, Education and Welfare; Environmental Protection Agency; Law Enforcement Assistance Administration; Housing and Urban Development; and Office of Economic Opportunity) to locate their regional field offices in the same ten cities in the United States and to use the same geographical boundaries for the responsibilities of those offices.[59]

There were obvious reasons for the action. The governor of Kentucky had discovered that to speak to regional officials of HUD, he had to visit Atlanta. The HEW office was in Raleigh, Labor had an office in Chicago, and OEO handled everything in Washington.[60] Regional officials were reluctant to meet with the governor at a single location, but all realized that any comprehensive plan for the region required the involvement of all of them. The problem had been under study before Nixon came to office, since the expansion of social programs in the 1960's had made it clear that restructuring was needed. The problem, however, went beyond the relocation of field offices, as was demonstrated by the President's parallel actions.

He enlarged the role of the Budget Bureau, changed its name to the Office of Management and Budget (OMB), and handed it broad responsibility to evaluate all ongoing programs of all government agencies. This seemed to place OMB above all Cabinet agencies, and those who advocated regionalization seemed to have this in mind. They wanted to put an OMB official in each regional grouping of offices, designate him the "President's man," and give him authority to make budgetary decisions binding not only upon federal agencies but upon states and other entities to which funds might be allocated.[61] If this had been done, the OMB official might have seemed a "regional President" standing between elected governors and an elected President. But it would have raised political questions; hence the President designated a separate Assistant Director of OMB as coordinator for each set of regional offices, then prohibited the Assistant Directors from moving permanently to the regions. They were to live in Washington and to travel only occasionally to their regions. This design led to predictable results.

In conversation with the author, a high-level OMB management expert admitted that the agency felt it must proceed cautiously in implementing its role in the ten federal regions. To do otherwise might lead to a confrontation between the OMB and a Cabinet officer who felt his autonomy threatened. With the Assistant Directors remaining in Washington, the White House looks to individual agencies to provide strong leadership on a project-by-project basis,[62] but this hierarchical approach not only makes other federal agencies wary of intensive involvement but scares off state and local officials for the same reason. The outlines of a viable policy system are visible, but conventional wisdom prevents further articulation. Those in the system cannot yet see that as they increase their reliance upon hierarchy, less and less is accomplished.

It is more important to sketch the conceptual outline of a revised policy process, or series of processes, than to fill it in. Indeed, the conscious adoption of a theory of this sort would be only the beginning of continuous change; individuals and groups (including all those we now define as government agencies, interest groups, and private organizations) would enter and leave specific policy processes in accordance with the situation at the moment. If one reflects on it for a moment, the framework in Figure 6 simply

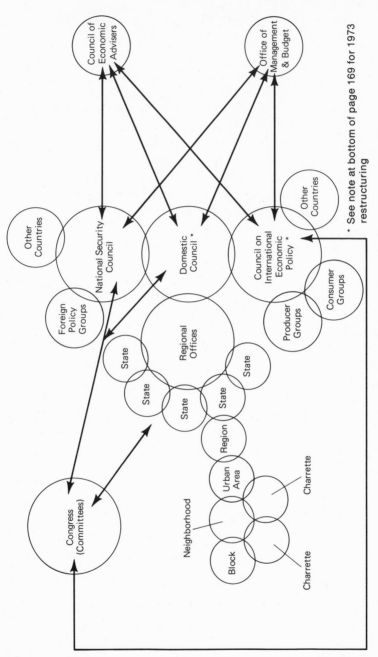

Figure 6: Redesigned U. S. Policy Process

* See note at bottom of page 169 for 1973 restructuring

formalizes numerous linkages already in existence, drawing upon widespread trends in organization theory and practice to obliterate distinctions between the formal and the informal. As outlined here, the policy system begins with the three councils already officially in existence, the most recent addition (Council on International Economic Policy) reflecting Nixon's conclusion that we must approach such issues systematically. Given the impending debate on economic growth, this new sub-Cabinet will become a focal point of Presidential attention before long. As presently constituted, both it and the Domestic Council (each council is assigned an Assistant to the President) are unwieldy; they are too large, each having a formal membership of approximately ten.[63] Groups of five or so principals would be more desirable—even if that requires breaking up large groups into smaller ones and then setting up linkages between them. The lack of emphasis upon the President as an individual will be unacceptable to some, as will the formal overlapping of governmental and nongovernmental organizations, and of urban areas, substate regions, states, and federal regional offices.* The diagram outlines a system which has no single focus of authority, responsibility, or sovereignty, and which explicitly allows for an overlapping of the policy processes of other nation-states with ours. If the idea of having outsiders (the draft-eligible youth) peruse "top secret" policy proposals seems startling, perhaps we should examine the assumptions on which we now exclude them. In operation, this policy system would resemble the Japanese approach to consensus, as did Truman's approach in 1947.

The Council on International Economic Policy provides the linkage mechanism for bringing together our supposedly separate

---

* The classic contradiction of conventional wisdom is perfectly reflected in a federal system. The national government and states (provinces) must interact in resolving common problems when both have Constitutional powers. If the state (province) is subordinate, the system no longer is federal but, if the state (province) can reject a national decision, the system becomes anarchistic.

political and economic systems. Worldwide planning on a product-by-product and resource-by-resource basis is inevitable, the only question being how long we shall resist. This means bringing together government and business. Initially it might become a partnership model which would "permit government and business to treat one another as allies associated in a common endeavor rather than as foes." This argument, outlined by a former counsel for the Senate Anti-Trust Subcommittee, recognizes the need for "institutional means that will permit the private and public sectors to coordinate . . . their objectives and requirements." [64] For practical purposes, explicit linkages have already been installed in rough form, since important price and wage decisions must be coordinated with a control apparatus that is likely to remain. With the United Nations holding conferences on the future of the world's environment, and with the recognized need to set about conscious planning for the development and conservation of seabed resources (to name but one area), the requirement for structured processes should be self-evident. Even now, the scope of the multinational corporation calls for the parallel development of transnational economic policy processes. Consider:

> . . . a supertanker that hauls crude oil from the Middle East to Belgium is built in Japan on behalf of a group of California investors, is financed by a syndicate of New York banks and is chartered on a long-term basis to a Dutch oil company. It flies a Panamanian flag, is manned by a Hong Kong–Chinese crew under a German master, and is insured by Lloyd's of London.[65]

Surely we must design policy systems to cope with such phenomena.

It remains to sketch one detail and make one broad observation concerning the unique qualifications of the U.S. system for this redesign. The Council of Economic Advisers and the Office of Management and Budget are portrayed as secretariat or service units, explicitly removing the notion they stand above any of the institutions depicted. Operationally, OMB experts might be attached to innumerable policy processes throughout the United

States, as they are now attached to the regional groupings of federal agencies. The OMB is a center of both managerial and budgetary expertise, but the President has elected to assign it a more hierarchical role.* The notion here is that the experts should be fully involved, but not as authority figures. If the hierarchical overtones were removed, the OMB Assistant Directors could move to the regional offices and go to work.

The U.S. Constitution is uniquely adaptable to the theory outlined here. The U.S. formula of divided sovereignty makes it easy to design planning processes without a central focus of authority. We remain temporarily stalemated only because our own addiction to conventional wisdom convinces us that joint planning by cities, states, and national government cannot be effective unless we become a unitary nation-state. As in the two-person family, we must realize that a democratic policy process is possible only if we rid ourselves of the notion that an organizational pyramid must be created. Our federal system gives us an opportunity unique in the West, if not in the world. All we need do is create policy processes which, by the terms of our own Constitution, could not be managed by a single decision-maker. And so we have before us the chance to operationalize the theory; all the processes envisioned here would be ongoing "sensitivity sessions," for none of the participants in any process would be able to rely upon his or her formal authority over others. To put it even more simply, all we need do is *imagine* that a President is always as weak as Truman was presumed to be in 1947, then design policy processes on that premise.

It will not be an easy task to decide in each specific instance

---

* As 1973 began, Nixon named four Cabinet members "policy" Counselors (Treasury for "economics," Health, Education, Welfare for "human resources," Housing and Urban Development for "community development,". Agriculture for "natural resources"). Widely interpreted as a "Super-Cabinet," the design can be viewed as restructuring the Domestic and Economic Policy Councils into manageable (and necessarily overlapping) sub-groups. All we need do is view the structures as *nonhierarchical and collective* and, critics notwithstanding, avoid dismantling them (as Kennedy did with the NSC).

which individuals and groups should be included and why. We can only begin by linking together what we now perceive as the separate sovereignties of the federal system, separate branches of government at all levels, and other autonomous organizations. While conventional analysts cannot yet understand how coherent policies, plans, and programs could emerge from such processes, it is time to operationalize the merger of politics and administration we have sought only in rhetoric up to now. The designs of the processes, and the procedures used within them, are crucial; given the designs, those within specific processes could not be excluded from any deliberations. *Ex parte* meetings would be out of order, as would failure to invite a Secretary of State to a foreign policy meeting and to include young people who might be drafted. This is the most necessary aspect of merging the formal and the informal, for the casual style of some administrators who believe they encourage openness and participation is the enemy of the theory argued here.

Even if we cannot now discern the ultimate shape of a redesigned system, by implication a global one, it is time to experiment. The circles in Figure 6 represent actual or potential processes with which we already have experience; all that remains to do is formalize the arrangements. The longest experience we have has been with the NSC, and it seems self-evident that the foreign policy process, whatever its systemization up to now, needs further opening up. Despite apparent successes, as in the summit meetings in Peking and Moscow, the closed nature of the processes we now use blocks the credibility and trust we must seek. The distinctions between political and nonpolitical actors will disappear anyway; the only question is when.

From an administrative standpoint, implementation of this scheme will require changing the way we look at paperwork and information systems. To assert that "government" includes us all is to lay the base for a more elaborate information network than we ever considered in the past. If neighborhood groups and other outsiders are to be brought inside, we must expand what we call the red tape of bureaucracy rather than seek to eliminate it. A theory of extended face-to-face discussion within an almost infinite number of small groups requires the wherewithal to deal with huge numbers of written documents. This substantial "institutional memory" will be needed if any of us, newly assigned to a policy process, are to bring ourselves up to date. While each group engaged in the development of a particular policy will use intensive verbal interaction, it will also need to *write things down,* which sensitivity groups (as we now know them) usually do not do. This is but another example of the conceptual shift we must experience. We will have to be precise, and this will require both verbal and written skills. Our current problem, then, is not an overabundance of red tape; rather it is a perversion traceable to hierarchy. What we now define as red tape frustrates us because it seeks to make certain that we *obey,* instead of facilitating our involvement in decision processes.

As indicated in the outline, all sorts of organizations we now regard as nongovernmental will be seen instead as operational parts of political government itself. Yes, General Motors will be a part of political government, but so will community groups and families, for the removal of distinctions between governmental and nongovernmental will be complete. This leads to one of the most interesting paradoxes of all, but it is simply another aspect of the future we must face. We have been living for years with a theory which assumes that all social organizations must be designed around superior-subordinate relationships. The new theory will adopt one part of this assumption: it will indeed be necessary, as it always has been, that the organizational structures of society be compatible with one another. The future will be one of compatible *nonhierarchies.*

Simplifying the Model

As argued thus far, this policy process model may seem too confusing to be understood. But it can be simplified so as to indicate how policy documents could be formulated and the *collective will*

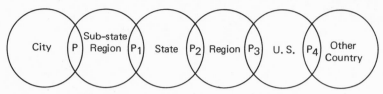

Figure 7: The Policy Process Simplified

reflected within them. Assume for the moment that overlapping circles (Figure 7) represent the policy processes of the governmental entities so indicated. Assume also that each policy process contains approximately five individuals, and that each is interlocked with a number of other processes. Individual P is a facilitator, or linking pin, who serves as a member of both the city's policy process and that of the substate region of which the city is a part. Similarly, individuals P_1 through P_4 function in the same overlapping manner.

Beginning from the left, the operational rule is that the city and the region must develop a consensus plan of what is to be accomplished, and the plan must include all appropriate subplans; both city and regional officials are involved in the designing of the subplans, as are individuals from neighborhood groups, economic groups, etc. Individual P, fully involved in the proceedings of the two policy processes, keeps them linked together, making certain that disagreements and conflicts are resolved at each stage; the consensus plan stands as the *collective will* of the city and region. This scheme continues, each consensus plan involving at least two levels of government, the facilitating mechanisms P_{1-4} performing the same conflict-resolving roles.

It can be seen that P deals face to face with individuals from three levels of government. He is a member of both city and regional processes, and his latter role puts him in a face-to-face relationship with P_1, who, in turn, is a member of the state's process. In this sense, P has a direct involvement in the state process and, presumably, a direct influence on its policy outputs. P's relationship with the multistate regional policy process is an indirect one which follows from the face-to-face interaction of P_1 and P_2. All this, it should be noted, is *formal* involvement in policy processes which must produce consensus outcomes, not the traditional form of "access" wherein one individual attempts to persuade another who retains sole authority over the outcome.

Because no policy process can produce a decision of its own, and because of the multiple overlapping, all the consensus plans so produced can, over time, become the *collective will* of *all* those involved in *all* the processes. The model explicitly requires us, of course, to abandon the notion that any single unit of government (and any organization) can produce a suitable plan for its own future that is not interlocked with those of other units of government (and other organizations). Stated more simply, we must abandon the notion of organizational autonomy.

The individual's influence in a scheme of this sort would be much more far-reaching, as a quick look at the diagrams indicates. In the simplified model, the individual directly influences three small-group processes; if we assume for the moment that an individual could be a member of, say, five such processes, then that individual directly could influence fifteen groups. The indirect influence would be considerably greater, even if we could not measure it with precision. Suppose, for example, that each small-group process contained five individuals and that each was a member of five processes. The interaction among the five individuals could have considerable influence upon at least seventy-five processes. This form of access would go far beyond anything we know now, for no decision could be implemented by any group without the agreement of the groups linked to it, which in turn would be linked to other groups. Thus, in situations such as the one outlined in Figure 7, individuals tied to the city's policy process (including those in neighborhood groups) would affect the U.S. policy process, even though that influence could not be discerned with precision.

As an organizational design, these outlines depart only slightly from our experience with policy-making processes. That is because we have no choice but to violate conventional administrative theories to get anything done at all. That we have not examined the deepest implications of the methods we actually use is another manifestation of our fear that our dominant theories will not stand up under close inspection. If a group process is to reach effective consensus, voting can play no part, for voting only perpetuates conflict and makes it impossible to find a basis for agreement. But voting is only one of the cherished traditions we must challenge; another is our fascination with political parties as agents of change and democracy.

Parties are especially significant because they are a tradition which few thought necessary when the United States was formed. One of the questions we might ask is why the founding fathers did not build parties into our Constitutional system. We have contented ourselves with the absurd notion that parties were necessary to complete the outline of the "democracy" the founding fathers handed us. Suppose, however, that it is the other way around. Suppose that parties and everything associated with them are a violent departure from our Constitution? As it stands now, we cannot deal with political party structures at all, for it is argued seriously (as during the 1972 political conventions) that political parties cannot be made subject to any rules other than those they enact for themselves. They are, for practical purposes, extralegal, perhaps because they have never made sense within our Constitution. This is the type of question we must ask if we are to survive, and a final chapter is reserved for wider speculation about the future.

6 It is time to be more futuristic. This chapter is speculation, some of it frightening even to the author, about changes in individual life-styles, organizations, politics, and economics that make sense in terms of the theory outlined in the last two chapters. The changes initially will bring some pain and fear, for most of us probably are afraid of being released from the repressive bonds of hierarchy; we are afraid we might not like what we discover about our*selves*. Hierarchy, after all, gives us a built-in rationalization for not being creative, for not fully developing our talents; it enables us to tell ourselves we have talents we may not have at all. We need have no fear, however, for the new paradigm of mutually supportive interaction will not require that individual contributions be evaluated, one against the other; *all* contributions will be valued. All groups, in other words, will have as an important responsibility the allaying of the fears of their members.

On balance, we have reason to be optimistic, even if those addicted to conventional wisdom will make things painful for a time as they make their final attempts to solve problems they cannot solve and to prevent changes that must come. Crisis will bring out the best in us, not the worst, as New Yorkers discovered during the power blackout a few years ago: citizens suddenly found themselves cooperating with each other, aware of their mutual dependence and happy to discover it within an uncertain environment. A little-noticed 1949 novel makes a parallel argument.[1]

The novel opens in 1960, then eleven years in the future. An international group of astronomers, a Soviet among them, discovers a new planet, and by the group's calculations, the planet will come very close to Earth by Christmas Day 1962. While the

A SENSUOUS FUTURE OR NONE?

planet already is responsible for some earthquakes and other disasters, these are attributed to Soviet and American launchings of secret weapons against each other. The world stands on the brink of nuclear war; many cities already are evacuated. The astronomers decide to announce that the planet will not merely come close to Earth, but will *collide* with it on Christmas Day 1962. Confronted with this "knowledge," the Soviets and Americans conclude that there is little point in destroying one another. All governments use whatever resources they have to alleviate human distress, and transform economic systems into engines of distribution. Since hoarding for further growth no longer is relevant, they are able to provide reasonable standards of living for all citizens. Governments agree to form a Federation of the World; one subagency, the World Conservation Commission, plans economic activity so as to ensure everyone's survival—until the collision. The mysterious planet comes close to Earth on Christmas Day and, when it veers away, everyone interprets the near miss as a miracle which gives the world a new opportunity to benefit from its lesson in how to cooperate for survival.

The fictitious astronomers designed an environment encouraging individuals and organizations to change their behavior toward one another. They performed as "behavior engineers," in B. F. Skinner's terminology. (Skinner, of course, argues that *all* human behavior is determined by the environment in which the individual is situated at the moment.) Like Skinner, the novelist assumed it valid for elites, astronomers in this instance, to manipulate information so as to achieve a larger objective; the goal of humane behavior and survival justified the means of false announcements. To some degree, the arguments in this book resemble Skinner's approach, in that they seek consciously to design social systems which permit individuals to interact creatively with each other, but there is one major difference. The argument here is that values, goals, or objectives can *never* be set *before* creative interaction begins, nor legitimately imposed upon others by elites—whatever the attractiveness of the ends they seek. Furthermore, and unlike

Skinner, *group* creativity will be the fundamental process of the future, not the reactions of individuals to "reinforcements" tested out by "behavior engineers." [2]

If organizational pyramids are, for practical purposes, to vanish, the nation-state cannot stand as an exception. Nationalism, despite its popularity in societies newly liberated from their colonial pasts, is a dying creed, even if nation-state policy processes currently are so important in the scheme of things as to be a focus of discussion here. The end of hierarchy and competition will mean the end of war as a social institution; speculation begins on that issue.

The Decline of the Nation-State and War

Some necessary preliminaries to the discarding of war are under way, even if they are not yet widely recognized. As in the 1949 novel, we will perceive before long that the growth crisis offers us the truly "great enterprise not involving war" [3] needed to bring our collective talents to bear upon objectives not requiring widespread destruction. President Nixon's quietly expressed doubt in March 1971 that "we will ever have another war" [4] seems not at all wide of the mark. Publicly reported fifteen months later, when his decision to mine North Vietnamese harbors and step up the bombing of that country had incited renewed criticism of his policies (including an attempt by some Congressmen to impeach and try him), the observation hardly was noticed. Yet, the winding down of the Vietnam War makes the comment believable; the same goes for his constantly reiterated objective of a "generation of peace." The Vietnam War may be the concluding chapter in the United States' glorification of war as religious crusade, a possibility worth exploring.

The Vietnam War can be traced in part to the feeling of many Americans that emotional all-out wars no longer were possible in an era of thermonuclear arsenals. It is almost as if we deliberately constructed new theories of warfare enabling us to preserve war as an institution without devastating the world in the process. We stumbled upon the concept of "limited," or "brushfire," wars; almost inadvertently, we defined "small" wars as "good" wars, providing us with the opportunity to display our virility as a society —within limits. The thinking was fuzzy, in that we redefined World Wars I and II as "limited" wars, but we were too busy convincing ourselves our concept was valid to notice the fuzziness.[5] But then we discovered in Vietnam that unemotional, cold-blooded, or "rationally calculated" warfare is psychologically damaging to those who wage it. We learned that there is little satisfaction in going to war with other nation-states when we cannot bring ourselves to hate them. The Vietnam War, then, seems to have closed the logical circle; with emotional wars out of the question because the destruction would be intolerable, and with small wars unacceptable because of their sterile premises, we probably have reached the end of the road for this central preoccupation of nation-state hierarchies. Like other organizational elites their principal task has been to command the struggle for "victory."

As of 1973, most critics of U.S. involvement in Vietnam have not quarreled with U.S. participation in World Wars I and II. To be sure, we have asked ourselves upon occasion if it was necessary to rain fire bombs on Dresden, Hamburg, and Tokyo, and to test atomic bombs on Hiroshima and Nagasaki. Quite aside from these questions, however, and despite the continued presence of U.S. troops in Europe at a time when nation-states seem genuinely to be groping toward some new future, we would have difficulty sustaining another wave of euphoria like the one accompanying World War II. Following Winston Churchill's blazing rhetoric, and reinforced by the Japanese attack on Pearl Harbor, we went on a binge that required us to make caricatures of Nazis, Fascists, and Japs. We manufactured the same hate which carries us through Presidential election campaigns, and we overlook to this day (save for some revisionist historians) the probability we enlarged that war well beyond any necessity to do so. We developed an earlier version of the "domino theory" which accompanied our later involvement in Vietnam; we convinced ourselves in 1941 that Hitler would overrun New York and that the Japanese would capture Hawaii and San Francisco if we did less.[6] The point is, if war as an insititution is near death, so is the nation-state as we know it.

Whatever the community-building activities of nation-states, their principal undertakings involve competition with other nation-states for territory, markets, "power," and "influence," the typical win-lose confrontations which lead to wars. In the search for planetary survival, war will be perceived as activity which works only against that objective; hence it is time to say "Farewell to the Nation-State," [7] and to think about the systems that will replace it in our thinking. We will find that the only overall system which must survive is the planet itself, and that the significant subsystems are small face-to-face groups bringing *selves* together. Intermediate groupings may persist (cities, nation-states, regional groupings), but their linking responsibilities will be designed only to ensure the viability of important systems—small groups and Earth. The important conceptual shift will remove the nation-state from its status as an organization "above" other organizations.

Further Organizational Change

There is little need for wholesale formal restructuring of social organizations, at least not now. All we need do is *remove* from individual administrators *everywhere,* whether elected or appointed, *all formal authority to make decisions binding upon others.* This does not require the removal of any official, just as revisualizing the Presidency does not compel the removal of Presidents. Change must begin, to put it simply, where individuals are *now.* This is happening everywhere, even if we hesitate to make explicit the demise of hierarchy. To formally remove the authority of individuals to make decisions by themselves is an obvious first step toward ending the repression inherent to a system in which some individuals are permitted to destroy others. With hierarchy removed, other changes logically would follow.

Salaries. Formal organizations still control the economic resources individuals require for survival, but there is no compelling reason for this. There can be little doubt that some combination of guaranteed income and employment is part of our near-term future and, if we are to overcome alienation, income and employment will have to be separated. If individuals are to realize a "psychic intimacy" with their work, then work should be defined in terms of what people *want* to do, not what they must do in order to live.[8] Anything short of such an arrangement will not suffice, nor will it do to perpetuate the old notion that individuals left to themselves will do nothing. Even a primitive sense of equity requires immediate partial implementation of this objective.

At present, universities recruit more candidates for doctoral degrees and teachers' certificates than the market can absorb; many of the universities, moreover, are themselves members of government. If state governments charge individuals for educations they cannot use, the result must not be brushed aside by referring to "buyers' markets." The same can be said for other professions, e.g., the aerospace engineers thrown out of work in Cape Kennedy, Seattle, and the suburbs of Boston. The problem, of course, is a much older one; craft union members have high wage rates but very uncertain work schedules, so they expand the time needed for the tasks assigned to them. We use the derogatory term "worker sabotage," forgetting that we compel individuals to do this to pay their bills. Individuals become apprentices in unions or students in universities, because *society* has suggested a need for their services. Accepting enrollment of such individuals, regardless of whether training is conducted under governmental or nongovernmental auspices, amounts to a promise that must be kept; once acknowledged, it is up to society to provide opportunities. On that basis, these arrangements seem immediately necessary:

1. Salary scales should be developed nationally for all occupational groups and, as the remainder of the argument will point out, this should be seen as the beginning of a wider scheme of salary equalization.[9]
2. Those unemployed but possessing the skills of a given occupation should be added to that occupation's work force and salaries then reequalized.[10]

The broader objective we must attain over time, and not much time, is the *equalization of all salaries everywhere;* there is no escaping the logic of the objective.* If the president of a corporation or the governor of a state is only one member of a group process which must reach decisions through conflict resolution and consensus, there is no reason for salary differentials within the group. That group, however, also must overlap other groups, so that members of the first function as members of others as well; if we retain salary differentials *between* groups, this will result in unequal salaries *within* a single group. To ponder the organizational outlines in the previous chapter is to realize that there is no logical argument for any salary differential between the member of a neighborhood block council and the individual designated President of the United States. To grasp this is to understand how work and income will not be related, *an absolute necessity if we are to end alienation.***

Promotions. In the absence of hierarchy, and with work separated from income, traditional concepts of "promotion" will disappear.

---

* Despite our relatively continuous "prosperity," a recent Labor Department survey concludes that we are undergoing a "persistent trend toward inequality" in the distribution of income throughout the United States. Relatively speaking, in other words, the poor become poorer every day, a trend that cannot improve things.

** Later in this sequence, I emphasize the coming erasure of boundaries between an individual's work, love, and play activities. "Workload," as we use the term now, will be a meaningless concept; the total range of activities will only be understandable as a "living load," unrelated to economic income.

What an individual does, and where he or she does it, will not be left to formally designated superiors who write efficiency reports. The notion of dispensing with traditional superior-subordinate evaluation systems is not new, but it receives less attention than it deserves.[11] Within socially organized processes, a vacancy in one group should be filled, not by conventional promotion, but by consensus decision of those in the groups linked to it; those involved, of course, could decide to bring in an outsider. It is worth emphasizing that this method of moving individuals from one group process to another bears some resemblance to the *indirect* election processes written into the U.S. Constitution, those we decided later to reject.

There can be no way of knowing now whether the outcome will be greater or less social mobility than we have thus far experienced. A rough guess is that opportunities for mobility between processes will remain, but that as individuals discover the group memberships most comfortable to them, they will decrease the frequency with which they relocate. Many corporations tie mobility to promotion; the professional moving up the ladder must relocate as part of the promotion. This is done to alleviate the problems that arise when one suddenly is elevated above former colleagues; corporate hierarchies seek to maintain the social distance they deem necessary for effective superior-subordinate interaction. In the future, social distance between those at work will disappear, and we will not perceive mobility as only a means of "exit" from distasteful situations. Admittedly, this raises yet other questions.

Sex in Organizations. One observer, concluding that the future will combine pain and joy, speculates that all interpersonal relationships will involve eroticism and sexuality. The end of hierarchy will, of course, remove superior-subordinate relationships between males and females, will make it clear to us that humanity itself is a total unity, and will encourage us to "not hesitate to touch what is really ourselves"; in the family, even the arguments supporting the incest taboo may be swept away.[12] Another observer, noting that boundaries between work, love, and play are increasingly blurred, argues that play is the only one of those functions performed from the beginning for itself; its self-validating aspects, which we now transform into the deadly competition of organized sports, must be maintained in original form.[13] It seems to follow that we must transfer to work and love the behavioral skills of play, and so we come to the possibility that all boundaries between them will be erased. The retention of boundaries between work and love depends upon whatever future we assign the nuclear family. From the perspectives of this book, all social organizations (including the family) are subject to the same general rules of operation; the potential disappearance of the incest taboo is frightening at first glance, but what about other taboos?

Anyone who has been involved in sensitivity training, T-groups, or similar undertakings can testify that once hierarchical relationships are removed and individuals truly "open" themselves to each other within a mutually supportive environment, the atmosphere can become erotic. Organizational decision processes will resemble ongoing sensitivity sessions. While this does not mean that we are entering an age of continuous orgies in office buildings, it is not difficult to visualize nonrepressive sexual relationships among individuals who work together. Indeed, if individuals "open up" to each other in truly meaningful ways, it will be impossible to suppress sexual overtones. To repeat, the current problems of "office sex" are those of hierarchy, not sexuality.[14] Thus, it will make sense for McDonald's to remove restrictions preventing couples from using the water-bed room.

Lest there be any misunderstanding about this speculation, it is not intended to be one-way in implication, i.e., the absurd "double standard," wherein men at work declare themselves free to engage in sexual liaisons but condemn women (whether at home or at work) for doing the same, must go. The woman who becomes involved in activities other than raising children and keeping house enters the typical organizational world and, in a nonhierarchical environment, she probably will be more open than men to erotic overtones. We know that there is some correlation between organizational achievement and sexuality in relation to women; the most successful and involved women have their first orgasms at an earlier age and, overall, are more sexually active than women not so involved.[15] Indeed, if sex were a yardstick of individual ability, the sexual capacity of women would transform them into the leaders of hierarchically structured society. This would be just as repressive as what we have experienced, but it follows also that if we are to experience nonrepressive revolution, it must be managed so as to avoid damage to individuals involved or affected.

There can be little doubt that we are headed in this direction. Articles and books describe the experiences of women in political campaigns and other undertakings, where intensive involvement brings sexual excitement.[16] We have discovered, if not quickly enough, that permitting conjugal visits to inmates is better than accepting the repressive homosexuality that runs rampant in prisons. Outside of prisons, those openly declaring their homosexuality gradually find increasing acceptance by society at large. Older Women's Liberation, a group of five hundred who so define themselves, have come together in convention, and, because they feel society is rejecting them, have seriously considered such alternatives as group sex, lesbianism, searching for younger men, masturbation, and numerous consciousness-raising sessions.[17] Despite its reluctance, the Catholic church will have to abandon its rule that priests and nuns remain celibate. The most explicit and detailed motion pictures of sexual congress are not shown on Times Square in New York City, but in church programs on sex education; perhaps they will next be shown in homes.* Whether, as part of Leonard's prediction that the incest taboo will disappear, families

---

* Nothing is more typical of the dying theory than our glorification of violence in movies and television, and the concurrent police raids on theaters showing "pornographic" films which are, by comparison, beautiful.

should teach sex to their children, and even demonstrate it to them, is another question, because teaching children to obey is no longer a reason for preserving the nuclear family.*

This speculation follows logically from the premise that all organized social processes will become systems of mutual dependence and caring, yet many will perceive the speculation as advocating promiscuity, rampant immorality, and the rotting away of society. If it is already recognized that "we seem to be moving in the direction of at least tacit, if not as yet formal, acceptance of extramarital relations," [18] if the plea of young people that we "make love, not war," has more significance than we yet accord it, and if those young people are comfortable living in coed university dormitories where they share bathtubs, books and, quite often, beds, something deep and profound is happening. This example may be as significant as any, for male-female involvement in universities comes close to combining those aspects of work, love, and play that seem on the verge of coming together. Individuals accustomed to such relations will not accept in organizations the old competitive struggle for status, dominance, and victory. They will bring with them what they have learned in churches and schools.

Technology and Unalienation. It was earlier indicated, especially in Chapter 1, that we must intensify our research, and quickly, not only into the redesign of conventional industrial technology, such as assembly lines, but also into more precise applications of technology which are just as assembly-line oriented, even if they do not so appear at first glance. Part of what we must do is reflected in the McDonald's office building, and all office buildings certainly are a first order of business. Perhaps the problem of mass transportation can illustrate the tasks ahead.

Every form of public or commercial transportation we use, ex-

* I am, of course, not equipped to deal with the genetic issue. The question itself, however, is tied to the traditional view that sex has no purpose other than procreation and that abortion is criminal.

cept perhaps for the surface or air taxicab, violates the philosophical premises of this book. When an individual boards a commercial airliner, a bus, a train, a subway, or even an elevator, he (or she) is subjected to a *process* over which he can exercise *no meaningful influence*. In almost every instance, the individual is one member of a much larger group: there is a "driver" or "pilot" who is "in command" and to whom the traveler must entrust himself; the route traversed and the stops made are predesignated and subject to change only for reasons the individual cannot influence (unless he becomes ill, say, on an airplane, and the pilot lands to send him to a hospital). The only partial exception is the elevator —but in most cases it is not enough of an exception to enable the individual to be *unalienated* in the process of traveling. Elevators customarily carry twelve to twenty individuals and, when they do, each individual plays no significant part in the routing of the one he rides. Oddly enough, however, the elevator is being used as the basis for futuristic designs in urban transit systems, and the following paragraphs suggest an unusual explanation for this development.

The addiction to automobiles and car pools may be symptomatic of a deep-seated urge to escape alienation, at least during periods of travel, by using a means of travel which the individual passenger can significantly influence. Similarly, the "horizontal elevator" (Personal Rapid Transit—PRT—as it is known in transportation jargon) may also be an attempt to escape alienation. Briefly, PRT comprises relatively small vehicles (one to six passengers) operating at very frequent intervals; individuals indicate upon boarding (by pushing buttons) the destination each seeks; the combination of buttons pushed by all passengers (including those waiting to board) determines the route. To emphasize that PRT *may* be a symptom is to suggest that, because designers do not yet realize the connection between travel and alienation; they have not gone far enough. Suppose for a moment that in an urban community, each computerized vehicle could carry *only* five or six individuals, and suppose further that this would require transit systems to have thousands of such vehicles and an almost infinite number of possible routings from a passenger's boarding point to his destination (inner city to recreation area, outer city to work, etc.). This implies vehicles available to board on almost any normal street, and it implies an end to massive "stations" used now (as in subways). In any such arrangement, each individual would significantly influence the route of a vehicle each time he boarded one because, as in any small group process, his input would be important to the output (and he would realize as much). This suggests that "horizontal elevators" carrying more than say, six individuals, are out of tune with our future, while smaller ones are harbingers of that future.

The argument can easily be summarized. In an unalienated future, it will be important to *maintain a state of unalienation at all times.* How could an individual unalienated at "work," "play," or "love" be expected to accept a social design which reinstates alienation during the time he spends moving between processes? This suggests we need PRT systems to replace such dehumanizing experiences as riding in subways (even the newer ones) as well as "three-dimensional" elevators to replace 747's. It suggests further that we face an exciting challenge in attempting to combine technology and unalienation, in that we must think seriously about the detailed requirements of unalienation. While even this bare outline falls well within our technological capabilities, it falls outside our current philosophical capabilities. Perhaps this nexus of technology and unalienation can be left to another book.

Further Political Change

When George McGovern accepted the Democratic nomination for President in 1972, he referred to the struggles within his party which had left it in disarray. He advised convention delegates not to underestimate the contribution President Nixon would make to the reunification of Democrats. This was a normal campaign statement, typical of what we must reject if we are to survive; it defined unity as something attained through hate. The task here is to suggest how to get rid of hate by integrating the U.S. Constitution with the theory argued in this book. As suggested in the previous chapter, the U.S. political system is uniquely adaptable to the future; because it has no clear focus of *command* (though we have been attempting to so transform the Presidency), we easily can design policy processes which explicitly provide for sharing governmental "powers."

If we are fortunate, redesigned processes will enable us to articulate truly *collective will* while we dismiss present electoral processes as relatively unimportant. Our addiction to hierarchy has encouraged us to define elections as the *ending* of *political* processes rather than the *beginning* of *policy* processes. The revised theory should enable us to perceive democracy, for the first time, as *continuous, challenging,* and *involving,* not something which formally includes us only for a few seconds each time we enter a voting booth. With elected leaders unable to make unilateral decisions (the suggested abolition of individual authority certainly applies to Presidents), elections would get much less attention—deservedly so. The function of those we now elect to command us would be to act as members of policy processes which include both legislative and executive branches, as well as others. Elected leaders would be relieved of the monumental contradiction which compels them to submerge themselves *within* political parties in order to win, then attempt to rise *above* parties to function in office.

Because the processes of organized public action are centered in the structures attached to elected executives, we must set about directly attaching legislators to those processes. As in the case of the foreign and military affairs committees mentioned in Chapter 5, we already have the framework; legislative committees exercise "supervision" and "oversight" of executive agencies. This is the most important of a legislator's duties, but we often look upon it as almost improper. As in the prominent case of the Army Corps of Engineers, we view the interactions of agencies with legislators friendly to them as something intended to subvert the executive branch by perpetuating "pork-barreling." * The argument here is precisely the opposite; any consensus-building process will have to include agencies, appropriate legislators, and individuals from, say, the Office of Management and Budget; furthermore, it will have to be linked ultimately to citizens affected by decisions.[19]

The committee or group processes envisioned herein for legislators would be more time consuming and intensive than those in which they currently engage. While almost everyone acknowledges some degree of importance for committee assignments, a Congressman faces a wide range of demands. If some estimates are credible, he spends 75 per cent of his time on "casework," the problems posed by individual citizens who either seek the reversal of some administrative decision or who must find out where to go for help.[20] This workload, important as it is to citizens, is the obvious consequence of relatively closed administrative processes which compel individuals to press their legislators into service as "ombudsmen." We must strip away the walls between "professionals" and "citizens," and use the policy processes outlined in Chapter 5 to link citizens directly with the decisions affecting them. Some of this is under way, as when public agencies set up "storefront" offices in neighborhoods to deal face-to-face with individual problems. Before long, all sorts of structures (schools, health centers, etc.) will become multi-functional, with neighborhood groups and administrators using them as conference centers almost daily. All this goes hand in hand with the notion of the "professional citizen" who has the same status as the administrator with whom he deals; "participation and partnership" replace the bureaucratic tradition that administrators are "servants of the people" [21]— which too many administrators interpret as placing them "above" those they "serve."

Superficially, this might seem an argument that administrators

---

* Actually, we approve legislative intervention when we agree with its objectives.

and businessmen be turned loose to negotiate their own "division of the spoils." Admittedly, those we now term "businessmen" will be *inside* public policy processes, but only in the company of other individuals and within a rubric that prevents any accumulation of "spoils." Were the processes already in existence, both Ralph Nader and the head of General Motors would be explicit members of at least one such process. Multiple and overlapping memberships, not to mention the assignment of individuals with conflicting perspectives, will make the processes uniquely self-auditing. The only reason for the General Accounting Office's present status in Washington is that closed and autonomous decision processes must be counterbalanced from outside, the undesirable result of the traditional notion that "authority" must be clearly defined. We should be able to visualize policy processes in which legislators would spend significant time each day in face-to-face interaction with groups comprising administrative officials and individuals outside government—not in the ways they interact now (often with just those individuals), but in explicit and detailed policy formulation. Logistically speaking, this would require legislators to work inside executive agencies, for that is where conference rooms and associated facilities are located.* That is where legislators are needed, where they must operationalize a new definition of legislative responsibility, and the outcomes could be far more useful than those usually sought by advocates of Congressional reform.

Most attacks upon Congress are aimed at its senior citizens (especially from the South) who, by virtue of long service, chair influential committees. While it doubtless is necessary to limit the time individuals can serve in Congress and to compel retirement at some age, reformers aiming at committee chairmen miss the point. Whatever its defects, the seniority system enables legislators to conduct business over a considerable period without ceaseless competition for "leadership." If committees had to elect new

---

* Parliamentary systems are ahead of us on this score, even if they are more monolithic overall.

chairmen each session, Congressmen would campaign and vote almost constantly against each other, and scars would be lasting. After all, why do you suppose that whenever elections are held for posts of "leader" or "whip," it *never* is possible to discover which Congressmen voted for which candidate? Congressmen indicate they will vote for one candidate and then secretly vote for another, because they must avoid creating new enemies. We accuse them of "deception," but they have no alternative if they are to work together. We are also learning that Wilbur Mills and John Stennis, to name but two senior legislators, are more capable of dealing with certain problems than those who remain in the executive branch for only a brief period. This argument expands upon the accepted idea that an important financial measure requires the involvement of Congressman Mills, as much (or more) an acknowledgement of his expertise as of his authority.* Only the conventional wisdom which dictates perpetual separation of branches stands in the way.

The broadest aspect of theory change will be disappearance of the idea that some citizens "speak for," or "represent," others, an automatically alienating idea. Those in one policy process will arrive there as the outcome of earlier associations with related processes, and it will make little difference whether they began as legislators, administrators, or individual citizens. Each will have an expertise which spans both the substantive issues and the skills of group interaction. Extensive linkages will make all decisions an expression of *collective will,* and "representation" will lose meaning. Wilbur Mills, once again, is an example; his expertise is not related to the rural area he "represents," but to the process including him. Once we see the end of representative government as an emerging reality, there will be no need for the political parties which blight our lives and which, in retrospect, never belonged in our system.

All this will be helped along, of course, by the separation of

---

* Senator McGovern admitted as much during the 1972 campaign, when he announced Mills as his choice for Secretary of the Treasury.

work from income and the redistribution of income and wealth. These outcomes will remove status distinctions we know now, and we will recognize concepts of the "decisive man of action," the man at the top who gets things done," and "the strong and dynamic leader" as preposterous misrepresentations dismissable as anachronistic folklore.[22] This will provide yet another solution which eludes us to date; we attempt to make public office financially attractive enough to lure somebody other than the rich, but without real success. The cost of getting elected largely restricts politics to the offspring or captives of the rich, and the upgrading of public salaries increases social and economic distance between public officials and fellow citizens. This brings us to the broader aspects of economic change.

Further Economic Change

The theory outlined here will not mesh with our historic notions of ownership and private property, but neither will it be compatible with conventional—and hierarchical—socialism. The trend toward consumerism in most socialist countries seems to reflect a subconscious premise that citizens should accept products in lieu of democratized social processes. In all probability, however, we probably will have to limit production in order to control pollution, accommodate ourselves to a global energy problem, or overcome congestion. Even if one problem is solved, it is unlikely we can solve all three without instituting some limits. It seems likely that even the consumption of energy within households will be curbed before long, just as we are realizing the impossibility of airconditioning every room in every office building. If you and I are neighbors, we may be able to figure out ways to *share* the use of items which consume energy. In areas that might not be provided with the more futuristic transit systems mentioned earlier, or in the period preceding their arrival, we might design neighborhood car rental systems, each individual scheduling the needed share of vehicle use. Clearly, the automobiles could not be the "private property" of individuals, so *collective ownership* becomes the logical model. How this might work in detail hardly can be outlined now, though the increasingly popular no-fault automobile insurance (drivers reimbursed for damage without regard to "blame") is itself a step away from traditional ownership and responsibility. It is sufficient to suggest that we face the issue, and at every level.

Proposals to make the stock market a public utility managed by government [23] reflect not only fear of dangerous instability, but also subconscious admission that the entire economic system must be transformed. Would government, for instance, guarantee every investor a certain amount of safety for investment, as in the case of bank deposits? If so, government might have to guarantee the survival of all businesses in which *it* invested funds on behalf of stockholders, a fundamental change in our ideas about stock markets. If this happened, businesses not handed such guarantees automatically would be doomed. If government, conversely, did not guarantee the survival of its favored businesses, would individual investors be expected to accept their losses when government market managers guessed wrong about certain stocks? If so, this would tie the fortunes of government itself to a competitive system which, in terms of the argument in Chapter 3, is nonrational by definition.

The average consumer, as already noted, is implored by government to spend all he earns for the sake of keeping the economy at full production; it is deemed almost subversive to save. Despite campaigns to attract small investors into the stock market, most stock is owned by the very affluent; they remain the only ones able to pass large accumulations of wealth from generation to generation. Yet the notion of stock ownership cannot stand scrutiny at all; when General Motors makes a profit higher than is normal for the money market, those who purchase automobiles perform the same act as those who buy stock, but only the latter are handed official shares. In a future of limited growth, the hoarded wealth of large shareholders will not be legitimate. In today's language, this appears as the advocacy of "confiscation"; in tomorrow's language, the action will be normal.

We cannot shrink from the demonstrable reality that when a businessman and the stockholders of his corporation realize very high profits and dividends, they *steal* from consumers. This is what less affluent citizens have been telling us, and one need not be a Marxist to agree. As outlined in Chapter 3, success or failure is traceable not necessarily to the businessman's efforts but rather to the overall market situation. It is not the businessman's fault when he "fails," but neither does he "succeed" because of his acumen; what happens to consumers, then, is "accidental" stealing. When industrialist Henry Ford II and economist Milton Friedman argue that the social responsibility of business is to make money, they forthrightly advance a case that can no longer prevail. This is not to suggest that those in business intend anything improper when they seek high profits. This is what society instructs them to do, it is what laws encourage them to do, and they merely operationalize our theory of economic citizenship. We must design a system which enables them to perform some function other than well-intentioned thievery. The most inadvertent thieves, of course, are stockholders, a reason why government cannot become the middleman of such action.

There is little doubt that global market systems, perhaps on a product-by-product basis, will have to be created, but they cannot be structured along hierarchical lines. The organizational point of entry probably will be the network of multi-national corporations already in being. They are political and governmental systems, and we should so recognize them. As for all other corporations, we will have to operationalize the notion that they are not "private property" but resources which belong to us all.[24] This will at least make it possible to interact with noncapitalist societies, but it is only a first step toward global planning for the use of resources, the production of goods and, most important, their distribution. Among other vanishing concepts will be "favorable balance of trade," so historically important to international economics. Each nation-state attempts to make sure the financial results of exporting some goods and importing others are favorable, in that the nation-state "makes money." Every nation-state, however, cannot have a favorable balance; when a national government takes pride in its balance, it knows other societies have been damaged, even if the precise extent and location of the damage are unknown.

These things are not going to happen overnight, but the growth crisis will, by 1975, have us looking back to 1973 in wonderment at the distance already traveled. If we were to select an initial short-term target for testing the propositions in this book, a likely candidate would be the competitive waste of oligopoly. We might well impose a heavy tax upon network television advertising during prime-time hours, those dominated by the largest companies, and tax as well the promotional expenditures of the five hundred largest corporations; this would transfer the taxing powers of television networks and corporations to government itself. We might simultaneously designate one industry a "pilot project," bring its producers together, and see how we could design the highest-quality standardized product at a reasonable price. It would be surprising if we did not discover that costs are two to three times what they should be. As a next step, we might begin redistributing wealth by heavily taxing capital gains, an idea that surfaced during the 1972 elections.

Some who admit the need to limit growth are pessimistic about our ability to manage the economic future, but the pessimism is due solely to a conventional wisdom which enshrines hierarchy and competition, thus preventing otherwise astute observers from perceiving how easily we can manage *if* we change theories.[25] The first requirement is an intellectual one; when we remove wealth and property from the list of things individuals legitimately accumulate, we will take a long step toward emptying our prisons.*

* Just as obviously, our adversary system of dispensing "justice" cannot survive.

Summing Up

Those wedded to the ethic of individualism will have difficulty grasping the arguments in this book. But the unadorned ethic legitimizes the repression of some citizens by other citizens. It presumes that those designated "superior" by virtue of talent, organizationally assigned role, or wealth are turned loose to dominate others. Those who cling to the ethic often forget that the game they play cannot be defined other than in terms of "winners" and "losers." The success of one individual can be described only by the failure of others. Most people understand this, if only subconsciously, and "success" is uncomfortable; those who win are damaged psychologically by what they must do to win, for they *know* they inflict costs upon others.

The contrast between old and new is exemplified in part by the competitive sports to which we are addicted. In the United States, baseball and football vie for designation as the national pastime. Because the new theory is just as much associated with our history as the old one, it is not surprising that baseball, the older of the two sports, seems more in tune with our future. Football, of course, is military-type conflict; small wonder that famous coaches of football have been avid students of military history and military leaders. Not only is football a game of violence, if controlled (at least in some cases), it is also difficult to describe except in terms of dominating and being dominated, repressing and being repressed. The individual can express himself only by subjugating the man opposite him, the most important aspect of the game; whatever the thrills associated with nimble running backs and skillful passers and receivers, the game is won or lost in the "pit," where massive guards and tackles struggle to overpower one another.*

Baseball, conversely, combines individual contributions and co-

---

* We have much to learn from others. Those visiting the United States, many of whom are attuned to soccer, are appalled at the violence associated with our version of football.

operative group interaction. Any addict of the game will tell you the most exciting play is the three-base hit (triple), or its near-miss, often a symphony of interaction. As the runner races around the bases, two outfielders chase the ball, one infielder awaits a relay from one of them, and the third baseman readies himself for simultaneous arrival of ball and runner, the latter attempting a graceful slide designed to avoid even touching the third baseman. When the play approaches perfection, the two teams seem to co-operate in putting on a superior performance—this being more important than whether the runner is "safe" or "out." The unsatis-fying outcome is a play marred by a wild throw, the third base-man dropping the ball, or some similar imperfection.

This is not to argue that baseball (or soccer) is "perfect," and that football should be outlawed. Given the zealousness with which we pursue "victory," baseball players are taught to slide "hard" into the second baseman in order to break up a double play, even if this maims the fielder, and pitchers sometimes throw at batters either to intimidate them or to retaliate for the actions of opposing pitchers. As for football, there are many indications that if professional owners, university presidents, coaches, and players undergo theory change, it will become a sport in which opponents respect each other as human beings and deal with the game as more a cooperative than an antagonistic venture.[26] His-torically speaking, that was the olympic ideal, but it was corrupted by nationalistic competition. The point is that humane competi-tion, a form designed to stimulate excellence, not the defeat of others, is worth reinstating.*

"The only thing we have to fear is fear itself," proclaimed Franklin Roosevelt in 1933. The same can be said now, even if the task of digging out of the great depression was minuscule in comparison to what faces us today. The greatest opportunity in history lies before us, if we but have the courage to grasp it. What we need do is implement the third alternative to the conventional

* When all professional athletes are paid the same salaries, we will learn how graceful organized sports can be.

choice between unorganized anarchy and rigid bureaucratic control of everything. The third alternative offers social processes carefully designed to preserve the best of our past while casting aside the repression of hierarchy and the destructiveness of competition. Rousseau missed the point when he introduced his social theory:

Man is born free; and everywhere he is in chains. One thinks
himself the master of others, and still remains a greater slave than they.
How did this change come about? I do not know. What can make it
legitimate? That question I think I can answer.[27]

We *cannot* make it legitimate for one to be the master of others, and the time has come to stop trying.

Introduction

1. Kenneth B. Clark, "The Pathos of Power: A Psychological Perspective," *American Psychologist*, 26((12), December 1971, 1047–57. This problem is explored at greater length in two as yet unpublished essays: William G. Scott, "The Theory of Significant People," and Scott and David K. Hart, "Administrative Crisis: The Neglect of Metaphysical Speculation."

Chapter 1

1. The material on McDonald's is summarized from articles in *Building Design and Construction*, October 1971; *The New York Times* (January 31, 1972); and *Time*, February 28, 1972. Similar ideas (but without reference to water beds) are expressed by an editor-in-chief of Simon and Schuster, Michael Korda, in "Tear Down the Walls! No Private Offices," *Glamour*, July 1972.
2. This theme appears again and again in a series of tape-recorded interviews with women employed as secretaries and administrative assistants in a major New York corporation. Jack Olsen, *The Girls in the Office* (New York: Simon and Schuster, 1972). While a number of examples could be cited (pp. 31, 270, 277, 298), one is especially to the point. A woman who had turned down her boss's invitation for dinner, dancing, riding in the park, and then a visit to his in-town apartment, felt in the position of a "slave girl [who] had refused the pasha." See p. 354.
3. The literature is summarized in James H. Donnelly, James L. Gibson, and John M. Ivancevich, *Fundamentals of Management: Functions, Behavior, Models* (Austin, Texas: Business Publications, Inc., 1971), pp. 82–85.
4. Howard F. Taylor, *Balance in Small Groups* (New York: Van Nostrand Reinhold, 1970), Ch. 1 and sources therein.
5. Sociopsychologists define groups as ranging from two to twenty, but focus on two to seven; *ibid.*, p. 3. "Action-taking" groups average 6.5 members; "non-action-taking," 14. U.S. Senate subcommittees average 5.4; the House, 7.8; the Oregon state government, 4.7; the Eugene, Oregon, municipal government, 5.3. Groups of five boys performed more effectively than groups of twelve; Mancur Olson, Jr., *The Logic of Collective Action* (New York: Schocken Books, 1969), Ch. 2. Parkinson's observation is that five is the best size for a committee (or Cabinet); it invariably grows to a much larger size but when it does, the five "who matter" become a separate group; C. Northcote Parkinson, *Parkinson's Law* (New York: Ballantine Books, 1957), Ch. 4. When a legislature began functioning in Western Samoa between 1948 and

1951, the active participants in each session rarely exceeded four to six of a membership of twelve. This gradually increased as the Samoans "learned" parliamentary behavior; Felix M. Keesing and Marie M. Keesing, *Elite Communication in Samoa* (Stanford University Press, 1956), pp. 132–33. After writing this paragraph, I discovered that the numerical parallels had been outlined by Robert J. House and John B. Miner, "Merging Management and Behavioral Theory: The Interaction Between Span of Control and Group Size," *Administrative Science Quarterly,* 14(3), September 1969, 451–64. On hunting bands, see George B. Leonard, *The Transformation* (New York: Delacorte, 1972), p. 51. Also see note 10 below.

6. Barnard repeatedly used the example of five individuals working as a cooperative group. He assumed hierarchy necessary primarily because any organization "is always subordinate to some other formal organization directly or indirectly, being ultimately subordinate to and dependent upon either a church or a state or both." Chester A. Barnard, *The Functions of the Executive,* 18th printing (Cambridge, Mass.: Harvard University Press, 1968), Chs. VII–VIII (quotation, pp. 109–10). Urwick recommended four as best for span of control (a group of five), and emphasized the "interlocking" of the work. Lyndall F. Urwick, "The Manager's Span of Control," *Harvard Business Review,* 34, May/June 1956, 41.

7. The principle: "In a Hierarchy Every Employee Tends to Rise to His Level of Incompetence," from Lawrence J. Peter and Raymond Hull, *The Peter Principle* (New York: Morrow, 1969), Ch. 2. A pertinent response partly in accord with the arguments in this book is Lane Tracy, "Postscript to the Peter Principle," *Harvard Business Review,* 50, July/August 1972, 65–71.

8. James D. Thompson, *Organizations in Action* (New York: McGraw-Hill, 1967), Ch. 1 and p. 157; "transorganizational" seems preferable to "multiorganizational" or "interorganizational" because it suggests a greater degree of interpenetration and because it also corresponds to the exciting concept of "transnationalism" which is becoming significant to students of international politics. Numerous economic, cultural, social, and other functional systems cut across, over, and around the nation-state system; ultimately we will perceive all of them as political systems, as in the case of major corporations.

9. Warren G. Bennis, *Changing Organizations* (New York: McGraw-Hill, 1966), Ch. 1. The most detailed study of such technological systems is Leonard R. Sayles and Margaret K. Chandler, *Managing Large Systems: Organizations for the Future* (New York: Harper and Row, 1971).

10. This line of thinking is well elaborated in Harlan Cleveland, *The Future Executive: A Guide for Tomorrow's Managers* (New York: Harper and Row, 1972). He also emphasizes the number 5.

11. Peter F. Drucker, *The Age of Discontinuity* (New York: Harper and Row, 1968), Chapter 8.
12. George S. Duggar, "The Relation of Local Government Structure to Urban Renewal," in Jewel Bullush and Murray Hausnecht, eds., *Urban Renewal: People, Politics, and Planning* (Garden City, N.Y.: Anchor Books, 1967), pp. 181–201.
13. Joan Cannon Feast, "The Multiorganizational Conjoin as an Administrative Collaboration: Development of the Concept and Application to the Golden Gateway Redevelopment Project," unpublished doctoral dissertation, GSPIA, University of Pittsburgh, 1969, pp. 135–38. This "conjoin" included one hundred and twenty-two private, thirty-five public, twenty-one voluntary, three quasi-public, and three nonprofit organizations.
14. Milton D. Esman and John D. Montgomery, "Systems Approaches to Technical Cooperation: The Role of Development Administration," *Public Administration Review,* 29, September/October 1969, 508–30.
15. My experience is that committees of middle-level officials produce many solutions which stand up, but only when top-level officials have not committed themselves to a position in advance. This means that solutions appear either when problems are relatively unimportant or when problems have not reached crisis proportions, even if categories are difficult to separate (solving supposedly unimportant problems may head off larger ones). Thus hierarchy prevents solutions to important problems that are recognized as such—unless the process permits those at the top to come together without prior individual commitment to a given solution. This holds true, it seems to me, for generals, Cabinet officers, university presidents, and academic deans.
16. More detailed reasons for this assertion are spelled out in my "Regional Administration: The Failure of Traditional Theory in the United States and Canada," *Canadian Public Administration,* 15(2), Fall 1972, 449–64.
17. W. Warner Burke, "A View of Organization Development," in *OD— Fad or Fundamental* (American Society for Training and Development, 1971), pp. 3–6.
18. Richard Todd, "Notes on Corporate Man," *Atlantic,* 228(4), October 1971, 84.
19. *Ibid.,* p. 93.
20. William B. Eddy, "Beyond Behavioralism? Organization Development in Public Management," *Public Personnel Review,* July 1970. "Management Issues in Organization Development," in Eddy, W. Warner Burke, Vladimir A. Dupré, and Oron P. South, eds., *Behavioral Science and the Manager's Role* (Washington, D.C.: National Training Laboratories, Institute for Applied Behavior Science, 1969), pp. 251–59.
21. Chris Argyris, *Management and Organizational Development,* (New

York: McGraw-Hill, 1971), p. 169. Warren G. Bennis, *Organization Development: Its Nature, Origins, and Prospects* (Menlo Park, Calif.: Addison-Wesley, 1969).

22. Abraham Maslow, "Self-Actualization and Beyond," in James F. T. Bugental, ed., *Challenges of Humanistic Psychology* (New York: McGraw-Hill, 1967), pp. 279–86.

23. Rensis Likert, *The Human Organization* (New York: McGraw-Hill, 1967), Ch. 4.

24. Samuel A. Culbert and Jerome Riesel, "Organization Development: An Applied Philosophy for Managers of Public Enterprise," *Public Administration Review,* 31, March/April 1971, 159–69.

25. Abraham Maslow, "The Superior Person," in Warren G. Bennis, ed., *American Bureaucracy* (Chicago: Aldine, 1970), pp. 27–38. Frank Goble, *The Third Force: The Psychology of Abraham Maslow* (New York: Pocket Books, 1971), Chs. 3, 11. This is a summary of Maslow's work which he approved.

26. Argyris, *op. cit.,* p. 6. Paul Blumberg, *Industrial Democracy: The Sociology of Participation* (New York: Schocken Books, 1969), Ch. 2.

27. Likert, *op. cit.,* p. 51. I have read the draft manuscript of Likert's forthcoming book. It will relate his organization theory more directly to political theory, and it probably will deemphasize the individual manager's unilateral authority.

28. "Brainwashing" remains difficult to define, but we have adopted the word from the Chinese experience. Likert's basic organizational design (Figure 2) closely resembles the "3 x 3" organizational structure of the People's Liberation Army of Communist China. Military squads of nine and ten are divided into groups of three or four, one member designated as leader of each group. Chinese soldiers are handed remarkably extensive information (by Western standards) about strategic operations—and "discuss" them. When this is combined with idolatry and charisma, as in the person of Mao, the structure becomes an effective means of totally submerging the individual in the achievement of organizational objectives he played no part in designing. See Alexander L. George, *The Chinese Communist Army in Action* (New York: Columbia University Press, 1967), Chs. 3, 7, and references therein.

29. Virtually every common-sense rule is broken by these undertakings, which might be labeled the equivalent of practicing medicine without a license and for very high fees. While consultants advertise "individual needs" and "self-development," this is tied solely to the needs of the corporation and the requirement that individuals prove themselves worthy by defeating their colleagues. Graduate students previously subjected to such exercises while employed by large corporations describe the sessions as frightening. For a positive view of an assessment practitioner, see William C. Byham, "Assessment Centers for Spotting Future Managers," *Harvard Business Review,* 48, 1970, 150–60. Another advocate of assessment centers traces the idea to German methods for

selecting intelligence agents in World War I. Dennis P. Slavin, "The Assessment Center: Breakthrough in Management Appraisal and Development," *Personnel Journal,* 51(4), April 1972, 256.

30. Marvin Dunnette, "On the Pros and Cons of Sensitivity Training," *Innovation,* September 1970. While I explore in Chapter 6 implications of removing "social distance," it is worth noting that to remove all hierarchical barriers while involving men and women together tends to make the atmosphere erotic.

31. Some of these issues are treated, if indirectly, in Argyris, *op. cit.,* Chs. 6–7. Also Martin Lakin, "Some Ethical Issues in Sensitivity Training," *American Psychologist,* October 1969, reprinted in James H. Donnelly, James L. Gibson, and John H. Ivancevich, *op. cit.,* pp. 180–87.

32. William B. Eddy and Robert J. Saunders, "Applied Behavioral Science in Urban Administrative/Political Systems," *Public Administration Review,* 32, January/February 1972, 11–16.

33. This is outlined in S. M. Miller and Martin Rein, "Participation, Poverty, and Administration," *Public Administration Review,* 29, January/February 1969, 15–24.

34. George Martell, "Parents in the School: Community Control in Harlem," *This Magazine Is About Schools,* 4, 1970, 98–99.

35. *The New York Times* (January 6, 1971).

36. Toronto *Telegram* (August 5, 1971).

37. "Charrette: Community Planning with Involvement," *HUD Challenge,* December 1971.

38. W. L. Riddick, *Charrette Processes: A Tool in Urban Planning* (York, Pa.: George Shumway Publishers, 1971), Ch. 1.

39. *Ibid.,* p. 83.

40. *Ibid.,* pp. 81–82.

41. *Ibid.,* p. 3.

42. Martin Rein, "Community Action Programs: A Critical Reassessment," *Poverty and Human Resources Abstracts,* 3, May/June 1968, 4. Community Action Programs, organized in more conventional ways, allow fewer outlets for involvement.

43. *The New York Times* (January 28, 1971).

44. Basil J. F. Mott, ed., "A Symposium: The Crisis in Health Care: Problems of Policy and Administration," *Public Administration Review,* 31, September/October 1971, 501–42.

45. U.S. military officers wrote articles praising "group consensus" as long ago as 1905. Charles Perrow, *Organizational Analysis: A Sociological View* (Belmont, Calif.: Brooks, Cole, 1970), p. 17 (citing Morris Janowitz). While split-second crisis might warrant exception, it is widely known that in the Vietnam War army units evolved a decision process which permitted soldiers to reject battle plans until they were handed one they considered acceptable. All sorts of explanations were produced to avoid having to try the men by courts-martial.

46. Ronald E. Jones, in an address to the opening session of the Ontario

Educational Association on March 21, 1971; cited in "Citizen Involvement," a working paper prepared for the Committee on Government Productivity, Province of Ontario, Canada (Queen's Printer, Queen's Park, Toronto, Canada), p. 7.

47. Amitai Etzioni, *Modern Organizations* (Englewood Cliffs, N.J.: Prentice-Hall, 1964), pp. 32–35.

48. Blumberg, *op. cit.*, Chs. 2, 3.

49. F. J. Roethlisberger and William J. Dickson, *Management and the Worker* (New York: John Wiley Science Editions, 1964), Ch. 21.

50. Emma Rothschild, "GM in More Trouble," *New York Review of Books*, 18, March 23, 1972, 18–24. Ruth Link, "Alienation and Participation," *Sweden Now*, 5, June 1971, 36–44. Richard E. Walton, "How to Counter Alienation in the Plant," *Harvard Business Review*, 50, 4, November/December 1972, 70–81.

51. On the discomfiture of organized labor, see Adolf F. Sturmthal, "Workers' Participation in Management: A Summary of U.S. Experience," *American Institute for Free Labor Movement Review*, 2, 1970, 3–14.

52. One example is a series of eight articles devoted to the subject, not a single one of which even mentions the connection between participation and factory design. See "Symposium on Workers' Participation in Management: An International Comparison," *Industrial Relations*, 9(2), February 1970.

53. Jay Hall, "Decisions, Decisions," *Psychology Today*, November 1971. Hall, who has done extensive research in group processes, reports also that mental patients who undergo training in such processes produce better decisions than untrained executives; in all cases, group decisions turn out to be better than individual ones. On this point, see also Edgar H. Schein, *Process Consultation: Its Role in Organization Development* (Reading, Mass.: Addison-Wesley, 1969), esp. Ch. 5.

54. For any given public problem, an "expert" analysis and recommendation could be prepared, followed by a more participative process designed to include those likely to be affected by the decision. The recommendation that emerges from that process could then be compared to the "expert" proposal—to discover whether costs and consequences not foreseen by the "expert" were avoided by the second proposal.

55. If we are to accept the most prominent definitions, political decisions are those which (1) affect the "authoritative allocation of values for a society," or (2) influence "the way in which society determines its fate." The first is from David Easton, *The Political System* (New York: Knopf, 1966 edition), pp. 129–34; the second is from Karl W. Deutsch, "On Political Theory and Political Action," *American Political Science Review*, 65, March 1971, 8. While we are coming to learn each day that almost any decision fits these definitions—in that the corporation

which builds a polluting plant obviously makes a political decision—our operational models of politics provide only that if the public interest is to be protected, the focus of decision authority should be shifted to elected leaders. This leads to the dilemmas explored in Chapter 2.

56. Peter Drucker, *Men, Ideas, and Politics* (New York: Harper and Row, 1970), pp. 205ff. The earlier observations on transagency decision processes parallel Drucker's argument: in an effective process, the decision evolves. Indeed, the Japanese do not even recognize the phenomenon of decision-making in the manner that we do. Where we separate decision and implementation, admitting the latter to be a problem caused by noninvolvement, the Japanese refer only to the "action stage"; once this is reached, implementation is no problem.

Chapter 2

1. Silviu Brucan, *The Dissolution of Power: A Sociology of International Relations and Politics* (New York: Knopf, 1971), Ch. IX. A former Romanian diplomat, Brucan resurrects the Marx-Engels notion of "self-administration of things and people" in a classless society, something requiring administration but not power. While this envisions the end of the nation-state, it is not at all clear that Brucan has in mind a nonhierarchical form of administration.

2. Holtan P. Odegard, *The Politics of Truth: Toward Reconstruction in Democracy* (University of Alabama Press, 1971), p. 288. The author's argument throughout, however, implies an authoritative role for relatively autonomous administrators.

3. Martin Albow, *Bureaucracy* (New York: Praeger, 1970), pp. 39–40.

4. Bertell Ollman, *Alienation: Marx's Conception of Man in Capitalist Society* (Cambridge: University Press, 1971), Ch. 18.

5. "It ought . . . to be plain that command depends not on ownership but on the division of labor in detail. . . . The command structure of a nationalized industry is, in essentials, no whit different from that of private industry, hedged about though it invariably is by the trappings of constitutionalism (joint consultation). It is at last plain to see that capitalism in industry is one thing, command in industry quite another." Graham Wootton, *Workers, Unions, and the State* (New York: Schocken Books, 1967), Ch. III. Wootton's view is that Engels grasped this point, Marx did not.

6. Robert Blauner, *Alienation and Freedom: The Factory Worker and His Industry* (University of Chicago Press, 1964), p. 17.

7. The quotation is from Ollman, *op. cit.,* p. 173. The outline of alienation is a composite of Blauner, *op. cit.,* Ch. 1, and Amitai Etzioni, *The Active Society: A Theory of Social and Political Processes* (New

York: Free Press, 1968), Ch. 21, "Alienation, Inauthenticity, and Their Reduction."

8. Jacques Ellul, *The Technological Society* (New York: Vintage Books, 1964), Ch. 1.

9. ". . . He creates a despair so profound as to render resistance hopeless, leaving many who accept what he has to say with the conviction that the only dignified thing left to do is await the end." Victor C. Ferkiss, *Technological Man: The Myth and the Reality* (New York: Braziller, 1969), p. 87.

10. Ollman, *op. cit.*, p. 213.

11. "If I had to describe in one word the general mood and tenor of the relationship between husband and wife in this country at this moment, I would choose, unhappily and unoriginally, alienation." Natalie Gittelson, *The Erotic Life of the American Wife* (New York: Delacorte Press, 1969, 1972), p. xii.

12. In describing why he wanted to act the title role in *The Godfather*, Marlon Brando observed, "The picture itself made a useful commentary on corporate thinking in this country . . . because the Mafia patterned itself so closely on the corporation. . . . Whenever they wanted to kill somebody it was always a matter of policy. Before pulling the trigger, they told him: 'Just business. Nothing personal.' " *Life*, March 10, 1972.

13. "Of all the corporate chores performed by executives, the most painful is firing other executives. . . . It is principally because of the 'democratization' of American business that this process is becoming more traumatic every year . . . in the modern corporation, increasingly dominated by humanist values and a democratic ethic, . . . it becomes harder all the time to view one's colleagues as just names on the table of organization—which means, among other things, that it becomes harder all the time to fire them." Judson Gooding, "The Art of Firing an Executive," *Fortune*, October 1972.

14. In recounting the debate over theories of prehistory and evolution, one author notes that defenders of the dominant theory successfully threatened textbook publishers with destruction of their university markets unless they removed from their book lists authors who did not conform. "The Galileos of today," he adds, "are not likely to be kneeling before cardinals and mumbling the truth under their breath; they will be kneeling before professors with tenure." William I. Thompson, *At the Edge of History* (New York: Harper and Row, 1970), pp. 128–32.

15. Dwight Waldo, "Some Thoughts on Alternatives, Dilemmas, and Paradoxes, in a Time of Turbulence," in his (ed.) *Public Administration in a Time of Turbulence* (Scranton, Pa.: Chandler Publishing, 1971), pp. 282–84. The conclusion came from Waldo's attempt to search out the longer history of public administration in the West.

16. Sheldon Wolin, *Politics and Vision* (Boston: Little, Brown, 1960), Ch. 10.

17. Albow, *op. cit.*, Ch. 2. In emphasizing the roles of professional managers, Michels did not note that even in their absence, hierarchy would obtain; those elected by members would be in command.
18. Richard Reeves, "Nixon's Secret Strategy," *Harper's Magazine*, December 1971; "The New Technology," *Time*, January 10, 1972; *The New York Times* (March 14, 1972). A scholarly approach which emphasizes how voters are manipulated like consumers is Murray Edelman, *Politics as Symbolic Action: Mass Arousal and Quiescence* (Chicago: Markham Publishing, 1971). One political consultant describes his task in these steps: (1) decide how you want the voter to react; (2) decide what you must do to make him react that way; (3) do it. Joseph Napolitan, *The Election Game and How to Win It* (Garden City, N.Y.: Doubleday, 1972).
19. Giuseppe A. DiPalma, *Apathy and Participation* (New York: Free Press, 1971), pp. 2–3.
20. This occurred at Attica Prison in New York, just a few months after an internal rebellion had been crushed at the cost of several lives. The quotation is from the warden. *The New York Times* (March 18, 1972).
21. When former union leader James Hoffa was released from prison, he announced he would become a crusader for prison reform because of what he had witnessed. He recounted an incident in which one inmate stabbed another seventeen times without any warning or apparent provocation. It turned out the attacker had constantly lost out to his victim in contests to determine who was the best athlete in prison. The stabbing was designed to remove the competition. *Pittsburgh Press* (April 2, 1972).
22. "The ideal of participation is stated supremely in Aristotle's definition of a citizen . . ." Emmette S. Redford, *Democracy in the Administrative State* (New York: Oxford University Press, 1969), p. 9.
23. Aristotle, *The Politics*, trans. T. A. Sinclair (Baltimore: Penguin Books, 1962), Book III, Ch. 4, pp. 109–10.
24. *Ibid.*, Book VII, Ch. 14, pp. 285–86.
25. *Ibid.*, Book I, Ch. 2, pp. 26–27; Ch. 5, pp. 32–34; Book VII, Ch. 9, p. 273.
26. The transition was bracketed by Montesquieu and Rousseau (pre–nation-state) and John Stuart Mill (nation-state), and it is outlined in Robert A. Dahl, "The City in the Future of Democracy," *American Political Science Review*, 61, December 1967, 953–69.
27. *The Politics*, Book III, Ch. 5, p. 112.
28. Jean Jacques Rousseau, *The Social Contract and Discourses*, trans. G. D. H. Cole (New York: Dutton, 1950), p. 57.
29. This would include breaking up New York City. Robert A. Dahl, *After the Revolution? Authority in a Good Society* (New Haven, Conn.: Yale University Press, 1970), pp. 160–66.
30. Harvey C. Mansfield, Jr., "Hobbes and the Science of Indirect Government," *American Political Science Review*, 65, March 1971, 107–08.

31. *Loc. cit.*
32. This is thoroughly documented in Frank Marini, "Popular Sovereignty But Representative Government: The Other Rousseau," *Midwest Journal of Political Science,* 11, November 1967, 451–70.
33. Rousseau, "A Discourse on Political Economy," in *The Social Contract, op. cit.,* pp. 285–87.
34. Quotations are from Madison's "Federalist 10," *The Federalist Papers* (New York: New American Library, 1962), pp. 77–84.
35. For a summary of the views of such theorists as Dahl, Eckstein, and Sartori, all of whom emphasize the need for hierarchy, see Carole Pateman, *Participation and Democratic Theory* (Cambridge: University Press, 1970), Ch. 1.
36. J. Roland Pennock, "Democratic Political Theory—A Typological Discussion," *The Monist,* 55, January 1971, 61.
37. Joseph A. Schumpeter, *Capitalism, Socialism, and Democracy* (3rd ed.; New York: Harper and Row, 1950), p. 269.
38. This is summarized in Roy Lubove, *Twentieth-Century Pittsburgh: Government, Business, and Environmental Change* (New York: John Wiley, 1969), Chs. 6, 7; and David L. Lawrence (as told to John P. Robin and Stefan Lorant), "Rebirth," in *Pittsburgh: The Story of an American City* (Garden City, N.Y.: Doubleday, 1964), pp. 373–456.
39. For an outline of these schools of thought and the course of the long debate among them, see David Ricci, *Community Power and Democratic Theory: The Logic of Political Analysis* (New York: Random House, 1971). On Dahl's use of his norms to evaluate the degree of democracy in many countries, see Robert A. Dahl, *Polyarchy: Participation and Opposition* (New Haven, Conn.: Yale University Press, 1971).
40. Political scientists, encouraged by the very definition of their discipline, have attempted to keep government a separate entity that can be analyzed by itself. In emphasizing process, conversely, Bentley removed all distinctions between groups *inside* government and those *outside:* ". . . no sooner do we attempt to study [political institutions] than we find we must take into account the various grades of political groups . . . which function through them. These range down from the political parties as organized in 'the government' through the parties outside of the government, to policy organizations, citizens' associations . . . *the governing body has no value in itself, except as one aspect of the process, and cannot even be adequately described except in terms of the deep-lying interests which function through it.* Arthur F. Bentley, *The Process of Government,* new ed. (Cambridge, Mass.: Harvard University Press, 1967), p. 300 (emphasis added). Bentley's outline of a network of activities seems to have been based on these assumptions: all organizations were political and engaged in continuous, undifferentiated process; the important organizations were the large ones; spokesmen for large groups did in fact speak for all members; and group

members had come to share the same views without coercion. This is similar to the emerging revisionist view of Bentley, as expressed in Henry S. Kariel, *Open Systems: Arenas for Political Action* (Itasca, Ill.: F. E. Peacock, 1969). The sociologists, in this sense, have been closer to Bentley all along, even if they are more critical of the process than he was.

41. "You know, we used to talk of college men. Then it was college boys. And now it's college kids. I remember reading one of the early diaries on the opening of the West; it mentioned that a wagon train was led by a 'man of fourteen.' I guess somebody fourteen could be a man then, and know all he needed to run a wagon train—which was plenty —because he had good models, and he could see people doing it, and it was taken for granted he was a man. But we keep introducing new metaphors. . . . We created children, and then we created adolescents; we created students in a classroom, and we call them college kids. They're supposed to act in certain ways. And one of them of course is quiet." Edward T. Hall, quoted in William Braden, *The Age of Aquarius* (Chicago: Quadrangle Books, 1970), pp. 104–05.

42. Given the behavior forced upon political operatives by the necessity to achieve success, it is already obvious that the mysteries of sophisticated computers can be used as a mask to hide new forms of "gerrymandering," whereby districts are carefully shaped to make things come out right. Terry B. O'Rourke, *Reapportionment: Law, Politics, Computers* (Washington: American Enterprise Institute for Public Policy Research, 1972), esp. pp. 96–98.

43. Mansfield, *op. cit.*, p. 108.

44. A. D. Lindsay, *The Modern Democratic State* (New York: Oxford University Press, 1947), Vol. 1, p. 134.

45. Quotations are from Alexander Hamilton's "Federalist 63," in *The Federalist Papers, op. cit.*, pp. 411–15.

46. Henry B. Mayo, *An Introduction to Democratic Theory* (New York: Oxford University Press, 1960), p. 124. On European experiences and their effect upon political theorists, and on the findings of social science research, see Pateman, *op. cit.*, Ch. 1.

47. All quotations are from Theodore J. Lowi, *The Politics of Disorder* (New York: Basic Books, 1971), pp. xvii–xviii, and Ch. 2; also see his *The End of Liberalism: Ideology, Policy, and the Crisis of Public Authority* (New York: W. W. Norton, 1969). The notion of "automatic" administration remains attractive. Redford joins Lowi and neoliberal economists (Hayek) in advocating such "stable rules," since "man is freer if he knows what rules he must adjust to," and Redford and Lowi praise the original social security system as a first-rate example. Redford, *op. cit.*, pp. 185–86; *The End of Liberalism*, pp. 217–25. Yet Lowi looks upon the agricultural subsidy system with disdain, in part because many farmers who don't need subsidies get them; *ibid.*, pp.

102–15. Any such system is bound to be inequitable in many cases if it is automatic. The affluent senior citizen living off dividends continues to receive social security, while the poor citizen who goes to work loses it. Automatic administration makes sense only when all recipients are totally destitute in the first place, so the argument amounts to saying they *should* be. For an impressive demolition of Lowi's argument that legislators should not delegate to administrators, see Carl A. Auerbach, "Pluralism and the Administrative Process," *The Annals of the American Academy of Political and Social Science,* 400, March 1972, 1–13.

48. Lowi's confusion is illustrated by the way he deals with foreign policy processes. He concludes that "our record of response to crisis is good," because *"crisis decisions in foreign policy are made by an elite of formal officeholders"* (emphasis his). *The End of Liberalism,* p. 160. Leaving aside the question of evaluation, his normative premise makes no sense unless we assume that crisis decisions in foreign policy correspond with whatever is demanded by other nation-states that precipitate crises. Surely he doesn't mean this, but it would have to be so if foreign-policy decisions were to correspond to his prescriptions for domestic policy-making. Lowi also seems to recognize that charismatic leaders concerned about their images are unlikely to even discuss with their followers the details of what they seek. He quotes with approval from Michels' description of behavior in large organizations: "As the organization increases in size, the struggle for great principles becomes impossible. . . . Every struggle on behalf of ideas within the limits of the organization is necessarily regarded as an obstacle to the realization of its ends, an obstacle, therefore, which must be avoided in every possible way." While Lowi refers here to permanent organizations, he fails to show how the charismatic leaders of social movements could fulfill their function in any manner other than by communicating highly simplified myths and metaphors. On this problem see Edelman, *op. cit.,* Ch. 5.

49. William A. Niskanen, Jr., *Bureaucracy and Representative Government* (Chicago: Aldine & Atherton, 1971), p. 222. This resembles Richard Neustadt's argument that a President and his closest advisers must carefully guard their power against bureaucratic encroachment. See his *Presidential Power: The Politics of Leadership* (New York: John Wiley, 1960).

50. Tullock credits the notion to James C. Miller. Presumably, the proxy notion would encourage legislators to conduct proxy-collecting campaigns in the manner of corporate America. Gordon Tullock, *Private Wants and Public Means: An Economic Analysis of the Desirable Scope of Government* (New York: Basic Books, 1970), pp. 112–13; the idea also is advocated in Zbigniew Brzezinski, *Between Two Ages:*

America's Role in the Technetronic Era (New York: Viking Press, 1970), p. 259.

51. Robert Sherrill, "Instant Electorate," *Playboy,* November 1968.

52. William C. Wooldridge, *Uncle Sam, the Monopoly Man* (New Rochelle, N.Y.: Arlington House, 1970). Peter F. Drucker, *The Age of Discontinuity: Guidelines to Our Changing Society* (New York: Harper and Row, 1968, 1969), Ch. 10; upset with the monopoly power of unions, a First Deputy City Administrator in New York City argues for widespread use of competitive bidding on public service contracts. E. S. Savas, "Municipal Monopoly," *Harper's Magazine,* December 1971, pp. 55–60.

53. If one looks at "public choice" from the perspectives of organization theory, the confusion appears in slightly different form. Decision-making approaches bring into administration the economic calculation of costs and benefits, with authoritative decision-makers seeking the alternative which will "maximize" or "satisfice" output (objectives) for a given cost (or "minimize" cost for a given output). This makes the individual "on top" the institutional source of "rationality" (the Niskanen model). Tullock turns this upside down by seeking to make each citizen a "rational" decision-maker who "maximizes" or "satisfices" *input* (the public services he uses) for a given output (taxes or the direct purchase of services). This nonsense runs throughout Vincent Ostrom and Elinor Ostrom, "Public Choice: A Different Approach to the Study of Public Administration," *Public Administration Review,* 31, March/April 1971, 203–15. It is worth noting that this approach would eliminate the distinction between private goods and those designated as public, or collective, goods. These are the goods which, if made available to one consumer, must be made available to all consumers. They are the common outcomes of political decisions, citizens often receiving them whether or not they individually want them. By the same token, citizens often will not buy them if the choice is left to them. Public regulations, for example, now prescribe certain safety features for automobiles; yet when automobile manufacturers attempted a few years ago to make safety a selling point, they failed. It does not follow, of course, that the designation of public goods always should be left to elite decision-makers, but this version of "public choice" would tend to completely eliminate the category of public, or collective, goods and, pursued to its logical extreme, would make *every* decision about public services a totally individual one.

54. This notion runs through the survey compiled in Terrence E. Cook and Patrick M. Morgan, eds., *Participatory Democracy* (San Francisco: Canfield Press, 1971).

55. Pateman, *op. cit.,* pp. 42–43. Her favorite theorists of participation are Rousseau, John Stuart Mill, and G. D. H. Cole.

56. F. M. Esfandiary, *Optimism One: The Emerging Radicalism* (New York: W. W. Norton, 1970), Parts 1–2.
57. Dahl, *After the Revolution?*, pp. 94, 120, 134–39. Ironically, Pateman joins Dahl in supporting worker self-management, even though he is her favorite target among contemporary theorists. Pateman, *op. cit.*, Ch. V.
58. Arnold Toynbee, *Surviving the Future* (New York: Oxford University Press, 1971), pp. 15, 106.
59. The definitions and judgments are those of Albert O. Hirschman, *Exit, Voice, and Loyalty* (Cambridge, Mass.: Harvard University Press, 1970), esp. Ch. 4.

Chapter 3

1. *Saturday Review,* January 22, 1972. The articles appeared in conjunction with the Committee for Economic Development. The author was Robert Lekachman.
2. *The New York Times* (January 25, 1972).
3. Philip E. Slater, *The Pursuit of Loneliness: American Culture at the Breaking Point* (Boston: Beacon Press, 1971), pp. 5, 100–18.
4. *The New York Times* (August 16, 1971).
5. I borrow here from Gardiner C. Means, *Pricing Power and the Public Interest* (New York: Harper and Brothers, 1962), Ch. IX.
6. Mark J. Green, ed., *The Closed Enterprise System: Ralph Nader's Study Group Report on Antitrust Enforcement* (New York: Grossman, 1972), pp. 5–6.
7. John Kenneth Galbraith, *The New Industrial State,* 2nd ed. (Boston: Houghton Mifflin, 1971), pp. 256–57.
8. *The New York Times* (December 5, 1970).
9. *Ibid.,* August 16, 1971.
10. U.S. Department of the Treasury, News Release, August 16, 1971 (mimeo).
11. Milton Friedman, perhaps the purest of conservative economists, condemned the controls as "deeply and inherently immoral." *The New York Times* (October 28, 1971). The business community did *not* condemn them.
12. John S. McGee, *In Defense of Industrial Concentration* (New York: Praeger, 1971), Ch. 8.
13. *The New Industrial State,* p. 180.
14. G. Warren Nutter and Henry Adler Einhorn, *Enterprise Monopoly in the United States: 1899–1958* (New York: Columbia University Press, 1969), pp. 7–8.
15. Arthur F. Bentley argued this in the 1920's. See his *Makers, Users,*

and Masters, Sidney Ratner, ed. (Syracuse University Press, 1969), Ch. 3, esp. p. 43.

16. *The New Industrial State,* Ch. 16. Gardiner Means chides one colleague for assuming it better to have five manufacturers of spark plugs instead of three, without producing evidence to show why. Means, *op. cit.,* pp. 166–67.

17. John Kenneth Galbraith, "The New Industrial State," in Edwin Mansfield, ed., *Monopoly Power and Economic Performance* (New York: W. W. Norton, 1968), pp. 125–33. This is a statement Galbraith made before a Senate committee, and it is the clearest argument of its sort.

18. In classic economics, each producer would operate his plant at economic capacity (the point where unit cost of production equals price in the market). The large industry regulates production in consonance with trends in sales, prices remaining substantially unchanged. This may or may not be close to the capacity of the plant. Means, *op. cit.,* pp. 199–205.

19. *Ibid.,* pp. 236–44; Means credits it to DuPont and General Motors executive Donaldson Brown.

20. It has become fashionable for government and business to insist that wage increases be tied to increases in productivity. James M. Roche, then chairman of General Motors, blames the "diminishing rate of productivity growth" for the weakened position of the United States in world trade; *The New York Times* (October 30, 1971). Big labor, knowing that corporations refused to grant equivalent wage increases in those years when productivity did increase at a fast rate, understandably objects. The problem is exacerbated as we become more of a postindustrial economy, with much employment concentrated in government and service sectors. Productivity increases in these sectors cannot parallel increases in industry, yet wage and price increases in industry force up all wages and prices; interview with John Kenneth Galbraith, *Business Week,* October 16, 1971.

21. Testimony before the Senate Subcommittee on Consumers indicated that one major cereal manufacturer charged 18 cents more for a twelve-ounce box of one cereal than for another, the only difference between them being the addition of 0.6 cents' worth of vitamins. *The New York Times* (March 3, 1972).

22. Means used the term "competitive waste" in relation to industries where it is easy to create new distribution outlets and where individuals easily gain franchises, his principal example being gasoline stations. I use the term to encompass everything associated with the costs of competition—and, moreover, gasoline station franchises are controlled by the giants of the industry anyway. Means, *op. cit.,* pp. 214–18, and note 26, below.

23. A "Premium Show" brings together in New York each year manufac-

turers seeking to sell their products as premiums; other manufacturers who might buy them to be sold in packages with their own (some manufacturers play both roles); and the middleman distributors who create the "incentive programs" for everybody. The 1972 show had 1,000 exhibits, a 10 per cent increase over the 1971 show. This was attributed by one expert to a tight economy, which forced manufacturers to go to greater lengths to make customers buy. One leading distributor has 8,000 items in his catalogue, and four of the exhibits promoted Bibles ("Let us help you increase your profits") which sell at $49.95 retail but at $9.95 in supermarkets when accompanied by $50 purchases of groceries. The net result of all this can only be higher prices. *The New York Times* (May 2, 1972).

24. Where banks are concerned, competitive warfare in Pittsburgh escalated in 1972 to the point where all major banks instituted free checking, i.e., no charges for checks, maintenance, or minimum balances. One banker estimated the top banks would lose 5 to 10 per cent of profits unless market shares increased. Since the scheme is doubtless attractive to depositors, the loss will have to be made up elsewhere. *The Wall Street Journal* (May 4, 1972). This is an unusual example which violates the normal behavior pattern of oligopolies, in that it amounts to price competition. If it is expanded, some banks will fail.

25. *Time,* October 25, 1971.

26. The individual gas station operator is like a tenant farmer. See "Angry Gasoline Retailers Boil Over," *The New York Times* (December 13, 1970). A graduate student, Peter Bouvier, grew up with a father who operated a station, and managed one himself for a year. He reports that what goes on resembles a chamber of horrors. A great many stations are merely leased to individuals. Often they must meet purchase quotas for oil, accessories, etc. Special promotions, including trading stamps, if not mandatory, are "strongly suggested," and the operator must bear much of their cost. He also bears much of the cost of periodic gas wars, in which his margin shrinks to virtually nothing. Stations are erected willy-nilly, not in accordance with what the market will bear, so station operators have little choice but to attempt to survive through adding repair services. These, however, are not supervised or guaranteed by the gasoline company. In a particularly clever decision in 1972, the major companies began requiring dealers to pay a surcharge on sales made by credit card. Dealers could escape the surcharge by encouraging customers to pay cash, but this would make them more vulnerable to robberies. New York *News* (June 8, 1972).

27. I have elaborated this argument elsewhere. See my *Air Transport Policy and National Security* (Chapel Hill: University of North Carolina Press, 1965), esp. Chapter 11; "Air Transport Policy: A Crisis in Theory and Practice," *Journal of Air Law and Commerce,* 36 (1970), 661–72; "International Air Transport: A Microsystem in Need of New

Approaches," *International Organization,* 25 (1971), 875–98; "The Empty Seat War or the Folly of Airline Competition," *Washington Monthly,* June 1972. On the conventional wisdom, a standard work is Richard E. Caves, *Air Transport and Its Regulators* (Cambridge, Mass.: Harvard University Press, 1962). The example of absurd expenditures in lobbying for a route is from William A. Jordan, *Airline Regulation in America* (Baltimore: Johns Hopkins Press, 1970), p. 242. If the airline industry seems not to be an oligopoly at first glance (there is a relatively large number of airlines), each particular route is an oligopoly (usually two to four carriers). Almost identical problems affect steamship companies. Seven of the big companies in 1972 sought approval from the Federal Maritime Commission to bring independent companies into discussions designed to head off a rate war. Rates were already at a money-losing point, but capacity was so great ("overtonnage" in steamship jargon) as to be disturbing; *The Wall Street Journal* (June 1, 1972).

28. K. William Kapp, *The Social Costs of Private Enterprise* (New York: Schocken Books, 1971), pp. 1–13.

29. When I suggested as much in a letter published in *The Wall Street Journal* (September 15, 1971), I was berated by the Vice-President for Advertising Sales of one of the most prominent U.S. financial institutions. Yet conventional wisdom makes no sense unless we assume that the amounts spent on products managed by the advertising agency would not have been spent at all if not on those products. On this point, see O. J. Firestone, *The Economic Implications of Advertising* (Toronto: Methuen, 1967, pp. 136–37).

30. One investigation disclosed at least ten such flights out of Washington National Airport in a three-day period. *The New York Times* (April 25, 1972).

31. Galbraith advocates such a tax in an interview in *Business Week,* October 16, 1971. This is how Arthur Bentley put it, in dealing with "atrocious abuses of advertising by the excess-profits-tax-dodgers in 1918, 1919, and 1920": ". . . advertising is not something academic, ethereal, a mere matter of dollar charges. It is trees, and men cutting down trees. It is pulp mills, and men working in them. It is paper, and railway transportation. It is printing presses, and printers, and circulators. And all of this wealth and these services might be producing real goods to use and enjoy." *Makers, Users, and Masters,* pp. 75–76.

32. The involvement gains significance as sports become a political and economic issue. According to one account, television investment in professional football is $40 million per year for broadcast rights. Given the connection, television pays scant journalistic attention to labor-management disputes, racial problems, and broader economic issues. *Pittsburgh Post-Gazette* (January 31, 1972). This is easily seen when network journalists interview the commissioner of a professional sport

(baseball or football) on panel shows. The degree of deference is unbelievable, and any practicing politician must envy it.

33. *Makers, Users, and Masters,* p. 80, in the chapter entitled "Waste and Welfare."
34. E. J. Mishan, *Technology and Growth: The Price We Pay* (New York: Praeger, 1970), Parts II–III. Kapp, *loc. cit.*
35. *The Pursuit of Loneliness,* pp. 74, 94. In his exploration of the psychological phenomena, George Leonard concludes that "civilization's most indispensable non-material endowment to its children is some type of neurosis/disease/discontent." George B. Leonard, *The Transformation* (New York: Delacorte Press, 1972), p. 71.
36. Means, *op. cit.,* Ch. 18.
37. *The New Industrial State,* Chs. 23, 24.
38. When Means advanced his recommendations, most corporations used profit-based bonuses to motivate their executives. It seems unlikely, however, that profits were then or are now the driving thrust; market shares and survival seem more significant. Even at the peak of target profits, companies could have set higher prices; moreover, the target-pricing formula does not even assume profit maximization. Galbraith, drawing upon his own experience in government, notes that "if a decision requires the specialized knowledge of a group of men, it is subject to safe review only by the similar knowledge of a similar group." But this, he adds, would introduce unnecessary duplication of effort "with adverse effect upon the good nature and sense of responsibility of the groups whose decisions it would override." *Ibid.,* p. 66. Galbraith knows well, in other words, what happens when hierarchies impose their views, and, in a sense, argues against unilateral decisions. His proposal, then, that unemployed scientists and engineers be designated a "specialist corps" assigned to do research into public problems—and the implication inherent in his own political activism that intellectuals who share his views become advisers to his favorite Presidential candidate so they can implement their own notions of good decisions—do not fit in his own theory. On the specialist corps, see *The New York Times* (April 27, 1972).
39. *The Closed Enterprise System,* p. 62 and Ch. 15.
40. Morton Mintz and Jerry S. Cohen, *America, Inc., Who Owns and Operates the United States* (New York: Dial Press, 1971); Nader's Introduction, pp. xi–xix.
41. Leading proponents are Walter Adams and Joe S. Bain. Useful summaries are in *ibid.,* Ch. 4.
42. *Can Regulatory Agencies Protect Consumers?* (Washington: American Enterprise Institute for Public Policy Research, 1971). Ch. 1 is a lecture by George J. Stigler, outlining the deficiencies in regulation in contrast to the "known" benefits of consumer sovereignty and competition.

43. A recent summary of the views of the experts is Robert G. Noll, *Regulation: An Evaluation of the Ash Council Proposals* (Washington: Brookings Institution, 1971). In summarizing the feelings of some thirty-one conferees, Noll reports in Ch. 11 that "much of regulation . . . is in deep trouble." Noting that a number of them advocated considerable de-regulation, he adds that ". . . proponents of deregulation did not claim that, in principle, price regulation of monopolies (power companies) was a bad idea on ideological grounds. Rather . . . regulation is expensive, ineffective, and even anticompetitive" (pp. 109–10). As if competition were not an ideology! A typical Nader volume is Robert Fellmeth, *The Interstate Commerce Omission: Ralph Nader's Study Group Report on the Interstate Commerce Commission and Transportation* (New York: Grossman, 1970), esp. Ch. 11.

44. This is borrowed from Mancur Olson, Jr., *The Logic of Collective Action: Public Goods and the Theory of Groups* (New York: Schocken Books, 1969), Ch. 1.

45. *Time,* March 27, 1972. After a slaughtering bill did not pass, the Agriculture Department advised everyone to reduce output by 2 per cent. *The New York Times* (August 6, 1972).

46. Lowi, *The End of Liberalism,* pp. 102–15. Presumably, Lowi would allow assistance to farmers in extreme difficulty, while denying it to those who are well off. This, in turn, would require a discretionary "nonautomatic" administrative process which Lowi disapproves of in principle. See above, Chapter 2, note 47.

47. *The New Industrial State,* pp. 190–91n.

48. Arthur M. Schlesinger, Jr., *The Coming of the New Deal* (Boston: Houghton Mifflin, 1959), Parts I–II.

49. Frederick Brooman and Henry D. Jacoby, *Macroeconomics* (Chicago: Aldine Publishing, 1970), pp. 409–10.

50. *The New Industrial State,* p. 222.

51. In correspondence I have had with the economic analyst of a leading U.S. newspaper, I was surprised at his assertion that "if prices and factors move freely, Say's Law does apply," and thus overproduction cannot be a problem. But this can mean only that everything can be sold at some price, even if disastrous to producers. The viewpoint has no ideological boundaries; one prominent socialist economist argues that a "shortage of demand" can never be a problem under socialism, for planners can "always cut prices to clear a market. . . ." Paul Sweezy, "Socialism and Communism as Ideals," in Tom Christoffel, David Finkelhor, and Dan Gilbarg, eds., *Up Against the American Myth* (New York: Holt, Rinehart and Winston, 1970), p. 419. The problem may be the internal logic of Keynesian economics used for policy-making, never analyzed in depth because it would suggest overproduction.

52. One example is Morton A. Kaplan, *System and Process in International Politics* (New York: John Wiley, 1957). "With five players of

roughly equal capabilities, one can play the role of the 'balancer' by throwing its diplomatic weight and influence to whatever side may appear to be weakening, strengthen that side, and thus 'maintain the balance' . . . the whole purpose . . . is to prevent the game from ending by preventing any clearcut winners and losers." Vincent Davis, "On Working a 'Balance of Power,'" *Christian Science Monitor* (January 14, 1972).

53. Daniel Bell, "The Cultural Contradictions of Capitalism," in Daniel Bell and Irving Kristol, eds., *Capitalism Today* (New York: Basic Books, 1970, 1971), Ch. 2.

54. In the early 1960's, electrical manufacturers had to submit sealed bids for government contracts involving unique equipment not sold on the market. Each, not having any idea what others would bid, felt trapped. The executives met together, and subsequently were convicted for it; *The New Industrial State,* pp. 192–93; "Collusion Among Electrical Equipment Manufacturers," *The Wall Street Journal* (January 10, 12, 1962). If General Electric and Westinghouse, for example, submitted sealed bids under such circumstances, one might consistently underbid the other, thus cornering the entire market for itself. National policy would intervene to prevent product monopoly. If the government tried to avoid this by accepting the highest bid upon occasion, this would violate the purpose of the bidding. And if the government announced it would divide the business, it would be accused of negotiating with the manufacturers. Thus, executives probably conclude they contribute to the public interest in such instances. Given the conventional wisdom, such situations can only recur—as when Senator William Proxmire and Admiral Hyman Rickover argue that steel companies engage in collusive bidding on defense contracts; Washington *Post* (December 19, 1971). All this has a revolving-door aspect. A federal grand jury indicted General Motors and Ford in May 1972 for conspiring (though not in face-to-face meetings) to refuse to cut prices for fleet buyers (rental companies, leasing companies, commercial accounts, state and local governments) while at the same time dealers sued Chrysler for setting lower prices for fleet customers and higher ones for individual buyers. The Justice Department admitted that all three companies might lose, two for not cutting prices and one for cutting them; *The New York Times* (May 2, 1972).

55. Quoted in *The Pursuit of Loneliness,* p. 41.

56. Japanese managers develop dependency relationships with other organizations (suppliers or buyers) so as to provide "ensured cooperation, firm organizational linkages, and precise systems of control." These relationships "tend to be incompatible with certain competition-oriented business practices." Thus, the Japanese recognize an obligation to provide work for those involved in these key relationships, and this leads them to mute the effects of competition. Americans, conversely, "seem to expect dependency and competitive behavior to somehow manage to

coexist." Leonard R. Sayles and Margaret K. Chandler, *Managing Large Systems: Organizations for the Future* (New York: Harper and Row, 1971), pp. 76–77.

57. Peter F. Drucker, "The New Markets and the New Capitalism," in Daniel Bell and Irving Kristol, *op. cit.*, Ch. 3.

58. This parallels what Donald Schon terms the evolution of corporations from enterprises which concentrate on products to ones which create larger business systems. These fit neither the traditional models of horizontal growth (merge with competitors) nor vertical consolidation (control raw materials). Thus, California firms contract to "keep customers in clean shirts" by supplying shirts in appropriate quantities and retaining authority to decide when old shirts should be replaced by new ones. Institutional feeding, geriatric care, the ventures of large firms into education and into the "city-building business" (Westinghouse and Walt Disney) are examples, many of them spurred by the example of NASA in organizing space operations. Donald Schon, *Beyond the Stable State* (New York: Random House, 1971), Ch. 3. While some conglomerates fit this pattern of a coherent system, it is not at all clear that most of them do.

59. Lawrence J. White, *The American Automobile Industry Since 1945* (Cambridge, Mass.: Harvard University Press, 1971).

60. Paul A. Samuelson, "On Mutual Funds," *Newsweek*, July 12, 1971; J. M. Kaplan, "Wall Street: A Radical Proposal," *The New York Times* (March 1, 1972).

61. Branko Horvat, "Yugoslavian Economic Policy in the Post-War Period: Problems, Ideas, Institutional Development," *American Economic Review*, 61, June 1971, 95.

62. Summarized in Carole Pateman, *Participation and Democratic Theory* (Cambridge: University Press, 1970), Ch. V.

63. Horvat, *op. cit.*, p. 96.

64. *Ibid.*, p. 104.

65. *Ibid.*, pp. 159–61; Deborah D. Milenkovitch, *Plan and Market in Yugoslav Economic Thought* (New Haven, Conn.: Yale University Press, 1971), Ch. 11.

66. Pateman, *op. cit.*, p. 95.

67. Horvat, *op. cit.*, p. 117.

68. Misha D. Jezernik, "Changes in the Hierarchy of Motivational Factors and Social Values in Slovenian Industry," *The Journal of Social Issues*, 24, April 1968, 103–14.

69. Paul Blumberg, *Industrial Democracy: The Sociology of Participation* (New York: Schocken Books, 1969), pp. 210–15.

70. Kevin Richard Kane, "Problems of Inter-Regional Disparities and Decentralized Socialist Development in Yugoslavia," unpublished Master's thesis, Graduate School of Public and International Affairs, University of Pittsburgh, 1971.

71. Milenkovitch, *op. cit.*, pp. 297–98.

72. Howard Sherman, *Radical Political Economy: Capitalism and Socialism from a Marxist-Humanist Perspective* (New York: Basic Books, 1972), pp. 287, 311.
73. Tokyo's Metropolitan Safety Council, concerned about pollution and traffic, has recommended traffic and ownership restrictions on "socially superfluous vehicles." *Parade*, July 16, 1972. George Leonard advocates a "transactional heat tax" to solve the energy crisis. At each stage in the sale of an automobile (producer, dealer, etc.), a progressive tax would be calculated from the amount of heat released by that transaction. Leonard, *op. cit.,* pp. 215–16. As a "sales tax" on heat, it would work against Leonard's larger objectives.
74. *The New York Times* (February 9, 1972).
75. *Ibid.* (March 30, 1972).
76. Jay W. Forrester, *World Dynamics* (Cambridge, Mass.: Wright-Allen Press, 1971), p. 2. I am indebted to a graduate student, R. L. Scott, for providing a more striking example of exponential growth. If one begins on the first day of a month with a single penny and postulates doubling the money each day, things begin slowly. By the tenth day, one has only $5.12. But from the twentieth day ($5,242.88) to the twenty-first ($10,485.76), changes certainly are significant; the thirtieth day's total is over $5 million!
77. Donella H. Meadows, Dennis L. Meadows, Jorgen Randers, William W. Behrens, III, *The Limits to Growth: A Report for the Club of Rome's Project on the Predicament of Mankind* (New York: Universe Books, 1972), pp. 34–35. See also *Population and the American Future: The Report of the Commission on Population Growth and the American Future* (New York: New American Library, Signet Edition, 1972).
78. Current world consumption is 6.5 billion metric tons of coal equivalent, of which the U.S. uses 2.2 billion. If China were modernized to U.S. standards, the Chinese alone would require 8 billion. Dennis Pirages and Paul R. Ehrlich, "If All Chinese Had Wheels," *The New York Times* (March 16, 1972).
79. Ralph E. Lapp, "We're Running Out of Gas," *The New York Times Magazine* (March 19, 1972). Renowned golfer Arnold Palmer has become the television spokesman for the industry, warning of higher prices ahead.
80. Aurelio Peccei, *The Chasm Ahead* (Toronto: Collier-Macmillan of Canada, 1969), pp. 241–58.
81. *The New York Times* (March 3, 1972).
82. *The Limits to Growth*, pp. 171–74.
83. Forrester, *op. cit.,* p. 120.
84. Malaysia might export not natural rubber but tires; India, not cotton but fabrics; West Africa, not palm oil but soap. Barry Commoner, *The Closing Circle* (New York: Knopf, 1971), pp. 289–92.

85. Richard A. Falk, "Adapting World Order to the Global Ecosystem," in John Harte and Robert Socolow, eds., *The Patient Earth* (New York: Holt, Rinehart and Winston, 1971), pp. 245–57. He argues for a world government, but with a conventional hierarchical structure.
86. "A Blueprint for Survival," *The Ecologist*, 2, January 1972.

Chapter 4

1. This is summarized in Nicos P. Mouzelis, *Organisation and Bureaucracy* (Chicago: Aldine Publishing, 1969), Ch. 1.
2. William I. Thompson, *At The Edge of History* (New York: Harper and Row, 1970), pp. 147, 151, 163.
3. Leonard, *op. cit.*, p. 2.
4. Thomas S. Kuhn, *The Structure of Scientific Revolutions* (University of Chicago Press, 1962, 1970), pp. 175–90.
5. *Ibid.*, p. 111.
6. Sheldon Wolin, "Political Theory as a Vocation," *American Political Science Review*, 63, December 1969, 1075, 1078, 1080. I have reversed the order in which Wolin's paragraphs appear in the original.
7. Arnold Toynbee, *Surviving the Future* (New York: Oxford University Press, 1971), p. 66.
8. H. Richard Niebuhr, *The Responsible Self* (New York: Harper and Row, 1963), pp. 71–73.
9. Paul Ramsey, "The Transformation of Ethics," in his *Faith and Ethics: The Theology of H. Richard Niebuhr* (New York: Harper and Row Torchbooks, 1965), p. 141.
10. *Ibid.*, p. 152; also James Gustafson, "Christian Ethics and Social Policy," in *ibid.*, p. 122.
11. H. Richard Niebuhr, "Theology—Not Queen but Servant," *The Journal of Religion*, 25, January 1955, 1–5.
12. *The Responsible Self*, p. 125.
13. John D. Godsey, *The Promise of H. Richard Niebuhr* (Philadelphia: Lippincott, 1970), pp. 106–08.
14. L. S. Halprin, "Toward a Redefinition of 'Radical,' " reproduced in *The MANAS Reader* (New York: Grossman, 1971), p. 258.
15. Mary Parker Follett, *The New State: Group Organization the Solution of Popular Government*, 5th ed. (New York: Longmans, Green, 1926), p. 62.
16. *Ibid.*, p. 59.
17. *Ibid.*, pp. 30, 271–74.
18. Arthur F. Bentley, *Makers, Users, and Masters*, ed. Sidney Ratner (Syracuse University Press, 1969), pp. 189–90.
19. Or so Holtan Odegard argues in *The Politics of Truth: Toward Reconstruction in Democracy* (University of Alabama Press, 1971), Ch. 10.

20. This summary is drawn from Anatole Shaffer, "The Cincinnati Social Unit Experiment, 1917–1919," *The Social Science Review,* 45, June 1971, 159–71, and Edward T. Devine, "The Social Unit in Cincinnati: An Experiment in Organization," *The Survey,* 43, November 15, 1919, 115–26.
21. Henry S. Kariel, *Open Systems: Arenas for Political Action,* (Itasca, Ill.: F. E. Peacock, 1969), pp. 96–98; and his "Creating Political Reality," *American Political Science Review,* 64, December 1970, 1083–98.
22. *The Greening of America* (New York: Random House, 1970), p. 285.
23. Rensis Likert, *Management of Crisis in Organizations* (draft MS). "Man was made for joy, for creation of meaning, for ritual and drama, for love, for poetry and mystery, for self-transcendence, and for union with all mankind. There is more, much more, to man than the narrow image of him that we have incorporated into our economic and political life." John Romanyshyn, *Social Welfare* (New York: Random House, 1971), p. 408.
24. L. J. Zimmerman, *The Propensity to Monopolize* (Amsterdam: New Holland Publishing House, 1952), p. 8. He adds that competition can work only when supply is limited and demand unlimited; this makes overproduction impossible, but it also totally depletes the resource (as in the case of whales).
25. John Kenneth Galbraith, *The New Industrial State,* 2nd ed. (Boston: Houghton Mifflin, 1971), pp. 358–60.
26. Admittedly, less than "perfect" planning resulted in some temporary shortages of telephone circuits but, from a cost standpoint, this is preferable to wasteful overproduction. Nor is this to argue that AT&T does not engage in its own form of competitive waste. Anyone who has been besieged by the drive to install seven telephones in a single home knows better; yet, the absence of the competitive struggle lessens overall waste.
27. Richard A. Posner, "Natural Monopoly and its Regulation," in Paul W. MacAvoy, ed., *The Crisis of the Regulatory Commissions* (New York: W. W. Norton, 1970), pp. 34–38.
28. E. F. Schumacher, "Buddhist Economics," in *The MANAS Reader, op. cit.,* pp. 180–86.
29. It went little noticed at the time *The Greening of America* was published but, while the intellectual community generally regarded it as empty of substance, one of the more favorable reviews was written by an editor of *Fortune;* he observed that *"in the past twenty years, the main institutions of American society have been moving very rapidly in the direction of the values and patterns of Consciousness III"* (his emphasis). Max Ways, "The Real Greening of America: A Fortune Editorial," *Fortune,* November 1970.
30. Herman E. Daly, "Toward a Stationary-State Economy," in John

Harte and Robert Socolow, eds., *The Patient Earth* (New York: Holt, Rinehart and Winston, 1971), pp. 245–57.

31. This view is at variance with that of the father of humanistic psychology, Abraham Maslow. See Chapter 2, note 23.

32. Philip E. Slater, *The Pursuit of Loneliness: American Culture at the Breaking Point* (Boston: Beacon Press, 1971), pp. 5, 26, 100–18.

33. Thomas E. Bier, "Contemporary Youth: Implications of the Personalistic Life-Style for Organizations," unpublished Doctoral dissertation, Case Western Reserve University, 1967 (Industrial Psychology).

34. Reich, *The Greening of America*, Ch. IX.

35. If "blue-collar" youth remain committed to the achievement ethic they will stand ready to replace those rejecting it. Peter L. Berger and Brigitte Berger, "The Blueing of America," *New Republic*, April 3, 1971.

36. William Braden, *The Age of Aquarius* (Chicago: Quadrangle Books, 1970), pp. 180–82.

37. Barbara Mikulski, "Who Speaks for Ethnic America?" *The New York Times*, September 29, 1970. The comprehensive proethnic argument is Michael Novak, *Politics and Culture in the Seventies* (New York: Macmillan, 1972). Elsewhere, Novak puts it this way: ". . . We think we are better people than the blacks. How much of all this we learned in America . . . is not plain to us. Racism is not our invention. . . ." "White Ethnic," *Harper's Magazine*, September, 1971.

38. Arnold Toynbee, "For the First Time in 30,000 Years," *Worldview*, 15, March 1972, 5–9.

39. Slater terms this the "toilet assumption"; Slater, *op. cit.*, pp. 15–20.

40. Antony Jay, *Corporation Man* (New York: Random House, 1971), Ch. III. This is remarkably similar to Leonard's observation that all the trouble began with agricultural surpluses which encouraged urbanization. Jay departs from the fascination with groups of five; his favorite is ten.

41. Odegard, *The Politics of Truth*, Ch. 11 and p. 217. The first four steps are adapted from Mary Parker Follett, the fifth from Horace Fries; I have done some rewording.

Chapter 5

1. Noting that among others, Benjamin Franklin favored a council rather than an individual executive, Leonard recommends we think now about a "group presidency." George Leonard, *The Transformation* (New York: Delacorte Press, 1972), pp. 189–90.

2. The Supreme Court is perceived as having performed a dialectical role in producing a "contemporary synthesis" of individual and societal val-

ues. Orion F. White, Jr., "The Dialectical Organization: An Alternative to Bureaucracy," *Public Administration Review,* 29 (January/February 1969), 41–42.

3. *The New York Times* (November 14, 1971).

4. To be sure, considerable Congressional activity is devoted to reversing Supreme Court interpretations of federal legislation, as opposed to Constitutional interpretations. Sheldon Goldman and Thomas P. Jahnige, *The Federal Courts as a Political System* (New York: Harper and Row, 1971), pp. 256–61.

5. Alexis de Tocqueville, *Democracy in America,* Henry Reeves Text (New York: Knopf, 1945), Vol. II, p. 280.

6. Warren E. Burger, "Foreword," *Public Administration Review,* 31, March/April 1971, 112–13. This issue contains a symposium on judicial administration.

7. Harry S. Truman, *Years of Trial and Hope* (Garden City, N.Y.: Doubleday, 1965), pp. 59–60. The formal reason for Presidential absence was "that the other members may have a free discussion without the premature expression of the President's personal views." Sidney Souers, "Policy Formulation for National Security," *American Political Science Review,* June 1949; reproduced in U.S. Congress, Senate, *Organizing for National Security,* Subcommittee on National Policy Machinery, Committee on Government Operations, 86th Cong., 2d Sess. (Washington: Government Printing Office, 1960), pp. 28–36.

8. Arnold A. Rogow, *James Forrestal: A Study of Personality, Politics, and Policy* (New York: Macmillan, 1963), Chs. II, IX, and pp. 267, 331, 344.

9. Walter Millis, with Harvey C. Mansfield and Harold Stein, *Arms and the State* (New York: Twentieth Century Fund, 1958), pp. 234–35.

10. Dean Acheson, *Present at the Creation* (New York: W. W. Norton, 1969), pp. 319–21, 373, 375, 441.

11. *Ibid.,* pp. 733–35.

12. Reproduced in Senator Henry M. Jackson, ed., *The National Security Council: Jackson Subcommittee Papers on Policy-Making at the Presidential Level* (New York: Praeger, 1965), pp. 96–97. Lovett's testimony was a curious mixture. His formal statement, prepared in advance, was highly critical of all committees and argued for "restoring the authority of the individual executive"; it has been widely quoted by anticommittee advocates. In answering questions, however, Lovett outlined in detail how effective the interaction within the NSC turned out to be.

13. This summary is drawn from the published materials of the Jackson Subcommittee of the late 1950's and early 1960's, especially its voluminous testimony. The perspective resembles that of Robert H. Johnson, a long-time staff member of the NSC, in his "The National Security

Council: The Relevance of Its Past to Its Future," *Orbis*, 13, Fall 1969, 709–35.

14. On Cutler's metaphors, see "The Development of the National Security Council," *Foreign Affairs*, April 1956; reproduced in *Organizing for National Security*, pp. 48–61; also his reproduced testimony in *The National Security Council*, pp. 111–39.

15. See letter from Presidential Assistant McGeorge Bundy to Senator Jackson, in *ibid.*, pp. 275–81.

16. Robert Cutler, *No Time for Rest* (Boston: Little, Brown, 1965), p. 312.

17. John Ponturo, "The President and Policy Guidance," in Keith C. Clark and Laurence J. Legere, *The President and the Management of National Security* (New York: Praeger, 1969), pp. 227–28.

18. Hans J. Morgenthau, "Can We Entrust Defense to a Committee?" *The New York Times* (June 7, 1959).

19. *The National Security Council*, pp. 35–37. For a further analysis of this report's conceptual deficiencies, see my "Presidential Policy Processes and 'New Administration': A Search for Revised Paradigms," *Public Administration Review*, 31 (September/October 1971), 554–55.

20. The concept is that Cabinet members and other advisers constantly attempt to have the President work for *them* instead of for himself (and, by implication, the country); thus he must carefully preserve his own power. See Richard E. Neustadt, *Presidential Power: The Politics of Leadership* (New York: John Wiley, 1960). Neustadt was, for a time, a staff member of the Jackson Subcommittee.

21. Theodore C. Sorensen, *The Kennedy Legacy* (New York: Macmillan, 1969), p. 218.

22. President Kennedy's statement, issued in conjunction with Executive Order 10920 abolishing the OCB, is in *The National Security Council*, p. 304.

23. Theodore C. Sorensen, *Kennedy* (New York: Harper and Row, 1965), p. 281.

24. From the remarks on Japanese experience in Chapter 1, it follows that implementation and evaluation would, in a revised paradigm, be less difficult problems than they are now. The mechanics of the OCB help make this clear. The Under Secretary of State, acting as OCB chairman, was hardly in a position to direct the activities of the Defense Department, or to prepare for the NSC a report critical of other departments. And he could hardly have been expected to criticize the Secretary of State. This same situation would confront any official, whether or not assigned to the White House staff, who attempted an evaluation. If he were to criticize departmental performance, officials would distort the information given him. Unless it was done with great secrecy, leakages could assist political opponents. Even with leakages,

accurate record-keeping by any administration would provide its successor with evidence useful in future political campaigns. These difficulties can be overcome, it seems to me, only by making policy processes more collective, to the extent that error can be diagnosed without attempting to apportion blame among participants.

25. Testimony of David Bell, reproduced in *The National Security Council*, pp. 216–17.

26. Sorensen, *Kennedy*, p. 284.

27. Bundy letter in *The National Security Council*, p. 277.

28. In 1962 I was permitted to peruse the NSC files pertaining to a topic of interest to me. All the files were in the Executive Office Building across the street from the White House. A few officials maintained custody of them, but no use was made of them.

29. Sorensen, *Kennedy*, p. 258; Arthur M. Schlesinger, Jr., *A Thousand Days* (Boston: Houghton Mifflin, 1965), p. 207.

30. All quotations are from Neustadt, *Presidential Power*, pp. 155–59. Neustadt relies heavily upon Schlesinger's analysis of the early Roosevelt years.

31. Sorensen, *Kennedy*, p. 285.

32. Henry L. Stimson and McGeorge Bundy, *On Active Service in Peace and War* (New York: Harper and Brothers, 1947), p. 564. I personally observed this reaction in the case of one high official in Washington during the mid-1960's. Some of us persuaded him that certain processes should be altered, but he declined to advance the suggestion because it might make him appear critical of the President. Indeed, he thought it inadvisable to even recommend that the processes be studied!

33. Schlesinger, *op. cit.*, Ch. X. One should especially note Schlesinger's objection that the Joint Chiefs of Staff "softly" voiced their preference for a different plan, and his conclusion that they neither approved nor disapproved the operation.

34. The details are in a series of articles by Edwin L. Dale, Jr., *The New York Times* (December 6, 12, 1966; January 22, 1967).

35. U.S. Congress, Senate, *The Secretary of State and the Problem of Coordination: New Duties and Procedures of March 4, 1966,* Subcommittee of the Committee on Government Operations, 98th Cong., 2nd Sess., 1966.

36. Edward Weintal and Charles Bartlett, *Facing the Brink* (New York: Scribner's, 1967), pp. 9–10. Because it is so difficult to describe a nonsystem, one must turn upon occasion to vignettes and metaphors. Presidential assistant Jack Valenti "carefully recorded in longhand" the opinion of each adviser during a 1966 meeting on the bombing pause in Vietnam; *ibid.*, p. 79. An experienced observer likened the Kennedy-Johnson years to a "cross between administrative touch football and a permanent cattle stampede," and described the behavior as typical of "the disarray and disorder of senatorial habit"; William D. Carey,

"Presidential Staffing in the Sixties and Seventies," *Public Administration Review*, 29, September/October 1969, 452–67.

37. I. M. Destler, *Presidents, Bureaucrats, and Foreign Policy: The Politics of Organizational Reform* (Princeton University Press, 1972), pp. 111–15.

38. Clark and Legere, *op. cit.*, p. 82.

39. *A Report to the Congress by Richard M. Nixon: Foreign Policy for the 1970s* (Washington: Government Printing Office, 1970), Part I: "The National Security Council System."

40. I. M. Destler concludes that Kissinger's personal relationship to the President and his institutional role as manager of the NSC machinery were incompatible. He spent so much time on "meeting the President's immediate, daily needs, on handling the President's own personal foreign affairs business" that he became distant and secretive with the NSC staff. Destler, *op. cit.*, p. 147. Alexander L. George concludes that while intensive interaction is desirable, the Special Assistant for National Security should perform as he did in the Truman-Eisenhower years, as a "neutral" or "secretarial" official; "The Case for Multiple Advocacy in Making Foreign Policy," *American Political Science Review*, 66(3), September 1972, 751–85. Both these analyses, focusing so closely on Kissinger as an individual, underemphasize the stark contrast between the systematic processes used by Truman, Eisenhower, and Nixon, and the total lack of any system at all in the Kennedy-Johnson years.

41. As a technique which depersonalizes the approach of any group to the problems before it, this corresponds to the recommendations of a number of analysts of organizational behavior, e.g., Rensis Likert.

42. Using all the sources he could find, Destler notes that Eisenhower's NSC met 51 times during its first year and 145 times during the first three years, as opposed to a total of 128 meetings during Truman's five years. Like most other analyses, Destler's does not distinguish between the two periods of Truman's Presidency, although it is noted that Truman's highest total in a single year was 34. Destler, *op. cit.*, p. 123n.

43. On the Cambodian speech, see *ibid.*, p. 126n, which draws upon *The New York Times* reports. There were some indications at the time of the initial incursions into Laos that final decisions had been reached after, not during, NSC meetings.

44. On the broad range of such proposals, see *ibid.*, pp. 26–28; they have been advanced by Herbert Hoover, Eisenhower, Nelson Rockefeller, and others. A recent proposal for an official "above the Cabinet" is Clark Clifford's in *The New York Times* (March 1, 1970). The "State Department should be dominant" theme is echoed in John Franklin Campbell, *The Foreign Affairs Fudge Factory* (New York: Basic Books, 1971).

45. The faulty logic is best exemplified in Destler's proposals for change.

The President, he argues, should want the Secretary of State to be "his pre-eminent foreign policy official," and the Secretary should "place top priority on making the State Department his own." Permanent career officials stand in the way of these objectives, because they are addicted to "pet bureaucratic doctrines"; hence the Secretary should rely upon the Assistant Secretaries, who in turn should be designated formally as having jobs of "Cabinet-level importance." The Secretary also needs a group of personal assistants, "in-and-out types . . . analytically oriented, more inclined toward aggressive involvement in issues and risk-taking." This "new blood" would collectively be known as the "Secretary's men," and they also would identify themselves as the "President's men." The NSC itself should decline in importance, although it should remain the "formal focal point for discussing issues requiring presidential decision." The principal body for making foreign policy would be a senior committee chaired by the Secretary of State, even if he might "choose to delegate much of its operation to the Under Secretary." Destler, *op. cit.*, Ch. 9.

It is one thing to define the Secretary of State as "first among equals," but something else to formalize his status as the hierarchical chairman of a "foreign affairs government," while insisting that his Assistant Secretaries have the same rank as other Cabinet officers. This implies that issues would reach the President only if some other Cabinet officer appealed them, but Destler's own evidence indicates this cannot work. (McNamara did not raise the Skybolt issue to top level because he did not want to criticize Rusk; *ibid.*, p. 115n.) To advocate primacy for a committee usually under the command of the Under Secretary of State is to argue for a return to the arrangements of Johnson's final years, though Destler concludes they did not work. To speak of the NSC as something less important implies that the President should be involved only in the unimportant aspects of foreign policy. This version of hierarchy, then, tends to remove the President from the process.

46. A summary of all proposals as of mid-1972 is in *Congressional Quarterly Weekly Report*, 30, May 13, 1972, 1054–55. The words are Senator John C. Stennis's.

47. This was the reaction of a member of that committee's staff, in conversation with the author.

48. This account is summarized from Joseph M. Jones, *The Fifteen Weeks, February 21–June 5, 1947* (New York: Viking Press, 1955). Jones was a State Department official at the time. June 5 was the date of Marshall's introduction of his famous aid plan.

49. Neustadt, *Presidential Power*, pp. 47ff.

50. Louis W. Koenig, *The Chief Executive* (New York: Harcourt, Brace and World, 1964), p. 352.

51. Sydney Hyman, *The American President* (New York: Harper and Brothers, 1954), pp. 295–96.

52. See Chapter 1.
53. The pattern has become relatively stabilized by now. At the most, key Congressmen receive only a last-minute briefing prior to a Presidential announcement, or a follow-up explanation by the President's principal advisers.
54. Henry A. Kissinger, *The Troubled Partnership* (New York: McGraw-Hill, 1965), pp. 225–48.
55. *The New York Times* (January 22, 1971).
56. Foreign policy officials, including many from other countries, speak off the record at Council meetings, and there is little doubt that it has been influential over the years. This has often been criticized, but the more logical approach would be to increase the interaction—and to include other groups.
57. Clinton Rossiter, *The American Presidency* (New York: Harcourt, Brace and Company, 1956), pp. 149–50.
58. Reorganization Plan No. 2, 1970, and White House Press Release, March 12, 1970.
59. White House Press Release, May 21, 1969.
60. John Fischer, "Can the Nixon Administration Be Doing Something Right?," *Harper's Magazine*, November 1970, pp. 22–28.
61. Two examples are James L. Sundquist, with David W. Davis, *Making Federalism Work* (Washington: Brookings Institution, 1969), pp. 244–45, 274–75; and Charles L. Schultze, *The Politics and Economics of Public Spending* (Washington: Brookings Institution, 1968), pp. 133–34.
62. One official, responsible for dealing with the Federal Executive Boards, those associations of federal officials connected with the regional offices of the major agencies, delivered a speech in Pittsburgh in December 1971, emphasizing the need for "leadership" and "initiative" by individual regional agency offices.
63. Destler, *op. cit.,* pp. 149–50, an analysis based only on the Council on International Economic Policy. The Domestic Council includes all Cabinet officers except those of State and Defense.
64. Richard J. Barber, *The American Corporation: Its Power, Its Money, Its Politics* (New York: Dutton, 1970), p. 297.
65. *Ibid.,* p. 270.

Chapter 6

1. Max Ehrlich, *The Big Eye* (Garden City, N.Y.: Doubleday, 1949).
2. In *Beyond Freedom and Dignity* (New York: Knopf, 1971), Skinner did not make clear the types of decision processes he had in mind. He later added clarifications which would install "behavioral engineers" as third-party adjudicators who would make definitive "judgments" about

how to resolve conflicts. *The Center Magazine,* 5, March/April 1972, 65.

3. In *The Transformation* (New York: Delacorte Press, 1972), George Leonard acknowledges that humans require some overall objective if they are effectively to come together in purposeful action. All too often in the past this has been war between nation-states (p. 206).

4. C. L. Sulzberger, "The Non-Allied Alliance," *The New York Times* (June 2, 1972).

5. Limited-war theories were originally based upon the premise that we and the Soviets might engage in land combat, short of nuclear warfare. While this had the initial effect of making limited war more attractive than all-out war, it tended to define Hitler's and Napoleon's campaigns in Russia as "limited." When it was understood that direct confrontation with the Soviet Union probably would escalate, and quickly, to all-out war, we became attracted to "counterinsurgency," "counterrevolution," and Vietnam. See Henry A. Kissinger, *The Necessity for Choice* (Garden City, N.Y.: Doubleday, Anchor Edition, 1962), probably the best known work which made small wars look attractive; and Richard J. Walton, *Cold War and Counterrevolution* (New York: Viking Press, 1972), Ch. 9. As this was written in 1972, many still believed that Americans and Soviets could engage in ground war in Europe, yet avoid the exchange of intercontinental missiles.

6. This is not intended to advance the old anti-Roosevelt argument that we should have permitted the Germans and Soviets to fight it out themselves. Yet the evidence is persuasive that Hitler had no plans for all-out war, and was in no position to wage it. See A. J. P. Taylor, *The Origins of the Second World War,* 2nd ed. (New York: Fawcett, 1968).

7. This was the title of Richard J. Barnet's article in *The New York Times* (June 19, 1971).

8. Roderic Gorney, *The Human Agenda* (New York: Simon and Schuster, 1968, 1972), pp. 352, 370–71.

9. Borrowing the idea of a member of the British House of Lords, one management consultant proposed in 1972 a national assembly of representatives of all occupational groups; they would develop guidelines for pay scales. While not identified as such, this would be an initial step toward Guild Socialism, and it would make sense only if professional membership, not current employment, were the determining factor. Edna Homa, "Power Bargaining Won't Answer Problems," *The New York Times* (December 12, 1971). Even *Fortune* argues that salary differentials between top-level executives and others are grossly out of line in modern corporations, where "the pyramid of influence on the formation of policy has flattened." Max Ways, "Business Needs to Do a Better Job of Explaining Itself," *Fortune,* September 1972, 198.

10. John Kenneth Galbraith suggested in 1972 that aerospace engineers

and other individuals who were thrown out of work because of cutbacks in defense spending be brought into a "specialist corps" to do research into public policy problems, each being paid according to the going rate in his profession. *The New York Times* (April 25, 1972). This resembles Donald Schon's notions of how to maintain the necessary "pools" of expertise; see his *Beyond the Stable State* (New York: Random House, 1971), p. 174.

11. "I would urge your organization to look with concern on any administrative device that encourages obeisance and bootlicking rather than independent expression and behavior. I have in mind especially the efficiency report. This device . . . accords to the superior in an organization far too much power over both the manners and thoughts of his subordinates. . . . Co-workers and subordinates are often in a far better position to judge a man's competence and his capacity for leadership than his boss." John Kenneth Galbraith, "Advice to the Foreign Service," *Foreign Service Journal*, December 1969.

12. George Leonard points out that most of the arguments supporting the incest taboo are either incomplete or wrong. Unable to satisfy himself as to the compelling reason for the taboo's survival, he admits that "in the simplest Freudian terms, mother-son incest would threaten . . . an authoritarian father." The taboo, in other words, may be nothing more than another protection of hierarchy. *The Transformation*, Ch. 12.

13. Gorney, *op. cit.*, pp. 332–35, 363, 402–03. Gorney concludes that both males and females seek to maintain boundaries between love and work; the suggestion here is that the end of hierarchy will tend to erase the boundaries.

14. This theme runs throughout the lengthy taped interviews with secretaries and administrative assistants (all women) in Jack Olsen, *The Girls at the Office* (New York: Simon and Schuster, 1972).

15. Barbara Seaman, *Free and Female: The Sex Life of the Contemporary Woman* (New York: Coward, McCann and Geoghegan, 1972), pp. 18–21.

16. Catherine Breslin, "Sex Life of a Political Campaign," *Cosmopolitan*, August 1972. This theme is implicit, if not articulated, in Natalie Gittelson, *The Erotic Life of the American Wife* (New York: Delacorte Press, 1969, 1972).

17. *The New York Times* (June 6, 1972).

18. Jessie Bernard, *The Future of Marriage* (New York: World Publishing, 1972), pp. 100–05.

19. While not publicized, the army engineers have employed the services of Rensis Likert's Institute for Social Research at the University of Michigan to help design more participative models for the development of local projects.

20. Walter Gellhorn, *When Americans Complain* (Cambridge, Mass.: Harvard University Press, 1966), pp. 64, 67. Charles L. Clapp, *The Con-*

gressman: His Work as He Sees It (Washington: Brookings Institution, 1963), p. 54.

21. Holtan Odegard, *The Policy of Truth: Toward Reconstruction in Democracy* (University of Alabama Press, 1971), p. 305.
22. John C. Ries, *Executives in the American Political System* (Belmont, Calif.: Dickenson Publishing, 1969), p. 125.
23. See Chapter 3, note 60.
24. We may learn something from the Chinese model, although we will have to become much more familiar with it before we so conclude. The Chinese have combined various forms of participatory management and the removal of status distinctions with wider processes of collective planning: individual industries can keep some of their profits for expansion, the remainder being transferred to the state. Louis Kraar, "I Have Seen China—and They Work," *Fortune,* August 1972.
25. One imaginative economist who now sees the extent of the problem remains pessimistic because he cannot escape from conventional wisdom. Robert L. Heilbroner, "Growth and Survival," *Foreign Affairs,* 51(1), October 1972, 139–53.
26. The point is made beautifully in an interview with George Sauer, an introspective and articulate professional football player who left the game at a time when he was regarded as one of its outstanding performers. "The Souring of George Sauer," an interview by Jack Scott, *Intellectual Digest,* 2(4), December 1971, 52–55.
27. *The Social Contract and Discourses,* trans. G. D. H. Cole (New York: Dutton, 1950), pp. 3–4.

ABOUT THE AUTHOR
Frederick C. Thayer, Associate Professor
at the Graduate School of Public and
International Affairs, University of Pittsburgh,
currently is Visiting Associate Professor
at the Maxwell School of Citizenship
and Public Affairs, Syracuse University.